P9-BYC-028

#55
Playa Vista Branch Library
6400 Playa Vista Drive
Los Angeles, CA 90094

World-Class Tennis Technique

Paul Roetert
Jack Groppel

Editors

796.1
W9275

Human Kinetics

Library of Congress Cataloging-in-Publication Data

World-class tennis technique / Paul Roetert, Jack Groppel, editors.
    p.   cm.
   Includes bibliographical references (p.) and index.
   ISBN 0-7360-3747-0
    1. Tennis.   I. Roetert, Paul.   II. Groppel, Jack
  GV990 .W67   2001
  796.342--dc21

                              2001024116

ISBN: 0-7360-3747-0

Copyright © 2001 by Human Kinetics Publishers, Inc.

All rights reserved. Except for use in a review, the reproduction or utilization of this work in any form or by any electronic, mechanical, or other means, now known or hereafter invented, including xerography, photocopying, and recording, and in any information storage and retrieval system, is forbidden without the written permission of the publisher.

Acquisitions Editor: Martin Barnard; **Developmental Editor**: Leigh LaHood; **Copyeditor**: Jennifer Merrill Thompson; **Proofreader**: Myla Smith; **Indexer**: Betty Frizzéll; **Graphic Designer**: Robert Reuther; **Graphic Artist**: Sandra Meier; **Cover Designer**: Jack W. Davis; **Photographer (cover)**: Lance Jeffrey; **Photographers (interior)**: Photos on pages 40, 42, 55 © Empics/Steele; photo on page 45 © Empics/Griffiths; photo on page 59 © Empics/Davy; photo on page 94 © Empics/Marshall; photo on page 123 © iPhotoNews.com; photos on pages 4, 11, 27, 28, 49, 68, 84, 104, 105, 107, 116, 158, 159, 172, 180, 181, 184, 194-197, 200, 201, 206, 208, 209, 216-219, 239, 252, 253 by Lance Jeffrey; all other photos by Tom Roberts; **Illustrator**: Robert Reuther

Human Kinetics books are available at special discounts for bulk purchase. Special editions or book excerpts can also be created to specification. For details, contact the Special Sales Manager at Human Kinetics.

Printed in England by Butler & Tanner, Ltd.   10   9   8   7   6   5   4   3   2

Human Kinetics
Web site: www.humankinetics.com

United States: Human Kinetics, P.O. Box 5076, Champaign, IL 61825-5076
800-747-4457
e-mail: humank@hkusa.com

Canada: Human Kinetics, 475 Devonshire Road Unit 100, Windsor, ON N8Y 2L5
800-465-7301 (in Canada only)
e-mail: orders@hkcanada.com

Europe: Human Kinetics, 107 bradford Road, Stanningley
Leeds LS28 6AT, United Kingdom
+44 (0) 113 255 5665
e-mail: hk@hkeurope.com

Australia: Human Kinetics, 57A Price Avenue, Lower Mitcham, South Australia 5062
08 8277 1555
e-mail: liahka@senet.com.au

New Zealand: Human Kinetics, P.O. Box 105-231, Auckland Central
09-523-3462
e-mail: hkp@ihug.co.nz

World-Class
Tennis Technique

Contents

Part Two

Perfecting Your Strokes

Introduction

Tennis players are bigger, stronger, and faster than ever. Rackets are bigger, wider, stiffer, and longer. Mark Philippoussis hits serves that fly at more than 130 miles per hour. Open-stance forehands like Venus Williams' are dominating the game. Andre Agassi and other top players are making swinging volleys more and more common. Two-handed backhands like Lindsay Davenport's are hit with incredible angles. Pete Sampras leads the way in slamming jumping overheads for winners. The game of tennis is definitely not the same as it was 25 years ago. New equipment, training methods, and techniques have changed the way tennis is played.

What are the causes of these changes in the game? Were any changes due to equipment changes alone? What was the impact of enhanced training techniques? And the largest question that looms: What about any technique differences? What is the contribution of technique changes to the overall changes seen in greater ball speed and spin? The quickness of the athletes around the court? The depth and power of the game seen in both men and women? These are questions that will be answered in this book.

Players serious about their game, as well as coaches and tennis teaching professionals, will benefit most from this book. The book features in-depth analyses of each stroke, presented with an incredible selection of sequence photographs taken by some of the world's greatest tennis photographers. Competitive players at all levels will find the most up-to-date information on tennis technique, based on solid scientific principles; however, the information is explained and described in an easy-to-understand, practical manner.

The contributors to this book are some of the world's top experts in the field of biomechanics, tennis technique, and coaching. The exciting part for us in assembling this great group of experts was that they were all very interested in contributing and being involved in a project with all the other authors. These are not just the top tennis people in the world who would only lend their name to a book. They truly were excited to help design and write the very best book possible. Each chapter features an expert with a scientific or technical background matched up with one of the top internationally known coaches. Many of the coaches also have played at a world-class level. We have assembled this group of experts based on their extensive backgrounds in the sport of tennis. They help explain the modern game and share from their research, knowledge, and experience. The sequence photographs in the stroke chapters make this an invaluable instructional as well as visual reference.

We all know there is no one perfect way to hit the ball; however, there are some common principles of each stroke shared by all top players. Through the analysis of the sequence pictures presented in this book, the authors share their knowledge of the proper fundamentals and techniques of the strokes. By understanding the scientific principles of stroke technique, players can improve both the efficiency and effectiveness of their strokes. This not only will affect the force with which a player hits the ball, but also the accuracy and consistency of each shot.

The first eight chapters of this book help prepare players for match play, and chapters 9 through 14 help in perfecting the strokes. Chapters 2 and 3 focus on the importance of proper equipment and the tremendous advances made in this area. Recommendations are made regarding the proper racket, strings, and string tension for a player's specific game and game style. In addition, the speed and future of the game in relation to court surfaces, tennis balls, and shoes are addressed. Chapters 4 through 8 help players understand the importance of proper technique and preparations before taking the court. Tennis-specific technique as it relates to training the appropriate muscle groups and movement patterns is highlighted. Chapters 9 through 13 describe the modern strokes, highlighted by sequence photographs for each stroke, whereas chapter 14 outlines the benefits of analyzing one's own game and provides the reader with checkpoints along the way.

Part One

Scientific Foundation

For years experts have felt that truly understanding how to play tennis is both science and art: science to know what really happens and art to accomplish the task. This section depicts the science of what actually occurs to make the game of tennis what it is and you the player you can become.

Historically, players have been taught tennis technique from coaches who teach the way they learned to play the game. This inbred form of teaching left much to the imagination and often developed techniques that were limited at best in the development of the player.

Over the last half of the 20th century the science of studying sport technique became popular. The former Soviet Union and Eastern Bloc countries spent huge amounts of money studying sport. These countries employed their best scientists in medicine, kinesiology, physiology, psychology, and nutrition to take their top Olympic athletes to superstar status. These are areas of each athlete's performance that received the most attention: what specific techniques were most effective, how the athletes learned their techniques most readily, how they developed their techniques through practice, how they exercised and trained to perfect their technique even more during competition, and finally, how the athletes performed their techniques under the stress of competition.

Unfortunately, tennis didn't become an Olympic sport until the latter part of the 20th century, so much of the attention from science went toward track and field and some of the other more popular Olympic sports.

Tennis techniques were first studied from a true scientific perspective in the 1960s. The late Dr. Stanley Plagenhoef was one of the first pioneers in the science of tennis technique. Plagenhoef used high-speed film and mathematical modeling to help educators and coaches understand the sport of tennis in greater detail. His ground-breaking work led many others around the world to study tennis from a scientific perspective. Many of Plagenhoef's successors are authors of chapters in this section.

Part I of this book is designed to take you on a journey of fundamentals. The top sport science people in their fields, along with coaches and former world-class players, will be your guides for the journey. The players and coaches will help you learn the material in a way that you can apply immediately to your game. The book opens with a chapter written by internationally recognized tennis educator Dr. Ron Woods and two-time Olympic gold medalist Mary Joe Fernandez showing you how players can most effectively and efficiently acquire tennis skills. This chapter is followed by an outstanding treatise on equipment by one of the world's top tennis physicists Dr. Howard Brody and tennis legend Stan Smith. Andrew Coe and Dave Miley, renowned scientist and coach educator, respectively, for the International Tennis Federation, will take you through the difference among court surfaces so you can not only apply it to your game but also more closely understand what goes on during televised matches from all over the world. Specific issues of training, footwork, and basic body mechanics are examined by some of the world's most experienced sports medicine specialists (Todd Ellen-becker and Drs. Don Chu and Ben Kibler) and coaches (Craig Tiley, Lynne Rolley, and Dennis Van der Meer). Richard Herbst, coach of many junior and professional players, and Patrick McEnroe, U.S. Davis Cup captain, discuss techniques for reaching the top. And this section concludes with a tremendous chapter by the world's top tennis psychologist, Dr. Jim Loehr, and former Davis Cup captain and Olympic coach Tom Gullikson.

When you finish this section you will be prepared to truly grasp the artistry required to play outstanding tennis. You will see how "the sport for a lifetime" is just around the corner for you.

Chapter One

Finding the Best Learning Style

Ron Woods

Mary Joe Fernandez

Whether you are a serious tennis player who is highly skilled or an occasional player who plays strictly for fun, you can improve your performance by understanding a few key concepts. Equally important, if you are a parent who hopes your children will learn tennis quickly and enjoy it for life, you will want to pay close attention to the advice that follows on modifying the game for kids.

Learning Styles

One of the enduring beauties of tennis is that people of all sizes, shapes, ages, and physical abilities can enjoy playing the game. All these people do not learn tennis in the same way. Here are a few generalizations.

Adults typically are more patient, like thorough verbal explanations, want to understand the reason behind suggested actions, and often expect mastery of one skill before moving on to the next.

Teenagers often are extremely self-conscious and live in fear that they will be singled out from their group of peers. They rely on looking, talking, and acting like their friends to "fit in," so a skilled instructor will respect their feelings and avoid putting them on the spot.

Kids often learn very quickly from simply imitating a movement and tend to be uninterested in lengthy explanations of any kind. They typically are impatient and anxious to move on to new topics.

Beginning players usually want to move quickly through the basic skills and on to playing the game, which seems to be more fun. Once a beginner successfully gets one good serve in the service box, he figures he is ready to play and keep score.

More advanced players have high expectations for their performance and often will spend an hour or more working on just one isolated skill such as deep crosscourt forehand drives. These players want to perfect the skill and ensure that it holds up even under the pressure of match play.

Other distinctions among types of tennis players are the preferences to learn visually, verbally, or using the kinesthetic senses. For the **visual learner**, a slow-

Pros such as Yevgeny Kafelnikov focus on perfecting each skill. This ensures that those skills will hold up during match pressure.

motion demonstration by a skilled player is essential and it might even be better to watch a videotape of the skill.

The **verbal learner** is comfortable with fairly detailed explanations of how to perform certain skills and may benefit from a printed explanation found in an article or a book. Probably the best advice for teachers and coaches is to "show and tell" so that both visual and verbal learners benefit from the same presentation.

Many learners also say that they need to "get the feel" of a motion or shot. They are using their **kinesthetic sense,** which is located in receptors in muscles, tendons, and joints throughout the body. The coach may emphasize the feel of a motion by helping the player through the correct path the racket should travel.

Proper Fundamentals

Tennis is a skill sport that is based primarily on learning to handle the racket in order to direct the tennis ball. Most people have the capacity to improve throughout a lifetime of play provided they have relatively sound tennis technique from the start. It doesn't matter whether you learn the skills as a child, a young adult, or a mature adult—you still want to start off with technique that allows you to improve for years to come.

Why do some people simply stop playing tennis? One of the top three reasons, according to research done by the United States Tennis Association, is their "lack of playing skill." It may just be that if people have a better idea how to keep learning and improving their skills, they will stay active in the game.

Here are some examples of poor technique that blocked further learning:

• When Sammy was 8 years old, he learned to serve overhand with a "frying pan" or western grip on the racket rather than the recommended serve grip, which is continental. He was successful as a young competitor and won quite a few matches in tournament play. As he got older, Sammy tried to hit his serve with more pace and, of course, with some spin on the second serve like other players. However, with the western grip, about all Sammy could do was hit a low-percentage, flat first serve and tap the second ball into play. Needless to say, it wasn't long before he was frustrated with tennis and resented the progress his peers were making as they passed him by.

• Anne Marie began playing regular tennis in her early 30s with a few lessons and then joined a regular team at the local park. From the start, she was very steady and could return every ball to her opponent. Anne Marie figured out that she could open her racket face a little and slice the ball on both forehand

Lindsay Davenport has worked on proper fundamentals, which are the basis for future improvement in technique.

and backhand and be very steady. The problem occurred when she wanted to move to a higher level of play in a very competitive doubles league. She found that net players loved to jump on her shots and no matter what she tried, it was tough to place the ball at her opponent's feet. If only she had learned a low to high swing when she first learned tennis, with a little practice she could have added some topspin to her shots to make them dip just over the net.

Most recommended tennis technique is the result of watching and imitating the best players in the world, studying their techniques to discover common movement patterns, and adapting those techniques to the age and experience of a new learner.

Simultaneously, laboratory research is helpful in assessing the best movement pattern from a biomechanical perspective. The science of biomechanics applies the laws of physics to athletic performance and helps us understand how to efficiently produce an optimal level of power and reduce the risk of injury.

A certified coach or tennis-teaching professional is the person who can distill the information gleaned from watching top players and research from a bio-

Watch and imitate the technique and movement patterns of the best professional players, such as Martina Hingis.

mechanics laboratory. An experienced coach will be able to apply that information to the age, skill level, and aspiration level of each beginning player and recommend a foundation of tennis skills to be pursued.

All is not lost if you don't have "perfect" technique or you have some peculiarities of style. An experienced coach will be able to help you understand your strengths, capitalize on them, and minimize the unnecessary movements in your swings. As well-known champion Fred Stolle used to say, "I'll take what you got and make it work better!"

Group Instruction vs. Individual Lessons

Many people have the mistaken impressions that private tennis lessons are essential for good instruction and optimize the learning process. Although a private lesson focuses the full attention on you, it is a costly process when compared with group instruction. In the United States, the typical costs for one hour of instruction may be $50 for a private lesson and $10 for a group lesson.

Another reason that people report that they stop playing tennis is the lack of playing partners. Group tennis lessons offer a built-in group of potential practice and playing partners who may become regular tennis buddies. Plus, learning tennis in a group environment is fun—you realize that you aren't the only one struggling to improve and the group camaraderie helps everyone enjoy the time.

It's a good idea to select a tennis program with coaches or teaching professionals who have the training and skills for quality group instruction. Every group member should be actively involved in learning tennis skills throughout the hour of instruction and each player should expect consistent, helpful feedback from the coach. If you get stuck in a class in which waiting in line for your turn is typical, look for a more effective instructor.

There is no magic number to the optimum size of a tennis class but it does depend on the number of tennis courts available along with the skill and training of the coach. Many experienced group teachers easily can handle six to eight players on one court and keep them all active. In the very beginning stages, having even more players per court is possible, although once you start to play points the number of players must be reduced.

Another good suggestion for groups of kids is to use the backboard for practicing good technique. The wall doesn't miss—and you really get a lot of hits in a short time. Some facilities also have automatic ball-throwing machines that are fun, too.

Tailoring the Game for Kids

A commonly asked question is, "When should I start my child playing tennis?" The first response is, "When a child shows some interest in the game." Naturally, if Mom and Dad or older siblings watch or play tennis, a young child is more likely to be interested.

A second consideration from a developmental perspective is to gauge the motor development level of your child. Children under 7 or 8 years of age should be learning basic locomotor and movement skills such as running, jumping, hopping, balance activities, eye-hand coordination skills, twisting, turning, and more. To be ready to start tennis skills, a child should have some skill in catching and throwing a ball. Without those fundamental skills, striking a tennis ball will be a challenge.

Some kids will thrive on a pre-tennis program that focuses on basic movement skills and gradually builds up to hitting the ball at the age of 4 or 5. Although their attention spans may be brief for one activity, a skilled instructor can maintain their enthusiasm with frequent changes of activity. Most children who have had some preliminary athletic development can achieve some success if they begin tennis activities between the ages of 6 and 8. The key is that it is an individual thing and the child has to want to do it.

Tennis for kids must undergo adjustment of certain elements for them to enjoy success and like the sport. The three things to adjust are the size of the court, the racket, and the tennis ball. Here's how to do it.

Until approximately age 8, kids ought to play on a tennis court that fits their size, strength, and speed. A mini-court with dimensions of 18 to 20 feet wide and 36 to 44 feet long makes sense. Your driveway or a nearby playground may have room for such a court, and mini-nets can be purchased to fit the court. If you go onto a full-size tennis court with a child, using only the service boxes to start will do.

The tennis racket should be light and have a small grip to fit a child's hand. Just as young baseball players use a smaller bat, your child needs a racket made for kids rather than your old hand-me-down. Now kids can get really good youth rackets that help them play better sooner.

Most important, the ball used for beginning children should be larger than normal and less lively when bounced. Balloons work well with very young children and you then can move to foam balls. A number of other lower-pressure tennis balls are now available. These balls slow the game down for beginning players and bounce lower to allow kids to stroke the ball that is at their waist rather than bouncing up around their eyes.

Every youth sport has modified the equipment so that kids can enjoy learning the game. Basketball hoops are lowered, dimensions of fields are reduced, and sizes of balls, bats, and sticks are adjusted to fit small bodies and less-mature physical skills. Tennis should be no different, and you can gradually wean kids from youth equipment as they grow and mature.

Early Success Is Key

It is no secret that people tend to choose activities in which they experience success. Both children and adults will stick with tennis if they feel the thrill of accomplishment at the start and continue to feel that they are improving their skills. In fact, one of the top three reasons people report they stopped playing tennis is their perceived "lack of skill."

Here's where an experienced certified tennis coach or teaching professional can really help. They typically know how to break the sport into manageable segments so that new players can learn quickly and retain that skill. At the same time, learning the skills and applying them to playing the game must be interwoven right from the start, because that is what attracts people to the sport in the first place. Endless hours of lessons without the thrill of playing games often deaden the enthusiasm of a novice player.

Learning to Play

As you are learning the basic skills of forehand, backhand, serve, and volley, you also should be learning how to "play the game." Even beginners should try to play a modified point as soon as they can. It may mean adjusting the rules a bit or modifying the shot, but if people wait until they master all the skills, learning to play will take years.

You should understand the basic strategy of tennis right from the start! Get the ball over the net, have it land inside the lines, and do it consistently. That simple strategy will get you started.

Next, hit the ball to the open court where your opponent has to chase it. You may not win the point outright but at least your opponent will have to work hard to return your shot.

As you play a bit more, you will discover that your opponent has a stronger and a weaker side. Guess what! If you hit more shots to the weaker side, your chances of forcing an error improve.

These basic strategic principles should be the foundation of your game and now you can see what skills you need to learn to execute your strategy. It's fun and easy to figure out what to do but it takes some practice to execute.

Mistakes vs. Errors

A good approach to the tennis court is to think of it as a "mistake center" where you can experiment with shots, try them in different situations, and test your consistency. Even the finest players in the world make mistakes as they try to counter the offerings from an opponent.

An "error" on the tennis court may be a lapse in judgment in which you try to play a shot that has very little chance of success. For example, trying to hit a hard, flat second serve would be an error in judgment. Most people figure out very early that if they want to be sure to get their second serve in, they have to increase the amount of spin on the ball or hit it more softly.

The point of the distinction between mistakes and errors is simply that if you tried the right shot and it made sense strategically, you shouldn't be too upset with the result even if you missed it. In fact, you should pat yourself on the back

Even pros such as Pete Sampras must experiment with shots according to different plays from their opponents.

and perhaps focus on an execution cue for the next time, such as "get into position a bit earlier."

On the other hand, if your choice of shots was faulty or you tried for a shot with a very low chance of success (such as aiming a forehand passing shot to land on the sideline), then you've clearly made an error. If you learn to cut down on errors, your percentage of points won will improve immediately.

Increased Margin for Error

If you choose the correct shot to hit and you make a mistake with that shot, it may be a good idea to take stock of your margin for error. If your shot landed in the net, try aiming your next shot several inches higher over the net. If your shot lands long or wide, you should consider using an aim point several feet inside the lines for all your shots. Then if you miss by a few feet as most of us do, the ball still lands in the court.

Another fundamental is to play a majority of shots crosscourt to take advantage of the fact that the net is six inches lower in the middle than at the sidelines and the diagonal flight of the ball is longer than for a shot hit down the sideline.

Learning From the Pros

Nobody would argue that if you want to play better tennis, it makes good sense to watch the best players in the world. In fact, most people are so excited to play after watching top players that they rush out to find an available court. What is even more interesting is that people often play a bit better after watching the pros, even though they are not sure what they are doing differently. Apparently there is some subconscious learning occurring as we watch a match.

It is easy to be distracted when watching the pros' particular style of play. Idiosyncratic movements often are copied but unfortunately they have little effect on play. All players have their own peculiar habits and rituals that are useless to imitate. For example, Pete Sampras typically clears his eyebrows of perspiration before serving, but players who have tried to imitate this move report no effect on their ability to serve like Sampras.

What to Watch

You would do better to focus on watching the feet of top players, how quickly they move into position, their poise and balance during the time they strike the

Notice Serena Williams' poise and balance as she strikes the ball.

ball, and how they recover quickly and anticipate an opponent's next shot. Notice how they take their time between points, using that time to recover from the last exchange and plan the upcoming one.

Watch their reactions after a missed shot as they quickly forget it and move on to the next point. You'll notice how they try to stay focused on the task at hand, remain fairly even-tempered with a positive outlook, and look confident and determined to their opponent and spectators alike.

Strategy and tactics also are fascinating to watch. You'll see players who attack at every opportunity, others who simply counterattack, net-rushers who serve and volley exclusively, and all-court players who can play all the styles and vary their play according to the opponent and the court surface. Faster surfaces such as grass, hard courts, or indoor courts favor the aggressive players who like to attack and end points quickly. Slower surfaces such as the red clay found in Europe and South America favor the counter-punchers and those who can rally from the baseline all day.

Imitate Patterns of Play

If you watch closely, you see professional players use certain repetitive patterns of play over and over again. They have developed certain combinations of shots

Lleyton Hewitt stays calm and focused.

from years of practice and they rely on those patterns when they compete. Of course, their opponents also have certain patterns of play and at the same time are trying to dominate points by controlling the sequences of shots.

A couple of simple patterns are all you need if you can execute them really well. For example, if you serve to the outside of the service box that opens up a whole side of the court, you easily can play your next shot to the opening. If you don't win the point outright, at least you have your opponent on the run.

Another effective pattern is to move your opponent deep to one corner near the baseline and then play your next shot short along the opposite sideline. This forces not only a side-to-side move but also deep to short. If your opponent reaches both those shots, it might be time to launch a lob to chase her from coming in.

Tim Gullikson was my coach for several years and he had an impact on my game by teaching me about 10 to 12 key patterns that I could use over and over. I learned a couple of basic patterns from each part of the court, and as I played, the shots became second nature.

—M.J.F.

When your opponent is serving, your bread-and-butter return ought to be crosscourt to take advantage of the low part of the net and the longer angle. Since the server theoretically has the advantage, your main objective should be to get the ball in play safely and begin the rally. Of course if your opponent's second serve is weak, the pattern should change and you can become the aggressor by attacking the weak serve with a forcing shot that wins the point or allows you to follow it to the net.

Getting the Most Out of Practice

If you want to improve your playing skills, some type of practice is a must. It may be as simple as playing a few sets with particular strategic goals in mind. Or it may involve hitting a succession of serves by yourself so you can concentrate on the technique and the result without worrying about the next shot. The following suggestions may help you get the most out of your practice sessions.

• Practice the way you want to play. Be just as aggressive, focused, and competitive as you are in match play.

• Set goals for yourself. Players such as Monica Seles and Lindsay Davenport have set goals from the start of every practice. One example is to run hard for every ball just as you do in a match. No second bounces—ever!

• Once you feel you own a shot, overlearn it by executing it 50 percent of the number of times it took you to learn it. In other words, if it took 100 trials to learn to hit the overhead smash with confidence, hit another 50 before you leave the court that day to set the habit.

• Overpractice. Most players overpractice rallying and neglect serves and returning serve. In Fed Cup practice, Billie Jean King always had players start every point with a serve, return, and then the rally just like a point.

• Break practice sessions into short, intense work sessions with full concentration for 15 to 20 minutes followed by a break. You'll produce better-quality work this way than if you move at half-speed for an hour at a time.

• Adjust practice according to your level. Beginning players thrive on frequent changes of activity, but more advanced players may be willing to work longer on one shot or series of shots because they are striving for a higher standard of performance.

• Add variety. Even for world-class players, variety is the key to making practice fun. Try learning a new shot, or a new pattern or sequence of shots, or practicing with different people, not the same partners day after day. And it is best if you like the people you practice with and enjoy being around them.

• Practice your strengths as well as your weaknesses . . . or they won't be strengths for long. Hitting your favorite shot to end a practice builds your confidence and keeps you coming back for more.

Monica Seles runs hard for every ball in practice as well as in matches.

• Try new skills early in a practice, not when you're tired or bored. Work on your physical training near the end of practice so that it won't interfere with your learning skills.

• Break down points into typical patterns of play and practice those patterns. For example, serve the ball to the outside of the service box to pull your opponent wide and open up the court. When the return comes back, direct your next shot to the open court.

• Have a plan for every practice session and reward yourself at the end by doing your favorite thing. If that is playing a set, do it.

• Set goals for every practice and every drill and use targets on the court. If you don't have a clear purpose for each practice, it's easy to waste your time. These things help keep you focused and performing at your highest level.

Practicing With Players of All Skill Levels

Players often say they just can't improve unless they practice or play with better players. Of course if that were true, better players would have a very tough time finding playing partners. The fact is, you can learn a lot from playing with all types of players. Here's how.

• If you are playing someone who is below your level: This is the time to work on your weaknesses, try some new patterns of play, come to the net more, or vary your style of play.

At times you might have to change your typical strategy because of your opponent. When I played Steffi Graf, I knew my chances were poor if I tried to outplay her from the baseline. So I tried to come in to the net more often and attack her slice backhand.
—M.J.F.

• If you are playing someone at your level: Concentrate on your competitive skills, play percentage tennis, and try to relax even under pressure. This is the time to play your best shots and force your opponent to work for every point.

• If you are playing a better player: Make sure you get the ball in play, cut down on errors on serve and return of serve, and play to your strengths. The tendency against a better player is to hit shots you don't really own and try to play up a level. If you do that, you'll only lose faster and your opponent won't even get a good workout.

Vary the types and levels of player you compete against and learn from each experience. If you play only with better players, before long you'll have a complex about losing. Likewise, if you play only people who are less skilled, you may develop an inflated opinion of your abilities.

Tennis—A Mind Game

Controlling your thoughts and feelings while learning or playing tennis is just as important as learning the skills correctly or understanding strategic options. Your mind and emotions can be a powerful ally or they can destroy your ability to compete once you lose control.

A good starting point to check is your breathing patterns, especially when you are feeling under pressure to perform. Take a deep breath, let it go, and then perform the skill. Some players get so tight and nervous at points in a match that they hold their breath and try to play.

Along with deep breathing, another helpful skill when you're feeling pressure is the ability to tense and then relax your muscles. A typical response to pressure is to limit the swing or cut short the follow-through. By relaxing your muscles between points and regulating your breathing, you can ensure a full, smooth swing during the point.

As the pressure rises during a match, players have the tendency to rush between points, particularly when things are not going well. It seems as if they think that speeding up the process will get them through a bad patch of play. Nothing could be further from the truth. In fact, you need to slow down between points and plan your next point.

When things go wrong during competition, it is easy to criticize yourself and adopt a negative attitude. For some players, to stay positive and confident is a real test of mental toughness. One trick to doing this is to portray that image of confidence to your opponent even if you don't feel it at the moment. Another helpful strategy is to treat yourself as you would your best friend or doubles partner. You would be supportive, encouraging, and sympathetic rather than critical or demeaning.

Focusing your attention on the right stuff during play also can be a challenge. It's easy to let the conditions, the crowd, your opponent, or your play distract you. You've got to practice blocking out distractions and learn to focus on the task at hand. Focus on your game plan and adjust your tactics as the match progresses. Resist the temptation to think about your technique; instead, concentrate on moving into position early and preparing to hit the shot.

Chapter Two

Revolutionary Rackets

Howard Brody

Stan Smith

If you look at a modern tennis racket, it is obviously a very different object from the tennis racket in use 30 to 40 years ago. It has a bigger head, it is lighter but stiffer, it has a split shaft, and it is not made of wood. While the tennis racket in use during the 1960s or 1970s can be shown to have slowly evolved from the tennis racket in use at the turn of the previous century, the recent rackets represent a revolution in racket technology. It also is interesting to note that the strokes in tennis and the style of the game itself evolved very slowly over the first two-thirds of the previous century, but during the past 20 to 30 years there has been a remarkable change in the way the game is played. One can only wonder whether the change in racket technology was the driving force behind the changes in the game of tennis (particularly at the highest levels) that occurred during the same period of time.

A hundred years ago, tennis racket frames routinely were made by hand out of wood. Strips of wood were steamed to make them flexible, bent into the form of a tennis racket frame, and then clamped, glued, and lashed in place to maintain their shape as they dried. Because of the inherent structural limitations of wood, the racket frame was made fairly thick to survive the forces that are present. These forces are caused by the pull of the strings under high tension and the constant pounding the racket undergoes because of the impact of the ball. Making the frame thick, however, required that it be heavy. It was not uncommon to have a tennis racket frame that weighed almost a pound (16 ounces or almost half a kilogram in mass). The strung area of the head was quite small (about 70 square inches). To some degree, this size also was dictated by the structural limitations of wood and the necessity of being able to swing the racket easily. The rackets were 27 inches long from butt to tip and the outer width of the head was 9 inches. By the middle of the century, these dimensions were so standard that one could check the net height at the center strap (36 inches) by using two rackets—one vertical (27 inches) and one horizontal (9 inches), giving a combined height of 36 inches.

There was some experimenting with racket weight, size, shape, balance, and so forth during the early to middle part of the past century, particularly by F.W. Donisthorpe. Donisthorpe, one of the best tennis players in England in the 1920s, constructed wood rackets weighing from 9 ounces to 36 ounces, with big heads, small heads, longer shafts, shorter shafts, and various balances. He eventually was able to construct a lightweight, oversize racket that he claimed

Today's players such as Marat Safin show a change in the way the game is played that may be related to changes in racket technology.

played better than the then-standard racket, but it was not structurally sound enough to survive the pounding that the ball impact imparts. When he tried to make rackets that had larger heads and were strong enough to play with, the weight of the resulting frame made them too cumbersome for most players to use. It was not until the latter part of the 20th century that the availability of new materials allowed racket designers the freedom to innovate.

With wood rackets having small heads and weighing up to a pound, a style of play and stroking developed. Because of the weight, it was not possible to quickly whip the racket around, and because of the small head, it was necessary to be quite precise in the ball impact location on the strings. To maintain good racket head control and to be able to accelerate the racket head up to the desired speed, players used the classic tennis stroke.

When you look at the great players from 1920 to 1970, they were playing exclusively with wood rackets and the emphasis was on a smooth, flowing stroke with great transfer of weight into the shot. With the heavy wood rackets, players needed to start the swing early with a good shoulder turn. Generally the shoulder turn was to a sideways position with the left arm more or less pointing toward the target on the forehand and the right shoulder pointing toward the target on the backhand. This created a long backswing basically pointing toward the back fence. From there the players tried to meet the ball in front of the body and follow through toward the target. With the classic forehand and backhand, the weight transfer was more linear than rotational. This meant that players did not use the excessive shoulder turn that we see in many players today. The idea was to use the weight of the racket and the forward transfer of body weight to generate power.

Players hit the forehand either flat or with some topspin depending on where they learned the game. Clay-court players from Europe and South America are more apt to hit with topspin on their forehands because they have more time to set up and get their racket below the ball on the backswing.

Almost all players hit a one-handed backhand and in most cases hit the ball flat or with underspin. In the 1960s, a few players started hitting with more topspin on the backhand. They imparted topspin by starting the forward swing below the ball and brushing upward to a high follow-through. As the wood rackets became a little lighter and then the nonwood rackets came into vogue, more and more players started hitting topspin with the backhand.

With the heavy wood rackets there was quite a bit of variety in the shot selection. Players would drive the ball hard and deep toward the baseline or slice the ball to take the pace off it for control. They also would chip the ball low at their opponents' feet when they came to the net as well as hit topspin passing shots. The style of play, starting with Jack Kramer in the 1940s, became more of a serve-and-volley game, especially on faster courts such as grass and

Venus Williams' forehand shows a more excessive shoulder turn than players demonstrated when using heavy wooden rackets.

hard courts. The wood rackets were effective in this game and passing shots were not as easy with the long, flowing strokes.

In the 1970s and 1980s, two new developments in tennis arrived on the scene. New-composite, space-age materials became available, and Howard Head successfully designed and marketed a racket with an oversized head. The new-composite materials, usually graphite fibers molded in an epoxy binder, were light and very strong. This allowed the racket designer and engineer to break free of the limitations that wood had forced them into. The familiar small, oval-shaped head, necessitated by the huge forces the strings produced, was no longer necessary. Stiffness of the frame, a requirement for control and power, no longer had to pay a weight penalty. As design, engineering, and manufacturing technology improved, it became possible to produce an oversized, very stiff, durable racket that was very light yet had excellent playing characteristics. The latest technology allowed the construction of durable frames as light as 7 ounces, which raises interesting questions.

Is it possible that a racket can be too light? Is there an optimum weight for a tennis racket? As a racket is made lighter, it becomes easier to swing, is more maneuverable, and can be swung at a higher speed. At the same time, a lighter racket (for the same racket head speed) will propel the ball at a lower velocity. When rackets weighed 15 ounces, a reduction of several ounces still gave you a frame that was heavy compared to the 2-ounce ball, and the weight reduction led to very little loss of inherent racket power. This slight loss of inherent racket power could easily be made up by swinging the lighter racket just a bit faster. When rackets are in the 7- to 8-ounce range, the power loss is greater, and it may not always be possible to make up for the loss by swinging faster. For each player and each style of play there is probably a range of racket weights that will optimize one's game. For the serve, an analysis of the ball-racket interaction shows that the resulting ball velocity is relatively insensitive to the inherent racket power and very sensitive to the racket head speed. Therefore, a lighter racket usually will give the ball more speed on the serve. For a ground stroke, it can be shown that the resulting ball speed depends a great deal on the inherent racket power. In addition, when hitting ground strokes, most players do not swing the racket at full speed (as hard as they can), so a somewhat heavier racket may be optimum.

The lighter weight of the racket makes it more maneuverable, but there is not as much mass behind the ball at contact so that the racket can turn in the

Generally, a lighter racket will give the ball more speed on a serve.

hand on miss-hit shots. This can be uncomfortable and may cause some arm injuries. You have to swing harder to get the same effect as you would obtain with a heavier racket, but there is less effort to get the racket started. So there are trade-offs with the weight issue.

The lighter rackets have enabled players to get more racket head speed and have created a different type of game with more power and less finesse. Instead of the smooth, long-flowing strokes, we now see very aggressive and almost violent swings. Players are able to hit harder and more accurately with the lighter, stiffer, and stronger rackets than with the wood rackets. The style of play has changed from either the serve-and-volley style or a patient strategy waiting to set up the point to a consistent, hard-hitting style from every position on the court. There is less variety of shots with more hard serving and aggressive re-turning of serve. The most common strategy is to hit the big first serve, look for a short return, and go for a winner on the next shot.

With the lighter rackets, many players whip the racket into the ball, finishing across the body instead of toward the target. This not only creates more speed but also the opportunity to apply more spin. This spin not only controls the ball; it also causes the ball to dive down, then jump up when it hits the ground, making it a more difficult shot to return.

The larger head size that is now available has several distinct advantages over the old small ovals. With the head made wider (for example, going from 8 to 10 inches), the rotational stability of the racket increases, which is impor-tant when a shot is hit off the principal axis of the frame. This extra stability means that the racket will twist less when an off-axis impact occurs, and there is less loss of power when the ball does not hit exactly on the axis. The stability factor is proportional to the weight of the racket multiplied by the head width squared, so an increase of 25 percent in width (from 8 to 10 inches) will increase the stability by over 50 percent. This means that you can miss-hit the ball a bit more and not have to pay the severe penalty that a small-headed racket would exact. The racket is more forgiving and the margin for error has increased. The result of widening the racket head is that strokes do not have to be as precise.

As the head is enlarged and elongated, its center moves closer to your hand (if the overall racket length remains constant). This means that two of the sweet spots (the point of minimum vibration and the point of minimum shock or jar to your hand) end up close to the center of the head. With the old smaller head, these sweet spots were close to the racket's throat. If you want to hit the ball at these locations (and most players do), the enlarged head gives you more margin for error.

Determining the location of the third sweet spot (maximum power) is a complicated matter. Let's assume that the racket is moving forward in a straight

Serena Williams finishes the swing across the body, creating speed and spin.

line rather than being rotated during a swing. Then the region of maximum power (highest ball rebound speed) is close to the racket's balance point, which is usually near the throat. If the racket is swung, the top of the frame is moving faster than the throat, and consequently the maximum power region moves up higher into the head. It would be desirable to have this greatest power region close to the other sweet spots and close to the center of the strung area of the head. This can be accomplished by swinging the racket with a very wristy swing, modifying the racket design, or both.

To move the power point of a racket up higher in the head, you can make the frame head-heavy (or handle-light), make the head stiffer, change the basic head shape from oval to triangular, or fan out the strings toward the racket tip. To make the racket stiffer, either graphite fibers with higher moduli can be used or the thickness of the frame can be increased. Since the stiffness of a beam goes as the cube of that dimension, a doubling of the frame thickness (from 19 millimeters to

38 millimeters, for example) will increase the stiffness by a factor of eight, if all else is held constant. If the maximum power point can be moved to near or at the center of the head (by some combination of racket design and stroking), then the variation of power you get as the ball impact point moves around somewhat is greatly reduced. This allows you to hit the ball on the strings slightly closer or farther from your hand and still have the result be a good shot. Again the margin of error has increased and the precision of stroking has been relaxed. The racket is more forgiving.

If the head is enlarged, the strings get longer. As the strings get longer, the racket tends to produce more power. Racket designers and manufacturers always are looking for ways to increase the power of their rackets. However, the International Tennis Federation (ITF) has a rule about the maximum size of the hitting area of a racket (11.5 inches wide, 15.5 inches long), which clearly limits what a racket designer can do. To get a little more string length and still stay within the strung-area limits, racket designers have made the inside of the string grommets quite large so the string is supported by the grommet strip at the outside of the frame. This effectively adds length to the strings and also produces a somewhat better response to shots that are miss-hit and impact near the frame.

The larger racket has brought more parity to the game. Because they don't have to be so precise hitting the ball in the "sweet spot" to be effective, more and more players are competitive in today's style of play. Of course, the best players today do hit the ball in the sweet spot more often than those who are ranked lower.

The racket has made a big impact on both the men's and women's game. The men are hitting serves consistently in the 120- to 130-mph range and the top women are hitting them in the 100- to 120-mph range. The forehand has evolved most of all. The players are hitting the forehand with a semi-western grip and an open stance. The swing starts with a big shoulder turn that rotates beyond sideways to the target and a "loading" of the weight on the back foot. The contact point is way out in front of the body. The follow-through is across the body with so much acceleration that the hip rotation actually brings the back foot forward with the finish of the swing. This motion coupled with the upward swing creates heavy topspin and makes the modern forehand a real punishing weapon.

The two-handed backhand has made some players equally explosive on both wings. A player such as Andre Agassi is hard to play against because he can hurt you on both sides. The international game on the men's side has about an equal number of players using a one-handed backhand and a two-handed backhand. Today's one-handed backhand is hit with more power because of the grip (to be discussed later).

Andre Agassi's powerful two-handed backhand creates difficulty for his opponents.

When you hit a typical ground stroke, you have a certain margin of allowable vertical error, which may be thought of as a window at the net through which your ball must pass if the shot is to be good. The lower edge of the window is the top of the net itself, and the upper limit of the window is that height at which a ball's trajectory will cause it to land just on the baseline. The larger this window, the easier it is to get the ball to go through it and the less likely you are to make an error on that shot. For a typical flat shot (no spin) leaving the racket at 65 mph, the window at the net is somewhat over 8 inches. If you put topspin on the ball, the window opens up, and with a ball spin of 50 revolutions per second, the window is 15 inches high. If you could maintain the same racket head control on a topspin shot as you can on a flat stroke, the enlarged window would mean fewer errors would be committed, because it is much easier to get the ball through a 15-inch window than an 8-inch window.

However, topspin does not come free. You must swing the racket 50 percent faster to hit a typical topspin shot, compared to the racket head speed on a flat shot. This is because the ball, on its way to the player, bounces and this causes it to acquire its own topspin. To return such a shot with topspin means that both the ball's direction and its spin must be reversed. To obtain this topspin, a much greater racket head speed is required, which can be accomplished more readily with the new lightweight rackets. But a high-speed swing may lead to some loss of racket head control, possibly enough to negate the increase in window that the topspin gives you.

Heavy topspin on the ground strokes is generated by using the legs effectively. On the big forehands, the good players will plant their back leg with a good knee bend and then thrust themselves up and forward into the shot. At the same time they usually will take the racket back with a looping swing so that when they are about to come forward the racket is well below the ball. The racket is accelerated by the legs and hips so that the upward and forward movement is reaching maximum speed by the time contact is made. This is the kinetic

Gustavo Kuerten plants his back leg firmly and takes the racket back with a looping swing to create topspin on his forehand.

link system working along with the light racket that can make the swing look like a blur. For more on the kinetic link system, see chapter 6.

The only problem with this topspin shot is that if it is hit with too much topspin and not enough forward thrust, the ball will often land short and be vulnerable to an opponent's attack. Most of the players with good topspin forehands like the high balls. The low balls (particularly when playing on a dead surface such as grass) are difficult to handle for most of these players. The reason is the type of grip that is used. With the semi-western or western grip the hand is over to the right and even underneath the racket. With the hand in this position it is very difficult to get below the low ball and hit it over with any kind of power.

Another big change is with the extreme backhand grip often referred to as a semi-western backhand grip. This grip, used by players such as Gustavo Kuerten, allows one-handed backhand players to hit the ball very hard and to handle those difficult high balls. This grip allows a player to hit with heavy topspin as well as flat. In order to hit a slice, the player must change to a continental or eastern grip. The extreme grip changes that are necessary for these players make it difficult, especially when they play on faster, low-bouncing surfaces.

The Grip

One of the interesting things in the evolution and revolution in tennis racket design that has escaped general notice is the change of grip sizes available to players in standard, off-the-shelf rackets. In the wood-racket era, it was possible to walk into a store or tennis shop and find on the wall a racket with a grip size (circumference of handle) of $4\frac{3}{4}$, or $4\frac{7}{8}$, or even 5 inches. Today, those grip sizes have disappeared along with the heavy wood racket. The light, composite frames that are available today allow you to swing with a more flexible wrist, whipping around the racket. A large grip size tends to lock your wrist a bit and prevents you from taking full advantage of the lighter rackets. If you want such a large grip, you must have the handle built up by a racket technician in order to meet your needs. An argument in favor of a large grip claims that the racket will be less likely to slip or rotate in your hands on off-axis impacts because a larger grip gives you more stabilizing torque for the same grip firmness. It is true that the larger grip gives you more torque, but whether it is necessary is open to question.

There is a great deal of contradictory information in the tennis literature about the necessity of firmness or tightness of the grip of the player's hand on the handle. In some articles it is stated that a very firm grip will add the weight of the hand and possibly the weight of the arm to the weight of the racket, giving more power. Some laboratory experiments show that the power of a racket does not depend on whether the racket is completely free or the handle is clamped in a vise. Some articles advocate a very firm grip to keep the racket from rotating or slipping in your hands. Other lab experiments seem to show that a racket, when hit by a ball (or hitting a ball), acts as if it were free and not gripped, independent of grip firmness.

The arguments for an exceedingly firm grip producing benefits are mostly anecdotal. Where experiments have been done and the results published, the conclusions tend not to endorse the firm-grip concept. In fact, there is some anecdotal information that the firm grip (bordering on the "death grip") eventually may cause arm injury. It is clear that a sufficiently firm grip is needed to be able to maneuver the racket into the correct position and have it moving at the correct speed, but beyond that, there seems to be little gain. Too firm a grip probably will inhibit a free swing and reduce the effectiveness of the stroke. The player will appear to be "muscling" the ball back rather than swinging the racket.

As an example, think of a 5-year-old child learning to play tennis. The kid hits the ball all over the face of the racket (clearly off-axis) and does not have a very firm grip on the thin handle, yet the racket rarely rotates out of the hand. What does happen to both kids and adults on off-axis impacts (as shown by high-speed video) is that the racket twists, as does the hand and the forearm, but not the racket relative to the hand. If the grip becomes very slippery and the hand is tired, then there is a chance of the racket slipping, but under most conditions, a softer but firm grip is best. One of the reasons the hand becomes tired while playing can be the continuous use of too tight a grip on the handle.

In summary, a somewhat relaxed grip seems to have many advantages over the extra-firm grip that often is advocated.

The size of the grip that most players use has changed as dramatically as the style of play. Pete Sampras, who has a more classic game, still uses a grip that is relatively big—$4\frac{5}{8}$. The smaller the grip the more there is a tendency to use the wrist and create more topspin. Ken Rosewall, who does not have big hands, used a $4\frac{7}{8}$ grip. With the smaller grip you will be able to whip the racket head around faster and therefore be more effective with topspin and be in tune with the modern game.

Most of the good players hold the racket relatively relaxed. It keeps the rest of the muscles in the arm more relaxed so that a player will have a better chance to time the ball more consistently, create more power, and have better feel. In addition, the player's arm will not tire as quickly when he doesn't have a death grip on the racket. At actual contact the grip is firm so that the racket does not turn in the hand.

Keeping the wrist firm at contact prevents the racket from turning in the hand.

Racket Vibrations

When you hit a tennis ball there can be a discomfort to your hand and arm because of the impact of the ball on the racket. One type of discomfort is the initial shock or jar your hand feels. This can be minimized by hitting the ball at a place called the center of percussion (COP), which is located near the center of the strings on a typical oversize racket. The farther the ball impacts from this COP location, the more intense that initial shock or jar is to your hand. The exact location of the COP sweet spot depends on where you hold the racket. If you choke up a bit on the grip, you can move the COP up farther toward the top of the head.

This shock or jar discomfort also can be reduced by various technical devices built into the racket shaft, by making the shaft somewhat more flexible, or by reducing the string tension. Another method is to use a soft, padded grip (which most rackets now come with) as opposed to just a thin layer of leather wrapped around the structural member of the handle (as is found on older rackets).

You also can feel discomfort caused by vibration. There are two types of vibrations that occur when you hit the ball: the frame can vibrate and the strings can vibrate. It is frame vibration that causes the major discomfort, while string vibration is annoying to some players and does not bother others at all.

When the ball impacts on the string bed, the strings deform and then propel the ball back. After the ball leaves, the strings overshoot their equilibrium position and a vibration begins. This vibration occurs regardless of how hard or where on the strings you hit the ball. If no effort is made to dampen out these oscillations of the entire string plane, they will continue to vibrate for a fraction of a second at a frequency of 400 to 700 Hz (vibrations per second). The actual frequency is determined primarily by the gauge of the string, the head size, and the string tension. (Rule of thumb: the higher the tension, the higher the frequency, and the bigger the head, the lower the frequency.) This vibration can be dampened out in a few oscillations by inserting a small, light device between the strings in the throat of the racket. You can tell that the oscillations of the string plane are dampened out by listening to the sound that is made at ball contact. If you hear a "ping" as opposed to a "thud," then the string vibrations are not strongly dampened.

Can string vibrations cause damage to your arm? Probably not. If the dampener that you insert, which has a mass of a few grams, can successfully eliminate the vibrations, then there is very little energy in those vibrations and they will not cause harm. Then why use the dampeners? Some players don't like the feel of undampened strings and some don't like the sound of them, so it is a matter of personal preference.

Some players use them because they think they dampen out frame vibrations. They are mistaken. Experiments have shown that these dampeners in the

As the ball impacts the racket, the strings will deform and then propel the ball back, causing a string vibration lasting a fraction of a second.

string bed do a very good job dampening out string vibrations, but they do essentially nothing to reduce vibrations of the racket frame itself.

The vibration dampeners will make a thudding sound and make your racket feel different. This sounds unnatural but it really doesn't affect the playability of a racket. Some players are convinced that the vibration dampeners make a critical difference and will not play without a dampener. On the other hand, some will not play with one. One of us (Stan Smith) has played with and without one in the racket and likes the feeling of playing with the dampener, but it took a while to get used to it.

A modern tennis racket feels like a rigid body when you try to bend or deform it by hand. However, when a ball impacts on it, there is a deformation and a subsequent oscillation of the frame. Unlike the strings, where only 15 grams of mass are oscillating, the frame has a mass of about 300 grams, so there is much more energy involved in the frame vibration. The principal mode of this frame vibration can be eliminated if the ball impacts the strings at a location called the node. For a typical 27-inch-long racket, the node is located about 6 inches from the tip. When the ball is struck at this location, there is very little frame vibration, whereas ball impacts near the tip or near the throat of the racket produce large amplitudes of oscillation. For most rackets, the node (minimum vibration point) and the COP (minimum shock or jar point) are located very close to each other. If the ball hits one of these spots, it will impact sufficiently close to the other sweet spot so that the player gets the benefit of both.

For good players the difference between hitting the sweet spot and not hitting it is very apparent. The ball seems to come off the racket effortlessly with power and control. You do not have the feeling that you are working very hard. When you miss the sweet spot, the jarring that takes place makes you feel that you are having to work to muscle the ball over the net. If you have any pain in your arm then the miss-hit or off-center-hit feeling is terrible and it makes you want to guide the ball gently so as not to feel any pain. When you get into this mode of pushing or guiding the ball to protect your arm, then your effectiveness as a player is diminished.

Various methods for quickly dampening out these frame vibrations have been proposed and implemented, ranging from imbedding viscoelastic material in the frame to placing small bits of lead shot into cavities built into the racket frame. Many of these schemes do not work as well in dampening vibrations as the human hand that is holding the racket by the grip. The tighter the racket is held, the faster the vibrations dampen out—with the energy of vibration going into the hand and arm. However, as uncomfortable as these oscillations may feel, there is no clinical evidence that vibrations are or are not a source of injury to the hand or arm.

When a racket is made stiffer (and the ball impact misses the node), the amplitude of the oscillations decreases and the frequency increases. Typical racket

Martina Hingis hits this shot on the racket's "sweet spot," reducing the amount of frame vibration and thus creating more power, control, and arm comfort.

frames have a lowest frequency of oscillation between 100 and 200 Hz, depending on their rigidity and weight.

Racket Length

Throughout most of the 20th century, tennis rackets were 27 inches long. For most of this period of time there was no limit on the overall length of the racket frame. In the latter part of the century, a 32-inch length limit was imposed by the people who make the rules of tennis (the ITF). Starting in 2000, the longest legal racket is now 29 inches long. There are two obvious questions that this brings up: why did it take more than 100 years to impose these limits on the racket, and should every player go to the 29-inch-long frame?

When rackets were made of wood and were heavy, adding a few extra inches of length to the frame would produce a racket that was very difficult to swing.

The property that describes the racket's resistance to being swung is called swing weight or moment of inertia about the butt end. The larger a racket's swing weight, the more difficult it is to swing it. With the introduction of composite materials for racket frames, it became possible to fabricate a racket that was considerably lighter. As design and manufacturing techniques improved even more, it became possible to make a racket frame that was longer and stronger, yet easy to maneuver and swing (it had a low swing weight). Therefore, length limits were needed.

For the average recreational player, an extra inch or two may prove to be a slight advantage, but for an elite player, that extra inch or so may be the difference between winning and losing. For the elite player serving at 120 mph, each extra inch of racket length increases the acceptance window and can produce 5 percent more first serves going in (assuming the player takes advantage of the extra length by hitting the ball correspondingly higher). For a short player who is trying to serve "on the edge" (hitting hard, low-percentage serves), the extra inch or two is even more significant. For the recreational player who is not pushing the envelope on the serve, the increase in window may be useful, but serving at full extension usually will produce better results.

For all players, a longer racket means a longer reach on ground strokes, which can be useful. It can mean greater racket head speed at the ball impact point (which could translate into greater ball speed) if you swing the longer racket at the same speed as the shorter racket and you hit the ball farther from your hand. A longer racket also may mean some loss of ball control, but there is no evidence of this reported in the tennis literature. However, a number of the top players complain that they feel they lose control when they use the longer rackets and therefore have stayed with the 27-inch length. There is also no evidence that a longer racket can cause arm, hand, or shoulder problems, probably because no carefully controlled studies have been done.

Just as rackets can get too light, racket length can go too far. However, the 29-inch length rule keeps the racket close to what has been used for the last century. There is no overall best length ordained by the laws of physics and biomechanics, just as there is no best weight for tennis rackets. There are some advantages and possible disadvantages to a longer racket, and each player should try to find the length that optimizes his or her game.

For most players, it takes a while to get used to the longer length, and at first, contact is made a little off center and closer to the hand. The adjustment to hitting the sweet spot farther away from the hand does not take very long, especially if you approach this change with the right attitude. The benefits of more reach, more racket head acceleration, and more spin, using a racket with the same swing weight and an inch longer, seem to outweigh the possible loss of control and occasional jamming when your opponent hits the ball into your body.

Strings

Regardless of how high-tech your racket frame is or how much you paid for it, the ball contacts only the strings and not the frame holding those strings. Players have a choice between gut (beef intestines) and synthetic strings. Although there has been a revolution in racket frames and a major improvement in synthetic strings, there has been only a slow evolution in gut strings. A major change in gut has been the improvement in durability with respect to wear and the environment. Gut costs considerably more than synthetic strings to install in a racket, but many players feel that it is worth it in playability.

The major purpose of the strings in a tennis racket is to convert the incoming energy of the ball into string deformation and then convert the energy stored in that deformation back into the ball's outgoing energy. This energy conversion is to be done as efficiently and quickly as possible while also allowing the shot to be controlled. A second purpose of the strings is to allow spin to be imparted to the ball. How efficiently and accurately these are done depends on the type of string, the string tension, and the string spacing.

Many pros such as Nicolas Kiefer use gut strings.

While most players think about strings in terms of tension, it is actually the string plane deformation that determines how a racket plays. Sixty pounds of tension in an oversize racket will play differently than 60 pounds of tension in a midsize frame. As a general rule of thumb, when comparing tensions in different size rackets, divide the tension by the head size (width, for example) to get a comparable feel. If the string spacing is different, then the racket with the larger spacing will play softer (or as if it were at a lower tension) when the two rackets are strung at identical tensions. Most of this is of academic interest only, because players usually don't switch to a racket of a different head size or string spacing very often.

Today, the accepted wisdom is that tighter strings give you less power and more control. It is of interest that about 30 years ago, the conventional wisdom was just the opposite. The incorrect logic went like this: the best players generally string their rackets at high tension and these players generate high ball speed; therefore, tight strings produce high ball speed.

What is actually happening is the following. Strings absorb the incoming ball energy by deforming and then return 95 percent of that energy back to the ball. At the same time, the ball deforms, but it only returns about half of the energy it absorbs (this is set by the rules of tennis). To get the maximum energy back into the ball's speed, you want the deformation of the strings (which returns 95 percent of the energy it stores) to absorb as much of the ball's incoming energy as possible and have the ball deformation (which loses 40 to 50 percent of the energy when it deforms) absorb as little as possible. Therefore, you string the racket at a lower tension to allow the strings to absorb more energy, and the result is an increase in racket power. There are limits to this, because you cannot play tennis with a butterfly net. As the tension is decreased the strings start to move within the string plane, rubbing on each other and dissipating energy. There is also some evidence that as the string tension is decreased, there is some loss of control over where the ball travels.

One of the principal qualities desired in a string is elasticity. The more elastic a string is, the more energy it absorbs from the ball, the better it plays in the racket, and the better it feels to the player. Many synthetic strings begin to lose their elasticity as the tension is increased. This is particularly important when the ball is hit hard. The strings around the ball impact region are forced to stretch and the local tension increases a great deal. If the strings become much less elastic as the tension increases, the hit will feel "boardy" or stiff and it will not be a pleasant sensation. If, as the tension is increased, the strings remain elastic (such as gut does), then the impact will cause the strings to "cup" the ball and the feeling will not be as harsh or jarring, but soft.

Strings are made of various materials and of different thicknesses (gauges). The inherent strength of a string depends on the material it is made of, the method of construction, and its cross-sectional area (which is proportional to the square of the string diameter). On the other hand, the elasticity of a given string goes inversely as the cross-sectional area. Therefore, a thicker string is less elastic. So going to a thinner string (larger gauge number) means a more elastic, better-feeling string, but one that is not as strong and is more likely to break. A change of string diameter of 10 percent results in a change of string cross-sectional area of 20 percent and a corresponding change in the elasticity of the string.

Once strings are in place, they immediately begin to lose tension. Playing with them or subjecting them to high temperature will accelerate the loss of tension. The tension will eventually stabilize at a value from 10 to 30 percent below the original value. This loss of tension is associated with some loss of elasticity of the strings, but because the string tension is now lower, there may not be any power loss associated with it.

Playing with a newly strung racket can be a nice feeling because hopefully it's exactly as you want it. The tension goes down a bit quickly, but you gradually will get used to it while you are playing. If you have a racket that has had string in it for a long time and it does not feel very good, it may not be the racket that is bad. The strings probably have lost both tension and elasticity and feel dead. If you have the racket restrung, you will notice a big difference in how it plays.

As a general rule, stringing a racket with a material that is more elastic and stringing at a lower tension should help to protect your arm from the damage coming from the repeated jars of the impacting ball. More elasticity of the strings and lower tension increase the ball dwell time on the strings and reduce the peak force that your arm will feel, which should lead to less injury.

If you can afford the cost and inconvenience, you should change your string tension to match the playing conditions. Clay courts are notoriously slow and rob you of ball pace. If you were to reduce the string tension somewhat, you could gain back some of the energy the clay takes away from you. Grass courts are known to be very fast, and extra pace from the racket is not needed. So, when playing on grass or other fast surfaces, string your racket a bit tighter, and enjoy the extra control it may give you. The pros will have their rackets strung at different tensions when playing on different surfaces, in dissimilar climates, with different balls, and at varying altitudes. All these factors make a difference on their string-tension preference, just as the size of their racket head makes a difference on how the racket plays. Bjorn Borg, the great Swedish player, used to string his wood rackets very tightly for more control. At night when he was asleep, sometimes the strings would break because of the high tension and probably a weakness in one of the strings. The breaking of the strings in his racket would sound like a gunshot, which needless to say scared anyone in earshot and would awaken Borg from his sleep. The morning of every match, Borg would take out a number of rackets all strung at different tensions. He would practice with all of them and then select the tension that seemed best for those particular courts, the weather that day, the balls, and the way he felt. He then would select rackets strung at that tension for use that day.

The strings provide the force needed to give the ball spin. To propel the ball back to the opponent, the strings exert a force on the ball perpendicular to the string plane. To put spin on the ball, the strings exert a force on the ball that is parallel to the string plane. To produce topspin, the racket trajectory has an upward component. For underspin, the racket trajectory has a downward component. The friction between the strings and the ball is responsible for most of the spin-producing force.

It is common lore that tighter strings allow you to produce more spin, as do thinner strings and greater spacing between strings. This again is a case in which the definitive experiment has not been done to prove or disprove the anecdotal information that exists. One attempt to modify the stringing pattern to allow players to put more spin on the ball was the "spaghetti" stringing in which rubber bands were woven into the string pattern to increase the friction between the ball and the string plane. This was so successful that it threatened to change the basic nature of the game of tennis, and because of that, it was subsequently outlawed by the ITF.

It is amazing to see what happens with strings and what some players will do to have the tension the same in every racket every day that they play. Pete Sampras gets every one of his rackets strung every day during a tournament with 16-gauge gut so that they will play exactly as he expects them to if he breaks a string or has to change rackets. He feels that the change in tension by nonuse for one day changes the tension enough to make a difference. Needless to say he goes through hundreds of sets of gut during one year. For the average player, this is not necessary and of course the cost is prohibitive. Once the string has been in the racket for a short period of time, it will play about the same as it slowly loses its life. Most of the time it will break before it goes dead if you play more than a couple of times a week.

Today, the good junior players, club players, and certainly the pros break strings very quickly and have to restring their rackets often. It is a little tricky getting rackets strung by different people on different stringing machines because every racket can come out differently, even though you ask for the same tension. It is always good to have someone else with the same size racket have his racket strung first and then you test the tension in his racket before you request a tension for yours. The other variables for the tension you should use are the string pattern and the gauge string that you put in your racket.

With the heavy topspin that some players impart today, the strings are moved around in their rackets dramatically. You will see the players adjusting the strings with their fingers in between points to get the strings back in their grooves. If the strings are out of alignment, they will not play as well as they should. In addition, the moving of the strings against each other will cause a sawing effect that will notch the strings and cause premature breakage.

Chapter Three

Adjusting to Different Surfaces

Andrew Coe
David Miley

Playing a tennis match is all about developing and implementing a particular game plan that can defeat the opponent on the particular court surface where the match is played.

This chapter identifies court surface characteristics as well as the most important skills of a successful professional player (tactical, technical, physical, and psychological) and outlines how these differ according to different court surfaces.

Introduction

There are few sports in which the surface that the activity takes place on influences the nature of that activity as the court surface does to tennis. There are no other major sports that are played on as wide a variety of surface types, including at the highest levels of the professional game, as with the sport of tennis.

The importance of the court surface to the nature of tennis is the very reason for the proliferation of tennis surface types, which have developed from the earliest days in the evolution of lawn tennis, when the game was indeed played on the garden lawns of Victorian England. The limitations provided by a varying climate, the seasons, and the maintenance demands required to produce a natural turf surface of acceptable quality soon led to alternatives being sought in the form of clay (originally crushed brick), followed by other granular mineral surfaces, cement, asphalt, macadam, and wood. As polymer and material technology developed throughout the 20th century, the introduction of new man-made, synthetic surface types accelerated—hard courts with polymer coatings, cushioned coatings, rubberized shock pads, textiles, rubberized sheet carpets, artificial turf, sand-filled artificial turf, plastic modular systems, and so forth. With an estimated three-quarters of a million tennis courts in more than 200 countries worldwide, few would dispute the inference that the liberalism that tennis has allowed, in regulating the type of material tennis is played on, has contributed to the growth of tennis internationally and greatly increased access to the sport.

Patrick Rafter playing on a clay court.

At a time when grassroots participation is being targeted for growth in most of the traditionally strong tennis nations, the necessity to innovate has never been more important. Major opportunities exist for the development of surfaces that are safer, more uniform and predictable in performance, more durable, have lower construction and maintenance costs, are suitable for multisport use, and so forth. Research and innovation are crucial in any industry, and without the commercial opportunity provided by new product development, an industry can stagnate and fade.

However, innovation always must be balanced against the need to protect the nature of a sport. In the interest of tennis itself and for the enjoyment and safety of those who play tennis, some limitations and definitions eventually must be placed on the nature and physical characteristics of the court surface. The governing bodies of many sports in which the surface plays an important role (e.g., soccer, field hockey, golf, basketball, cricket, and track and field) have introduced, or are in the process of developing, formal qualifications of one kind or another for the type of surface considered suitable for use at various levels of competition. Such qualifications primarily are designed to provide the players of such sports with improved performance, generally defined as being a more consistent or more predictable surface to play on. In tennis, the qualities of consistency and predictability in the bounce of the ball are important factors in ensuring high-quality play.

It should be no surprise, then, that the tennis industry recently invested in research programs designed to help characterize and define the nature of the interaction between the tennis ball and the court surface and also the tennis player and the court surface. Tennis court surfaces now can be classified according to their pace characteristics, which until recently was only possible through anecdotal reports from tennis players.

What Is Pace?

Tennis players use the term "pace." It is a term that is used widely, but perhaps not so widely understood. Players may define pace as a number of different things:

- The speed (velocity) of the incoming ball as delivered by their opponents
- A fast- or slow-paced surface
- Fast- or slow-paced balls
- Low-bouncing (skidding) balls

- High-bouncing (kicking) balls
- A combination of these

From the player's point of view it is important to understand more about what is meant by the term "pace" in order to predict how a surface is likely to play, and predict how a particular type of ball is likely to play on that surface.

As alluded to here, from a scientific viewpoint we need to understand more about pace in order to

- design, manufacture, and construct better-performing court surfaces, and
- design and manufacture better-performing tennis balls and shoes.

As already stated, the wide variety of surface materials that tennis is played on greatly influences the way the game is played. In its extreme forms this has resulted in the evolution of quite different styles of play, designed to take advantage of the differing "pace" of these various surfaces. More on this adaptation to the surface later in this section.

To help illustrate the key differences among three important surface types—grass, hard court, and clay—studies have been carried out to measure the rebound angle of a standard pressurized tennis ball on such surfaces. In all cases the ball was projected onto the surface at the same velocity (30 meters per second) and angle (16 degrees). See figure 3.1.

We can draw the following conclusions from the data:

- On slow-paced surfaces (e.g., clay), the ball rebounds at a higher (steeper) angle.

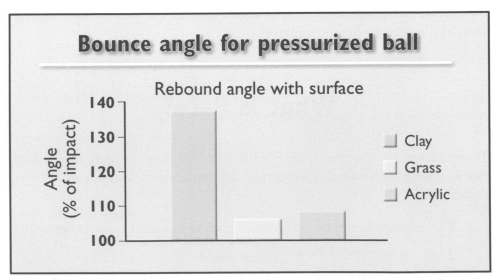

Figure 3.1
Comparison of rebound angles for different surfaces.

Cedric Pioline playing on a grass court.

- On medium-paced surfaces (e.g., acrylic hard court), the ball may be regarded as rebounding at a normal angle.
- On fast-paced surfaces (e.g., grass), the ball rebounds at a lower (shallower) angle.

At this stage it would be useful to introduce the concept of "response time." This is the time that a tennis player has to make a judgment about the speed, angle, and trajectory of the ball delivered by his or her opponent and to take the correct action to return the ball. The time taken for the ball to travel from the opponent's racket face to the point of impact with the court surface is, of course, the same on all surface types. The difference in response time between a surface that plays "slow" and one that plays "medium" or "fast" is a result of the interaction between ball and surface.

As a result of the differences in rebound angle described here, arising from the interaction between ball and surface, we can conclude the following:

- All other things being equal, a ball rebounding at a higher (steeper) angle from the surface (e.g., on clay) will give the player more response time.
- All other things being equal, a ball rebounding at a lower (shallower) angle from the surface (e.g., on grass) will give the player less response time.

Adjusting to Different Surfaces

How much slower is a "slow" court than, for example, a "medium-fast" court? What is the difference in response time between a clay court and an acrylic-coated hard court? Initial studies indicate the following response times for a typical 120-mph serve and using a standard-size, pressurized ball:

Clay court—0.678 seconds

Acrylic-coated hard court—0.640 seconds

Difference—0.038 seconds

At face value, these differences in response time—between surfaces that most players of any reasonable standard will readily acknowledge to have quite different playing characteristics—may appear to be very small. However, even given the fact that a good tennis player learns how to anticipate aspects of his opponent's play, any player receiving a 120-mph serve needs to make judgments about the speed, angle, direction, and spin of a ball as it leaves the opponent's racket.

The *effective* response time that a tennis player has when facing a serve therefore may be around 0.3 to 0.4 second. The difference in response time between a clay court and a medium or medium-fast hard-court surface is perhaps only 0.03 to 0.04 of a second, or little more than 10 percent of the response time.

Regardless of surface, players have to make judgments about the speed, angle, direction, and spin of the ball as it leaves the opponent's racket.

The Effect of Spin

Skilled tennis players will attempt to impart spin onto a ball to influence its trajectory in one way or another. To understand how a spinning ball behaves and is influenced by the characteristics of the court surface, we first must understand more about the nature of the ball-surface interaction.

Does a tennis ball slide or roll when it hits a court surface? A ball impacting a court surface will either slide, roll, or slide and roll in combination. In general, a tennis ball will slide at the beginning of impact. The ball will slide throughout the entire length of the impact if

- the impact angle is sufficiently shallow,
- the incoming ball speed is sufficiently fast, or
- there is sufficient underspin on the ball before impact.

The predictive model allows us to define under what circumstances a ball slides, rolls, or both slides and rolls during an oblique impact with the court surface. (See figure 3.2.)

For a given speed and angle, there will be one particular spin that corresponds to rolling. For a ball with a specific incoming rate of spin this means that the ball will be rolling at the start of the impact—marked on figure 3.3 as the "always rolling" point.

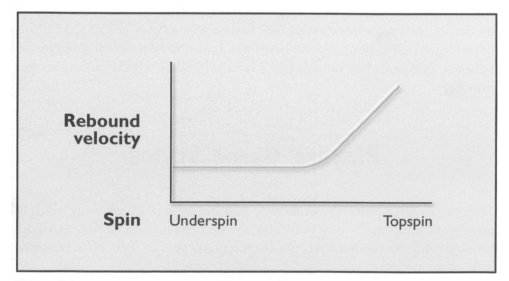

Figure 3.2
Relationship between rebound speed and spin rate for a given impact velocity.

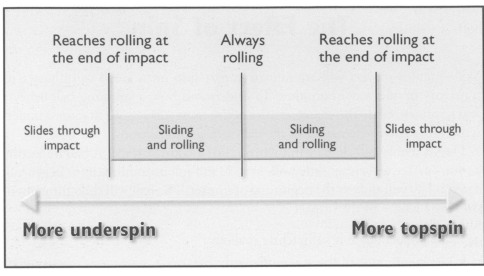

Figure 3.3
How the nature of the ball impact varies with spin.

A ball with a high rate of underspin will slide across the surface throughout its impact. As the incoming rate of underspin decreases, a point will be reached where the ball begins to roll across the surface at the end of the impact. With an increasing rate of incoming topspin the ball will impact with a mixture of sliding and rolling. At higher rates of topspin the ball will tend to roll more than slide. In reality, it is unlikely that a ball will ever reach the point where it is rolling throughout the impact, as this may require incoming spin rates in excess of 600 radians per second (5730 revolutions per minute). Elite tennis players have been found to impart ball spin rates of between 200 and 300 radians per second (1910 to 2865 revolutions per minute).

Players' Game Styles

Each player has a particular game style that can be recognized easily. Each of these game styles tends to be more effective on certain surfaces. The technical, physical, and mental characteristics of each player usually will define the game style of the player.

The main styles of play in professional tennis today can be summarized as follows:

- *The net rusher/serve-and-volleyer.* These players have the ability to combine both serve and volley and approach and volley very well and are continually trying to move forward to the net. When complemented by a high percentage of first serves, pressure is placed on an opponent who, in turn, will be forced to repeatedly produce an accurate pass. This type of player usually is more effective on medium and fast surfaces than on slow ones. The games of Pat Rafter and Jana Novotna are good examples of this playing style.

- *The aggressive baseliner/good returner.* This type of player plays close to the baseline and endeavors to take the ball early with powerful ground strokes. The forehand is usually the big weapon and he or she attempts to dominate the point from the backcourt, often using the inside-out forehand to good effect. Although proficient on all types of surfaces, these players are particularly effective on slower- and medium-paced ones. They have good returns but usually lack a dominating serve. Andre Agassi and Monica Seles are good examples of this playing style.

- *The counter-puncher.* These are usually defensive baseline players who react to their opponent's play. They tend to allow their opponent to dictate the play and take the initiative in the points. These players usually play a bit farther back from the baseline than an aggressive baseliner and they hit consistent ground strokes, often mixing heavy topspin with very high and deep ball trajectories. They usually are very physically fit, fast around the court, and mentally very

Andre Agassi is an aggressive baseliner/good returner.

strong. They tend to be more effective on slow surfaces than on medium and fast ones. Michael Chang and Arantxa Sanchez-Vicario are two players who adopt this type of game style.

• *The all-round player.* These players are capable of playing with and against all styles of play because of a good all-round technique and their ability to make use of a variety of paces and consistency. They are very effective on all types of surfaces because they can adapt their play to suit the surface, the opponent, or both. Pete Sampras in the men's game and Martina Hingis and Venus Williams in the women's game are good examples of this type of game style.

While the player's body type and mentality often help to determine the game style adopted, the court surface on which the player grew up and developed his game is perhaps the most significant determinant of an individual's playing style. Obviously the best type of player to try to develop is the all-round or all-

Martina Hingis is a good all-round player.

court player. In order to do so, the coach and, in turn, the player should ensure from an early age that the training sessions and private practice incorporate work on all five game situations: serving, returning, rallying from the baseline with both players back, passing, and approaching the net/volleying.

However, they should do so on a variety of court surfaces both in training and in matches. The player who develops her game exclusively on one surface is unlikely to develop an all-court game. In professional tennis today, the two most common (and successful) game styles and those most suited to the challenge of playing competitively on a variety of surfaces are the aggressive baseliner and the all-round player.

Match Strategy and Tactics

All players need to develop a specific strategy and tactics for each match. This should take into account many factors, such as the following:

- The player himself (e.g., his own strengths)
- The opponent (e.g., the opponent's weaknesses or style of play)
- The environment of the match (e.g., the surface, the altitude)

They also will have to be ready to adapt the tactics during the match according to the situations encountered. Irrespective of this, one of the greatest influences on the tactics chosen is the court surface the match is played on. Before looking at the tactical implications of playing on different court surfaces, let's look at some of the most fundamental tactics required for players to achieve success:

- *Play percentage tennis.* Eighty-five percent of tennis points are not won— they are, in fact, lost as a result of an error. There are some keys to avoiding errors: clear the net on every shot, use a margin for error, hit the ball high and deep to gain time, play the ball back in the same direction for safety, get into position early, work the point before attacking, and so forth.

- *Keep the ball in play.* This is the most obvious but also the most important tactic in tennis. You need to be consistent if you want to achieve good results in matches.

- *Analyze your opponent.* During match play, the player has to be able to (a) recognize and evaluate the tactical plans of her opponent, and (b) analyze the impact of her own tactics on the match. The player then will need to draw conclusions on what to do to overcome any negative situations.

- *Put your opponent under pressure.* Modern tennis demands that almost all successful players have an attacking mentality and continually try to apply pressure on their opponents. They are capable of taking advantage of half opportunities and attacking when an opening is created. The faster the surface, the more important this attacking mentality becomes.

- *Use your strengths.* All players have certain strengths that their game is based on. Some players have great serves, others have great forehands, some a good net game, and for others their passing shots are their strength. These players usually will construct their strategy and tactics around the strengths in which they have absolute confidence. The extent to which they can use their strengths will depend on the surface. For example, on grass a net rusher might serve and volley on all serves, but on clay he may do so only 50 percent of the time and only on first serves.

- *Exploit your opponent's weaknesses.* You should try to take advantage of your opponent's weaknesses by forcing her to play in more unfamiliar game situations or play her weaker strokes (e.g., draw an aggressive baseliner into the net with a drop shot to make her volley).

- *Play your own game/play the ball.* You should concentrate primarily on playing your own game and not change your style dramatically to suit either the opponent or the court surface. A good example of this occurred some years ago with Ivan Lendl. At Wimbledon he changed his game style dramatically (slicing backhands, serving and volleying on second serves, etc.) and never looked comfortable. However, Andre Agassi in the same circumstances made minor adjustments to his game but continued to use the game style that he was comfortable with (aggressive baseliner) on all surfaces. As we know, he has won grand-slam singles titles on all four surfaces. Many people believe that if Lendl had played with his normal game style at Wimbledon he might have won the title there.

- *Avoid unforced errors.* There are two types of errors: forced and unforced. Forced errors are the ones made by a player due to a forcing shot of the opponent. They are considered "good errors." An example of a forced error could be a mistake returning a good first serve. On the other hand, unforced errors are those made by a player when in control of the ball. They are considered "bad errors." An example of an unforced error could be a mistake made when returning a short second serve. On slower surfaces where there is more time to prepare and get in position there should be less of a necessity to take "risks," and therefore the number of unforced errors should be kept to a minimum. The mentality of the player on slower surfaces also needs to change, with patience (building the point, waiting for the opening) being the key to accepting the necessity for longer rallies and consistency.

• *Use the court space effectively.* You need to be able to use the court space as effectively as possible in order to win points. This can involve some of the following:

1. Hitting to the open court—the player should aim to hit the ball away from the opponent.

2. Hitting behind the opponent—this ploy is used to good effect against very quick players who tend to anticipate the change of direction of the shot, and it is even more effective on more slippery courts (clay).

3. Using angles and spin to open the court and then going flat down the line to win the point.

4. Using combinations of shots (e.g., ground strokes deep down the line, followed by a shot hit short and crosscourt; volley deep down the line followed by a short, angled volley crosscourt) to make the opponent move.

Tactical Patterns

In today's game, the successful players automate, through practice, a shot or a sequence of shots in an effort to repeat them with a high degree of consistency in match play. You should try to use the patterns of play most suited to your own individual game style and then adapt or modify them according to the court surface concerned.

For the player's self-belief and performance it is very important to develop patterns in which he has considerable confidence and where consistency is over 90 percent. Some of the most common tactical patterns for singles are summarized in table 3.1.

Effect of Court Surface on Play

As stated in the first part of this chapter, tennis is a sport played on many different types of surfaces (clay, grass, and hard courts). It also can be played indoors or out. We will now look at how these differences in court surface can affect the main psychomotor attributes (tactical, technical, physical, and psychological) that make up any tennis player.

Table 3.1

Common Singles Tactical Patterns

Game situation	Tactical pattern
Serve	Ace Serve direction: wide to open angles; to the "T" to close angles; to the body to avoid angles on the return Serve and volley Serve and attack with the strongest ground stroke to the open court, or behind the opponent Second serve and defend the point
Return	Attack a weak second serve with an attacking ground stroke Return and approach the net High deep ball to the weakest side of the opponent To the middle and deep against a big serve Short and low return to the feet of the serve-and-volleyer Block return
Playing from the baseline	Change directions (moving the opponent around the court) Hit with the best ground stroke (i.e., inside-out or big forehand) Hit to the open court Hit behind the opponent (to wrong-foot him) Play the big "X" (crosscourts) Make the player come to the net
Approaching and net game	Approaching: to the open court; to the weak side of the opponent; deep and low; short and angled; high (moon ball) and deep; to the middle Approaching as the ball is being played on the other side (as though sneaking in) Midcourt volley: deep and low, short and angled, topspin/drive volley Volley: to the open court, behind the opponent, hard and angled Smash: to the open court, behind the opponent, hard and angled
Passing the net player	Direct passing: short crosscourt, deep down the line, hard to the body Two-ball passing; making the net player volley up, then pass crosscourt or down the line Lob: deep and high, to the backhand

Tactical Differences

There are several tactical differences when playing on various surfaces. Clay courts are best suited to a more secure serve with heavy topspin. For the first serve, players tend to employ a variety of spins or angles rather than just going for power. Returns often can be aggressive since the receiver has more time to prepare for the shot. High, deep returns also are a very common pattern. The baseline game is the most-used game situation on this surface with the basic pattern of play consisting of quite long rallies with high and deep balls that try to keep the opponent behind the baseline. The midcourt game involves angled shots and drive volleys used to close out the point. Players tend to take advantage of short balls by approaching the net with hard, flat strokes or, alternatively, by hitting a winner from the midcourt. Players also can use a combination of high shots with a lot of topspin, and then semiflat shots, to finish the point

Gustavo Kuerten executing a forehand on clay.

or to advance to the net. The net game is used less than on medium and fast courts, with deep volleys or put-away overheads being the most common shots in this game situation. When passing the net player, players tend to use a two-ball passing-shot tactic with dipping topspin ground strokes in combination with topspin lobs to create an opening for the easy second pass. Players also should learn to use (with a similar preparation to the ground strokes for disguise) the drop shot as an offensive weapon and a winning shot.

Indoor and hard courts allow for flatter and faster serves than those typically done on clay courts. When returning, players should endeavor to attack yet be prepared to defensively block the more powerful serves as well as the serves hit right at the body. The medium to fast speed of indoor and hard courts tends to be preferred by players with an all-round game. The basic pattern of play consists of rallies with deep balls combined with approaches to the net and the net game. The baseline game demands that flatter strokes be played, whereas the midcourt game consists of low and midcourt volleys as a means of advancing to the net. Players should play short balls behind the opponent and continue to move forward when hitting the high volley. The net game—more pronounced than on clay—should involve volleying to the open court, with short angled

Jared Palmer blocks a serve hit right at the body.

volleys and aggressive overheads. Similarly, when passing the net player, players tend to use offensive lobs and to complement and add variety to the hard passing shots played with topspin or hit semiflat. Players should remember that different strategies are needed against different opponents and that they have to be prepared to use a combination of shots hit with different spins and heights.

Grass and very fast courts allow for both a faster serve with minimal spin and an angled serve with slice. With more slice applied to flatter shots, the ball passes over the net with a lower trajectory to further minimize the time an opponent has to prepare for the forthcoming shot. For returns, players should use abbreviated backswings to play the ball (a) high and deep to provide sufficient time for recovery or advancement toward the net (against a player staying back), and (b) low at the feet of their incoming opponent (against a serve-and-volleyer). The baseline game is the least-used game situation on this surface. The basic pattern of baseline play consists of very short rallies with fast and flat balls attempting to keep the opponent away from the net. Players should try to attack all short balls, be aggressive, and move in to close out the point as soon as an opening occurs. They should let the ball bounce as little as possible and volley crosscourt to the open court or, alternatively, use the drop shot. The midcourt game also is very important with numerous half volleys and low volleys being played as preparation shots for the net game to follow. The net game is the most common game situation on these surfaces with players often required to play all kinds of volleys and overheads. When passing the net player, players tend to use a variety of lobs and passing shots with a combination of different spins.

Technical Differences

There are several technical differences that are the result of playing or developing a game on various surfaces. Clay courts allow for more extreme grips (western and semi-western on the forehand and two-handed and extreme grips on the backhand) because the ball bounces higher. From a biomechanical perspective, these grips are the most suitable for hitting balls above shoulder height. The reduced speed of the ball on these courts also allows players to develop larger backswings on the ground strokes as a means of generating the greater racket speed required to apply more spin to the ball. Topspin is the most-used spin on clay courts since it helps to keep the ball bounce very high and deep. Players tend to use mostly ground strokes with the open stance, which facilitates the effective body rotation (angular momentum) necessary to develop optimal power.

Indoor and hard courts allow for intermediate grips such as the eastern and semi-western grip. The ball bounces are lower than on clay and these grips are the most suitable for balls played between shoulder and waist height. The medium speed of the ball on these courts also allows the players to develop more compact backswings on their ground strokes. Topspin is also the most often-used spin on medium-speed courts since a high and deep bouncing ball continues to be of considerable tactical importance. The stances used for the ground strokes tend to be more between open and semi-open.

Grass and very fast courts allow for classic grips such as the eastern or continental grips (less common today) on both sides. The ball bounce is quite low and these grips are the most suitable for hitting balls between waist and knee height. The fast speed of the ball on these courts also allows the players to develop very short backswings in the ground strokes. Topspin can be used on the ground strokes, but flat and slice shots are very common on these fast courts in that they help create a very low ball bounce. Players tend to play mostly serves and volleys. Less body rotation is required because players can use the pace of the court and linear momentum to help generate optimal power.

Physical Differences

When the game is played on clay, matches tend to be long and physically very demanding because the aerobic endurance of the player is challenged. Players often use the strategy of physically tiring the opponent, reasoning that the surface allows for the return of most shots. They also have to learn to slide on lateral and forward movements. In order to be successful on clay courts, players need to build a good level of physical fitness through physical preparation both on and off the court.

On slower indoor or hard courts it is generally the anaerobic lactic endurance system that is challenged during matches. On the other hand, players should use footwork effectively. They should try to prevent possible future injuries by using well-cushioned shoes and stretching before and after matches.

On grass or very fast courts it is generally the anaerobic alactic endurance system that is challenged during matches. Players need to be very fast, agile, and flexible to reach the net as soon as possible. They can practice two-on-one drills to help shorten their swing preparation and quicken their reflexes.

Psychological Differences

When playing on clay, you need to prepare mentally to accept long rallies. You also need to effectively use the time between points for recovery and to plan the next point. Patience is the key word on this surface.

When playing on an indoor or hard surface, you have to prepare mentally to accept rallies of different lengths. Adaptation is the key word on these surfaces.

Patrick Rafter demonstrates the need to be fast, agile, and flexible when playing on a grass court.

You also should be ready to play opponents with different game styles and thus be prepared to change your tactics according to the opponent, the strategy, and the score of the match.

When playing on grass and very fast courts, you should be prepared mentally to accept very short rallies. You need to concentrate very well since the percentage of "dead time" will be greater than when playing on other surfaces. Concentration is the key word on this surface because you need to be very focused on the match and to take advantage of the chances (which tend to occur less than on slower surfaces) when they come.

Adjusting to Different Surfaces

Chapter Four

Training Muscles for Strength and Speed

Todd Ellenbecker
Craig Tiley

The game of tennis has unique physical demands and requirements for successful players. Tennis stresses all areas of the body, with overuse injuries reported in the upper and lower body and trunk in both recreational and elite-level players. A tennis match can contain anywhere from 300 to 500 bursts of energy and it can last more than four hours. This requires not only elite levels of muscular strength, but also muscular endurance and both aerobic and anaerobic fitness. The purpose of this chapter is to outline the major muscles used during tennis ground strokes and serve as well as to provide information regarding tennis-specific training for strength and speed development. Also covered are important concepts of flexibility and actual tips for integrating these training methods into complete programs for players.

Tennis stresses every area of the body.

Types of Muscular Contractions in Tennis

There are three primary types of muscular actions that the human body is capable of, and all three are used to some extent in tennis. These three types are isometric, concentric, and eccentric. Tennis is a very dynamic or movement-dominant sport, so concentric and eccentric actions predominate; however, the stabilizing role of isometric muscle work cannot be overlooked. By definition, an isometric muscular contraction is one in which engagement or contraction of the muscle occurs without joint movement. An example of this type of contraction is a player pushing his hands together very hard with no movement

Ellenbecker and Tiley

occurring. Isometric contractions are used by the body to stabilize joints or hold a certain position or posture.

During tennis play, most of the muscular work is dynamic in nature and consists of concentric and eccentric actions. A concentric contraction occurs when the muscle contracts and actual shortening of the muscle fibers occurs. The origin and insertion of the muscle move toward each other. An example of a concentric contraction can be illustrated by the biceps muscle in the arm when an arm-curl exercise is performed. The hand moves toward the shoulder as the muscle shortens and a weight or object is raised toward the body. Concentric actions usually are used by the body in sports to accelerate a limb or body segment.

The opposite type of contraction is termed an eccentric contraction. During an eccentric contraction the origin and insertion of the muscle move away from one another while the muscle fibers lengthen. These types of muscular contractions typically are used by the body to decelerate limbs or body segments and to assist the body in shock absorption and stabilization.

Because all three types of muscular contractions are used by the body during tennis play, particularly both shortening and lengthening contractions of the muscle during dynamic movements, both of these types of contractions must be worked or emphasized in tennis-specific training programs.

Muscle Groups Used During Tennis Play

To better understand which muscles are used in tennis play, scientists use electromyography and high-speed filming to identify the amount of muscle activity during each phase or portion of tennis strokes. This allows sport scientists, strength and conditioning specialists, and coaches to focus on specific muscles and joint movement patterns that are inherent in tennis play. Tables 4.1 through 4.3 outline the activity of the major muscle groups during specific phases of each of the tennis strokes.

Several common activity patterns can be identified by reviewing these tables. During the forehand and serve, most of the muscles in the front of the chest and trunk serve as the primary accelerators or force generators (i.e., pectorals, abdominals, quadriceps, and biceps). Muscles in the back of the body primarily serve as decelerators for the body during the tennis serve and forehand (i.e., rotator cuff, rhomboids, and back extensors). Since these two strokes (tennis serve and forehand) are the primary power strokes in most tennis players' games, the accelerator muscles often become overdeveloped at the expense of the

Table 4.1

Muscular Activity
During the Forehand Ground Stroke

Action	Muscles used
Acceleration phase	
Lower body push-off	Gastrocnemius/soleus, quadriceps, gluteals (concentric)
Trunk rotation	Obliques, abdominals, back extensors (concentric/eccentric)
Forward swing	Anterior deltoid, subscapularis, biceps, serratus anterior, pectoralis major, wrist flexors, forearm pronators (concentric)
Follow-through phase	
Lower body	Gastrocnemius/soleus, quadriceps, gluteals (eccentric)
Trunk rotation	Obliques, back extensors, abdominals (concentric/eccentric)
Arm deceleration	Infraspinatus/teres minor, triceps, serratus anterior, rhomboids, trapezius, wrist extensors, forearm supinators (eccentric)

Table 4.2

Muscular Activity During
the One-Handed Backhand Ground Stroke

Action	Muscles used
Acceleration phase	
Lower body push-off	Gastrocnemius/soleus, quadriceps, gluteals (concentric)
Trunk rotation	Obliques, abdominals, back extensors (concentric/eccentric)
Arm forward swing	Infraspinatus/teres minor, posterior deltoid, rhomboid, serratus anterior, trapezius, triceps, wrist extensors (concentric)
Follow-through phase	
Trunk rotation	Obliques, back extensors, abdominals (concentric/eccentric)
Arm deceleration	Subscapularis, pectoralis major, biceps, wrist flexors (eccentric)

Table 4.3

Muscular Activity During the Serve and Overhead

Action	Muscles used
Preparation phase	
Lower body	Gastrocnemius/soleus, quadriceps, gluteals (eccentric)
Trunk rotation	Obliques, abdominals, trunk extensors (concentric/eccentric)
Cocking phase	
Trunk extension and rotation	Back extensors (concentric), obliques (concentric/ eccentric), abdominals (eccentric)
Arm motion	Infraspinatus/teres minor, supraspinatus, biceps, serratus anterior, wrist extensors (concentric), subscapularis, pectoralis major (eccentric)
Acceleration phase	
Lower body	Gastrocnemius/soleus, gluteals, quadriceps (concentric), hamstrings (eccentric)
Trunk rotation	Abdominals, obliques (concentric), back extensors (eccentric)
Arm motion	Subscapularis, pectoralis major, serratus anterior, triceps, wrist flexors, forearm, pronators (concentric), biceps (eccentric)
Follow-through phase	
Lower body	Gastronemius/soleus, quadriceps, gluteals (eccentric)
Trunk rotation	Back extensors (eccentric), obliques, abdominals (concentric/eccentric)
Arm deceleration	Infraspinatus/teres minor, serratus, trapezius, rhomboids, wrist extensors, forearm, supinators (eccentric)

decelerators. This leads to a muscle imbalance and can serve as an important factor predisposing a player to injury.

During the backhand, the opposite relationship is seen. The muscles in the back of the shoulder and trunk function as accelerators while the muscles in the chest and front of the body primarily act in a deceleration role during follow-through.

Another common activity pattern or combination is that while one muscle or muscle group is serving as an accelerator, its antagonistic (opposing) muscle group is working as a decelerator. An example of this can be demonstrated by analyzing the upper arm during the serve. As you straighten your elbow using

Training Muscles for Strength and Speed

Serena Williams uses the muscles of the legs, chest, and trunk to provide most of the force in forehands and serves.

the triceps muscle during the acceleration phase of the serve, the biceps muscle contracts eccentrically to help decelerate and control the straightening of the elbow to prevent injury and to control the position that is established before and after contact. This paired concept is important to remember when training muscles for strength and speed development.

Joint Kinematics—Speeds of Motion

Another important concept to consider when training is the enormous speed of the joints during tennis-specific movement patterns. For example, when you

Ellenbecker and Tiley

are walking, the knee joint moves approximately 240 degrees per second. The shoulder by comparison during a tennis serve actually rotates internally during the acceleration phase at more than 2,500 degrees per second. This occurs so fast it actually is hard to comprehend. To put this in relative terms, the rotation of the shoulder into internal rotation during the tennis serve occurs at approximately the speed of rotation of the wheels of a bike when it is going 32 mph, or more simply, 417 times faster than the second hand on your watch. To control this rapid motion, the muscles must work properly, both when shortening and lengthening, as well as at fast speeds repetitively. Table 4.4 contains information about some of the other angular velocities in tennis strokes.

Table 4.4

Angular Velocities of the Upper Extremity in Tennis

Action	Angular velocity
Serve Shoulder internal rotation Elbow extension Wrist flexion	1000-2500 degrees per second 1700 degrees per second 315 degrees per second
Forehand Shoulder internal rotation	350-750 degrees per second
Backhand Shoulder external rotation	350-650 degrees per second

Flexibility Training for Tennis Players

It is important to mention flexibility training before discussing specific aspects of strength training for tennis players. Flexibility is an extremely important aspect of training, and one that often gets overlooked and is underutilized. Flexibility is described literally as the ability of the muscles, tendons, and connective tissue around joints to elongate to allow range of motion. There are several types of flexibility exercises that can be applied to a tennis player's training program.

Mary Pierce's serve demonstrates the speed of shoulder rotation.

Types of Flexibility Training

There are two main types of flexibility exercises that can be used for tennis players. Each of these has distinct advantages and limitations.

Static Stretching

Static stretching is by far the most popular and most widely recommended form of stretching for tennis players. It is very safe and is effective when applied in a consistent and systematic way (Sobel et al. 1995). Static stretching involves isolation of a particular muscle or muscle group by using traditionally described positions. Once the player assumes a position that appropriately isolates the muscle group desired, tension slowly and gradually is increased by lengthening the muscle and then statically holding an endpoint position over a period of time. Although many different hold times have been mentioned in the sports science literature, hold times between 15 and 30 seconds have been recom-

Ellenbecker and Tiley

Monica Seles' flexibility allows her a greater range of motion.

mended most often. Holding longer than 30 seconds does not harm the body, but it also does not consistently increase gains in flexibility. Therefore, because time always is limited in a tennis player's training program, two to three repetitions of each stretch holding between 15 and 30 seconds are recommended.

Table 4.5 contains the recommended sequence for enhancing the effectiveness of a static stretching program. Care must be taken not to bounce or perform ballistic-type movement as this actually can activate the stretch reflex and hinder the relaxation of the muscle. A slow, controlled movement during stretching with normal, relaxed breathing also is recommended.

Dynamic Stretching

Dynamic stretching involves the simulation of sport-specific movement patterns without excessive impact or weight bearing. It is particularly effective immediately before performing an activity, either in training or tennis play. Examples of dynamic stretches include (a) making arm circles while holding the racket, (b) marching in place pulling the knees farther up toward the chest with each step, (c) butt kicks that involve jogging in place while kicking the feet up toward the buttocks, or (d) simulating tennis strokes such as ground strokes and serves with increasing intensity over a period of repetitions. Each of these dynamic stretches can be used after a gentle warm-up such as running in place, riding a stationary cycle, or doing calisthenics, as well as after a series of static stretches that prepare the muscles and joints for the dynamic movements.

Table 4.5

Components of a Static Stretching Program

Recommended sequence	Important points to enhance flexibility
General body warm-up (5-10 minutes) until you achieve a light sweat Perform static stretching of specific muscle groups using positions that isolate that group; use 2-3 stretches holding each 15-30 seconds Perform dynamic stretching with progressive increases in range and velocity of movements Play tennis Static stretching during cool-down	• Do not bounce • Don't stretch into painful ranges of motion; you should feel a moderate stretch only • Be sure to stretch after workouts or tennis play when your body is very warm • Do not lock your joints Emphasize slow, smooth movements and coordinate deep breathing • Stretch both sides of your body • Focus on tight areas; don't perform stretches only in areas you already have a lot of flexibility in

Recent research has questioned the use of static stretching immediately before maximal performance. These studies have measured the acute effects of stretching immediately before a vertical jump and other maximal-effort physical performance tests. Decreases in jump height and performance have been recorded in groups after performing a static stretching program. Though static stretching may prove beneficial for preventing injury and preparing the body for activity, it also may cause a short-term decrease in performance from muscles. Therefore, scientists have recently recommended static stretching after activity or, in this case, tennis play, as well as at least 20 to 30 minutes before actually playing tennis. Static stretching still can play an important role in prematch or pre-workout flexibility training; however, a period of 20 to 30 minutes may be a more optimal or appropriate rest period between pre-activity static stretching and maximal-level performance. The current pre-activity emphasis is on performing a warm-up followed by dynamic flexibility exercises immediately before tennis play based on this most recent research. Further research clearly is needed to provide guidance on the optimal flexibility programming to both prevent injury and enhance performance.

Dynamic stretching prepares your muscles for the type of movement used during play.

Integrating Flexibility Training Into Workouts: A Coach's Perspective

Integrating flexibility programming into workouts can be done using the example program to follow. This is similar to the program used at the University of Illinois. This program stresses an on-court warm-up sequence before stretching and emphasizes dynamic stretching immediately before tennis play. The post-practice or post-workout stretching program emphasizes static stretches to work on joint range of motion when the body is very warm and to help decrease post-workout stiffness.

Pre-Practice or Pre-Workout Stretching Routine

On-court warm-up

First lap

- Jog across baseline and sideline
- Shuffle, staying low across baseline

- Butt kicks to net
- High knees to starting point

Second lap

- Power skips across baseline
- Seventy-five percent effort across length of court
- Carioca step across baseline
- Jog back in

Stretches

1. Wrist and forearm stretches each way with both arms
2. Posterior shoulder stretches
3. Overhead shoulder stretch with racket
4. Hamstring stretch
5. Walking with high knees (hold at top) once across court
6. Walking with heel kicks (hold at top) once across court
7. Straight-leg front raises (right foot left hand, left foot right hand) once across court
8. Hip rotation (up and out) once across court
9. Forward-lunge right leg and right elbow to ground to left, and then other way (once across the court)
10. Leg swinging (10 per direction each leg)

Post-Practice or Post-Workout Static Stretching Routine

1. Circle up as a team (stretches 2 to 6 are done while standing up)
2. Groin stretch to the right
3. Groin stretch to the left
4. Posterior shoulder stretch
5. Right calf stretch
6. Left calf stretch
7. Butterfly (groin stretch)
8. Right leg out (hamstring)
9. Left leg out (hamstring)
10. Right leg to chest (ankle roll optional)
11. Left leg to chest (ankle roll optional)

12. Right quadriceps stretch
13. Left quadriceps stretch
14. Partner up and stretch hamstrings

Strength Training for Tennis Players

Properly training a tennis player to increase strength and muscular endurance takes a sport-specific approach. The information presented earlier in this chapter as well as throughout this book will enable coaches and strength-and-conditioning specialists to stress the appropriate muscles to promote muscular balance for both injury prevention and performance enhancement.

Muscle Groups to Emphasize

Arguably, virtually all muscles of the body are used during tennis play, and they do deserve some type of attention during training. The purpose of this chapter, however, is to highlight the most important muscles in the tennis player that should be trained and those muscles that need particular attention. A review of tables 4.1 to 4.3 will serve to highlight the major muscles and muscle groups that perform the essential acceleration and deceleration functions for the tennis player. Merely training the primary movers or accelerator muscles used in tennis can decrease performance and increase the risk of injury to the player. Therefore, careful balancing of muscular strength is of primary importance when training tennis players.

Training to Promote Muscular Balance

One of the best ways to present the concept of strength training to promote muscular balance can be achieved by citing specific examples in tennis players. For the purposes of this chapter, the shoulder and trunk will be used.

Shoulder

Several studies have been performed measuring shoulder strength in elite-level tennis players. One common finding is that the muscles in the front of the body including the pectorals and deltoids are very strong on the tennis-playing side, while the muscles in the upper back and shoulder blade such as the rotator cuff, rhomboids, and trapezius are relatively weak. This is particularly important since the muscles in the back of the shoulder provide stability and protection of the joint and act as primary decelerators of the arm during the follow-through phases of the serve and forehand. Therefore, exercises for the shoulder in tennis players should emphasize rotator-cuff strengthening, rowing, and other upper-back exercises in an attempt to balance these muscle groups. The rotator cuff is a group of four muscles and tendons spanning between the shoulder blade and head of the humerus or arm bone. Exercises are recommended for all levels of tennis play, and recent research has shown that just playing tennis does not develop these important muscles even in elite performers (Ellenbecker and Roetert 2000).

In addition to rotator-cuff exercises, exercises emphasizing the upper back and muscles around the shoulder blade are critically important. These include the seated-row, shoulder-punch, and step-up exercises, which are important for promoting upper-back strength and, ultimately, muscular balance.

Trunk

Similar to the shoulder area, the trunk is another area in tennis players where both muscular imbalances and injuries abound. Again research performed on

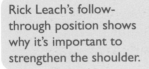

Rick Leach's follow-through position shows why it's important to strengthen the shoulder.

elite junior tennis players has helped to identify a strength imbalance between the muscles in the abdominal area and the lower back (Roetert et al. 1996). The abdominal muscles work to accelerate and stabilize the trunk during the serve and forehand, whereas the muscles in the lower back work very hard to both decelerate and stabilize the trunk during follow-through. Sports scientists and coaches for years have preached the importance of performing abdominal exercises and had their players literally doing hundreds of sit-ups per day. This research showed that elite-level players actually have greater abdominal strength than low-back strength. This creates an imbalance making the lower-back muscles seem weaker to the body. Therefore, you should include not only abdominal exercises in your strength training programs, but a series of lower-back exercises as well.

Several additional concepts regarding strengthening of the trunk should be considered. One of the most important new concepts regarding abdominal training is the "drawing-in" concept. This involves drawing or "sucking" in the abdomen similar to what is encountered when trying to get into pants with a smaller waistline than normal. This maneuver increases the activity of the main abdominal muscles as well as the obliques, which create and control rotation of the trunk. By performing the "drawing-in" maneuver, you can use virtually any exercise to strengthen the trunk. Combining this maneuver with traditional crunches, crunches with rotation, sit-ups over a therapy ball, or even bridging and other lower-body exercises is recommended.

This brings up several important points that must be discussed in any chapter about strength training. The first point is integration. Successful coaches and strength and conditioning professionals integrate several exercises and activities to achieve optimal benefit for the player with whom they are working. For example, having a player stand on one leg and perform a diagonal pattern with a medicine ball simulating the motion of the serve is definitely a good idea. However, placing the foot on a half foam roll to challenge the balance system as well as perform the "drawing-in" maneuver during the exercise increases the demands placed on abdominal musculature and greatly enhances the exercise.

The second point to consider involves the prevalence of trunk rotation in tennis training and performance. The use of trunk rotation is an example of how the human body applies the concept of angular momentum, and this angular or rotational momentum is an extremely important factor in power development in tennis. It is of paramount importance to train the muscles that provide and control rotation of the trunk. Again, clearly indicated is the integrating of an exercise that normally may involve only straight-plane or straight-ahead movements, such as a sit-up on a therapy ball, with a rotational movement to increase muscular activity by the obliques.

Strength Training Recommendations

One of the most difficult aspects of adding a strength training program for a tennis player is deciding the exact volume and intensity of strength training exercises to initiate. In general, several recommendations based on the specific demands of the game of tennis can provide valuable insight into this important step.

Intensity

Intensity is usually the most frequently asked question by the player. How much weight the player uses can be built nicely into the volume of the training session being designed. One of the most widely recommended methods for setting the intensity or amount of weight is the repetition maximum (RM) method. This method uses the number of repetitions performed each set as the factor for determining the resistance level. With this method, a weight is chosen that allows the player to perform the desired number of repetitions without substituting or breaking form, yet fatiguing the muscle or muscle groups involved by the final repetitions in that set.

For example, if the player is performing a 12- or 15-RM training program, one that often is recommended for tennis players for improving local muscular endurance and strength (Roetert et al. 1996; Roetert and Ellenbecker 1998; Fleck and Kraemer 1986), a weight would be chosen such that the player can perform either 12 or 15 reps in that set without breaking form. If that exercise is a bicep curl, a 10-pound weight may achieve this goal or two to three plates on an exercise machine. However, a 10-pound weight when used for a squat or calf raise may be entirely too light and not create muscular fatigue by the 12th or 15th repetition as desired. Strength training for tennis players often utilizes a 12- to 15-RM training intensity. Occasionally during a periodized training program, periods of training will be used focusing on strength and power with RM loading schemes of 8 to 10 repetitions per set. In general terms, the 12- to 15-RM loading scheme is an excellent guide for increasing both muscular strength and endurance in the tennis player.

Often players will try to use too much weight for exercises. This is where application of the RM system by the coach or strength-and-conditioning professional is essential. Providing the important framework for the player is an important part of a successful training program.

Sets and Reps

Equally important is the number of sets and repetitions, or volume of exercise. We just discussed how the volume of exercise directly affects the intensity of the load used during strength training. Again, in general terms, two to three sets of 12 to 15 repetitions often are recommended to encourage strength and endurance of the muscles being worked. Recent research supports this recommendation. Kraemer et al. (2000) compared a multiple-set resistance training program to a single-set resistance training program in female collegiate tennis players. Their findings showed superior gains in muscle strength and power as well as increases in serving velocity in the training group that used a multiple-set training program. Therefore, these recommendations appear to result in improvements in muscle strength power and endurance and have positive effects on tennis performance.

Timing and Periodization

Strength training exercises typically should be performed after skill-oriented workouts or tennis play. What is not considered optimal is to have the player working on court in a state in which the muscles already are fatigued from strength training. Therefore, most strength training should be performed after on-court or skill-oriented drills or match play. Often coaches have players perform their strength training on days when on-court play is minimized or decreased. This allows a greater emphasis on the strength training and does not interfere with on-court performance. Flexibility exercises should be performed after a copious warm-up and before strength training to optimally prepare the muscle for the challenges incurred during strength training and to minimize the risk of injury.

It is beyond the scope of this chapter to completely discuss the concept of periodization. Periodization consists of a long-term training program whereby the variables of rest and recovery, volume, intensity, frequency, and duration of performance and training are systematically manipulated and changed to allow an optimal adaptation to training and decrease the risk of injury or burnout. During a periodized program, several stages or cycles are utilized that have specific goals and activities. The preparation phase uses a great deal of strength training exercise with a goal of preparing the player for more tennis-specific training ahead. Lower-intensity training with higher volumes prevails during this cycle. The next phase is termed the precompetitive phase. This phase utilizes a greater number of tennis-specific training procedures and on-court performances as compared to the preparation phase. This phase also uses strength training but at a lower volume and greater intensity—for example, two sets of 10 reps as opposed to three sets of 15 reps in the preparation phase. Greater focus on power and strength is an inherent characteristic of exercises practiced during the precompetitive phase.

The competitive or peaking phase involves actual competition. Tennis matches and tournaments take place during this phase. Strength training plays a lesser role in this phase and typically consists of very light workouts to maintain strength levels and provide exercise between matches or on lighter days of performance. Finally, the transition or recovery phase includes a period of rest from tennis and high-level performance. Players often play other sports for fun during this time period, or they rest and rehabilitate injuries.

Tips for Integrating Strength Training

The strength training program included in this chapter is based on programming implemented at the University of Illinois. This program is performed three to four times per week in a gym, with each training session started by completing core strength work for the trunk and abdomen, followed by speed and power work, and then finishing up with stability exercises. Days one and two in the strength training sequence are used primarily for strength, power, and stability, with day three consisting of circuit training (muscle complex and medicine ball). This is an excellent example of how different types of strength training exercises can be grouped and varied to provide a training stimulus for the player, as well as to provide new challenges and changes in the training sequence to minimize staleness and boredom. Each workout is designed to last approximately 45 minutes to facilitate time management and allow other types of on-court training and tennis play. Each workout is preceded by 5 minutes of lower-body cycling or rope jumping as well as stretching.

Sample Workout

Day 1

Exercise	*Core program*
Back squat	Sit-ups 3 × 20
Bench press	Side bends 3 × 20
Dumbbell reverse fly	Reverse hypers 3 × 20
Seated rows	Reverse sit-ups 3 × 20
Dumbbell triceps extension	
Medicine-ball catches	
Four-way hip exercise	
Superman exercise	

Day 2
Exercise
Lateral lunges

Hammer curls

Three-way deltoids
  (raise to shoulder level only)

Shoulder external rotation

Lat pull-downs (behind head)

Dumbbell triceps kickbacks

Medicine-ball partner catches

Calves/shins

Core program
Sit-ups 3 × 20

Side bends 3 × 20

Reverse hypers 3 × 20

Reverse sit-ups 3 × 20

Day 3
Exercise
Muscle complex

Bent-over rows

Rotary torso

Four-way hip

Medicine-ball circuit

Core program
Sit-ups 3 × 20

Side bends 3 × 20

Reverse hypers 3 × 20

Reverse sit-ups 3 × 20

Additional Types of Resistance Training Techniques

In addition to the as-mentioned traditional exercises using dumbbells and weight machines, as well as the use of circuit training and plyometrics, another method of resistance training is recommended and implemented for tennis players. This method applies elastic resistance. The advantages of this type of resistance training are that (a) the exercise devices are portable; (b) resistance levels can be adjusted based on the density of the bands or tubes used, as well as the amount of elongation in the elastic device; and (c) research has shown positive changes in both muscular strength and endurance with their use. Again, several sets of 10 to 15 repetitions of elastic resistance exercises typically are employed and recommended for improving both strength and local muscular endurance.

Training for Explosive Power and Speed

One of the goals for training tennis players includes the characteristics of explosive power and speed. One of the common mistakes and myths about power and speed development is the thought that using a dumbbell or weight machine at fast speeds is all that is required. These traditionally applied methods are not appropriate at fast speeds and also may not be as safe. Therefore, coaches and strength-and-conditioning experts have used special types of exercises to improve speed and power development.

Technically, muscular power can be defined as the ability to perform work in a very fast or short period of time. An example of powerful movement patterns in tennis is the internal rotation movement of the shoulder during the serve, or the powerful drive forward by the legs after the serve as a player moves toward the net when serve-and-volleying before the split-step. If these movements can be performed only at slow speeds, performance clearly is hindered.

Plyometrics

Plyometrics is a type of training that has been used for years in many sports to obtain explosive power and speed development. This type of training was started in Eastern European countries and virtually has spread worldwide. Plyometric exercises begin with a stretch to the muscles through an eccentric or lengthening contraction. This eccentric contraction immediately is followed by a concentric or shortening contraction. The eccentric contraction serves to increase the strength and power of the subsequent concentric contraction and produces stronger and more powerful concentric contractions when compared to traditional concentric-only training programs (Chu 1992). The brief period of time between the eccentric contraction and the concentric contraction is called the amortization phase. It is the goal of plyometric exercises used for speed development to make this time period (amortization phase) as short as possible.

Plyometric-type training is very specific for tennis players and these types of muscular patterns are everywhere in tennis play. The quadriceps in the lower body, abdominals in the trunk, and shoulder internal rotators of the upper extremity are great examples of this patterning.

Application of Plyometrics to the Lower Body

As a right-handed player is pulled wide to hit an open-stance forehand, the right leg initially performs an eccentric muscle contraction with the quadriceps to absorb the force exerted by the body and decelerate the lateral movement to stabilize and balance the body for execution of the forehand. During the acceleration of the racket forward during the forehand, the quadriceps then immediately contracts concentrically to initiate the series of energy transfers to the hips, trunk, and, eventually, the upper body. This contraction sequence is typical of a plyometric activity.

Tennis-specific plyometric drills can be performed both on-court and in the weight room or off-court environment. An on-court method of plyometric training that serves to increase lateral speed and power is the "alley hop." This drill involves the player standing at one side of the doubles alley on the court and jumping or actually bounding back and forth as rapidly as possible, touching alternately the singles sideline and outer sideline of the doubles alley.

Typical lower-body plyometric drills performed off-court involve box jumps. In these plyometric drills, players jump from wooden or metal boxes 18 to 24 inches high. Upon the player's landing from the box, the quadriceps and calf muscles (gastrocnemius and soleus) undergo an eccentric contraction whereupon the player then immediately jumps up maximally performing a concentric contraction of the muscles. Many variations of these box-jump exercises have been used coupling the jump performance with a sprint or shuttle run to emulate various sport-specific movement patterns (Chu 1992). In general, plyometric exercises should be added or integrated into a total conditioning program for the tennis player and initiated only after the player has developed a baseline level of muscular fitness, because plyometrics utilize maximal levels of muscle work.

Application of Plyometrics to the Trunk

During the serve, players arch their backs into extension, which causes an eccentric contraction of the abdominal muscles that help to stabilize the spine. Immediately after this extension of the back, the player flexes or bends the spine forward contracting the abdominals concentrically. To simulate this type of contraction specificity, players and coaches can use a medicine ball to train the abdominals. Medicine-ball exercises can provide additional variety to the traditional sit-up abdominal exercises in a player's program.

Application of Plyometrics to the Upper Extremities

Following the examples mentioned earlier, the upper body functions in this pattern as the internal rotator muscles of the shoulder are eccentrically loaded during the cocking phase of the serve followed immediately by the powerful internal rotation before ball contact. However, since tennis players' dominant shoulder so typically contains a muscle imbalance with the internal rotators showing exceptional levels of strength and endurance (Ellenbecker and Roetert

Lleyton Hewitt shows how plyometric exercises can help players improve their speed when running for wide shots.

1999), additional plyometric training for the shoulder internal rotators typically is not performed or recommended. Plyometric exercises for the upper body, however, can be useful in the form of medicine-ball chest passes, side throws, and actual forehand and backhand ground stroke emulation. These passes can be performed with a partner or against a wall or angled trampoline to accentuate the rebound characteristics of the ball. Another plyometric exercise that can be used for general upper-body conditioning is the wall plyo. This partnered drill consists of one player standing about three feet away from a wall with the arms outstretched at shoulder level. A partner from behind pushes the player toward the wall. Upon contacting the wall, the player immediately and rapidly pushes back away from the wall, and the partner again pushes the player's back toward the wall. This is repeated to promote upper-body strength and power and especially helps to develop the muscles around the shoulder blade, triceps, and wrist flexors.

Additional Methods for Training Power and Speed

Several additional methods can be used to improve a player's speed and power development. One commonly applied method uses resistance cords (also called sport cords). These cords can be secured around a player's waist for both on-court and off-court speed and power development exercise. One typical drill emphasizes lateral speed development and consists of the coach holding one end of the cord while a player moves laterally at a maximum speed and with maximal effort. Resistance provided by the cord ensures that an overload is applied to the musculature that facilitates the development of speed and power.

Ellenbecker and Tiley

Another off-court method used in training and often in rehabilitation for power and speed development is isokinetic training. This type of training utilizes an isokinetic machine that, unlike other resistance training equipment, sets and holds constant the speed of the exercise, not the resistance. The isokinetic machines offer training at faster, more functional speeds and have been particularly effective in training the rotator cuff in elite-level tennis players.

Coach's Role in Integrating Speed Training

Many types of training techniques can be used to increase speed. Several key components should be inherent in the types of training drills used by tennis players. One of the most important components that must be considered is specificity. Does the drill specifically match the demands the player will encounter on the court? Speed training drills that utilize long spans of single-direction movement probably are not applicable to the tennis player. Therefore, the drills that coaches recommend and implement typically include multiple changes of direction, brief periods of maximal-effort movement, and work–rest cycles consistent with the physiological demands of the sport of tennis.

Summary

This chapter has presented information regarding the muscular demands and contraction types inherent in tennis-specific movement patterns. Training concepts for increasing flexibility, strength, and muscular endurance—as well as speed and power—have been presented. The integration of all of these training methods and concepts ultimately will enhance performance, prevent injuries, and facilitate proper tennis technique.

Chapter Five

Improving Footwork and Positioning

Donald Chu
Lynne Rolley

*"The whole movement potential of a tennis player is
determined by the individual conditioning and
coordination abilities, and that is why these abilities
must be continually integrated into tennis technique."*

Richard Schönborn, 1998
—Former head coach of the German Tennis Federation,
Davis Cup, and Federation Cup

Tennis is a sport that demands multidirectional movement capability. The tennis player must be ready and able to move in various directions quickly and instinctively. In order to be able to accomplish many rapid changes of direction during the course of a match, it is essential to understand the biomechanics of movement as well as the means of improving your power output. Balance and footwork drills that enhance movement learning skills should parallel the development of tennis skills. This will be emphasized throughout this chapter.

Balance

Balance is a word used quite frequently in teaching the tennis player the fundamentals of movement. The definition of balance has two forms; the first refers to "static balance." Static balance is the ability to maintain equilibrium; when your body's center of gravity (C of G) is over its base of support, you are in a

Richard Krajicek demonstrates the ability to change directions quickly.

state of balance. The base of support is formed by an imaginary base that connects the front of the toes and the backs of the heels, regardless of the stance you assume. This base can assume many shapes because the feet are placed in many different positions during the course of a match. The feet are sometimes side by side, staggered, or in line with each other. When the feet are side by side and about shoulder-width apart, you should flex the hips and knees slightly and keep the trunk in the erect position. This position maximizes this form of balance and is considered to be the essence of stability.

The optimal "ready" position includes the head up, trunk upright, hips and knees slightly flexed, feet placed slightly wider than shoulder width, and the body weight shifted to the balls of the feet.

It is important when receiving serve that you assume this "balanced" position so that you can be prepared to react to the type of serve your opponent uses. In order to be effective at returning serves you must have proper mental as well as physical preparation. You must believe you can return the ball, develop a ritual to help you prepare to react to the various types of serves, and learn to read your opponent's serve motions. Physically, the great tennis players actually

Anna Kournikova displays the ready position.

move into a position of greater stability as they prepare to receive serve. This is accomplished by a slight lowering of the C of G while in the "ready" position, and it makes the receiver even more stable in preparation for movement in any direction.

Drill to Improve Balance and the Ready Position

Stand opposite a partner with approximately 10 to 15 feet between you. Assume the ready position for serve-receive while holding a medicine ball in front of you.

Use the legs to initiate a "split-step" that is a little wider than shoulder width, and lower the center of gravity by flexing the hips and knees. Move in a specific direction by initiating movement with the outside foot in that direction. Keep the posture upright.

Turn the body as a unit, letting the hands, arms, shoulders, and trunk move the ball back toward the racket-ready position. Keep the hips pointed toward the target area of the return.

Uncoil the hips and initiate a throwing action with the ball, throwing it to your partner. Keep the head still and let the shoulders swivel. Attempt five to six throws with the medicine ball and then try it with your racket as you actually receive serve. Switch back and forth for 15 to 20 reps total.

Balance and Force Development for Ground Strokes

In order to forcefully put energy into the forehand and backhand ground strokes, you must assume a position of balance so you can push against the ground by way of the lower extremities. In this way, when you exert force against the ground, the forces are transmitted back from the ground through your legs and body into the stroke itself. This is known as Newton's third law of physics, "action and reaction." In order to keep the C of G over the base of support, you should work to keep the body erect in a "stand-up" position. This maintains the most stable position for initiating ground strokes.

The second form of balance is the ability to maintain the C of G over the base of support while the body is moving. This is known as "dynamic balance," and it is crucial to the tennis player. Running in any direction, and on any surface, requires that you bring the C of G to the edge of the base of support so that the body can become unstable or "out of balance." When you become unstable or out of balance, you can run in the direction that you have moved your C of G in—that is, moving the C of G to the forward edge of the base of support means moving in a forward direction. However, when you wish to be able to move in response to various cues—such as the ball coming off the face of an opposing

Here Kiefer's feet push against the ground to promote force in his forehand.

player's racket or reacting to the open area on the court—a different set of circumstances exists. The C of G cannot be so far outside of the base of support that you are unstable, or overcommitted. In tennis, the preparatory movement before such a quick change of direction is the "split-step."

This move allows you to momentarily achieve a position where the body is in its most balanced position. This can be considered to be a neutral or noncommitted position that then allows you to move the C of G in any desired direction. Training exercises and drills that can be used to improve the achievement of the split-step follow.

Strength Exercises to Improve Dynamic Balance

It is important to remember that strength training helps to develop two forms of strength that are vital to success in movement on the tennis court. The first is

Running for a wide shot while staying balanced.

eccentric strength, necessary to decelerate the body and responsible for controlling the lowering of the C of G. The reversal of deceleration is acceleration, and it is controlled by the amount of *concentric* strength you are capable of developing. These two forms of strength are developed as you "descend" or lower the resistance and then reverse the motion or "ascend" with the resistance. Thus, the following exercises for the lower extremities are excellent for the development of a strength base. See a certified strength and conditioning specialist for proper technique with these exercises.

- Back squats
- Front squats
- Front squat to a push-press
- Dumbbell split jerk
- Lunge series: front, 45 degrees, side, crossover

On-Court Drills to Improve Dynamic Balance

On-court drills that can be very effective at improving these skills include the following:

- Mini-tennis with a medicine ball
- Close and drop
- High-low drill
- Court drill 8

Chu and Rolley

Going beyond a preparatory movement such as the split-step, you should look to footwork for changing direction. A lateral change of direction is crucial on the tennis court, and an effort to improve it should be an integral part of any training program.

When we examine movement along the baseline during a game of tennis, two common techniques are most often used:

1. *The shuffle.* Move the feet in the same plane and then push off the outside foot to shift the C of G in the opposite direction.

2. *The crossover.* Slide the feet in the same plane; cross over with the opposite foot to plant and then push back to reverse the direction of movement.

As an example, Martina Hingis often can be seen using a crossover step to initiate movement to her backhand side. This results in the right leg moving in front of the left so that she saves time by immediately pushing off the left foot and using the swing of the right leg across her body to provide her body with momentum in the intended direction of movement. It may be noted that even while she is running she maintains an upright posture, which helps her to position her upper body and arms more easily for her two-handed backhand shot.

Hingis uses what amounts to a side lunge on her left leg to provide stability and force to her backhand. The planting of her left foot allows her to pivot into her shot with maximum force. She makes contact with the ball in this position so as to allow the most stable base for exerting force. She will maintain the upright posture, early turn of the shoulders, and preparation of the racket during this time phase.

At contact, Hingis pushes forward with the left foot to help put force into her shot. This allows her to develop maximum forces even with a compact stroke. After contact, she moves her right foot forward in order to begin the deceleration or slowing process that allows her to initiate a single recovery step with her left leg. At this time she plants the left leg and pushes from the outside back toward the center of the court.

Each movement requires focus and concentration of effort in pushing off the ground forcefully with one foot so as to pass the ground forces up the kinetic chain of the leg and into the body. This may require mental focus and concentration when you are first learning or improving in this area. Young or novice players should be instructed to build good habits and learn the proper mechanics of movement. Once the basic movement patterns have been established, the emphasis should be on frequency or number of steps per unit of time. Efficient, quick steps help in improving the speed of recovery between shots.

Martina Hingis maintains an upright posture that positions her arms and upper body for her two-handed backhand.

Exercises and Footwork Drills to Improve Lateral Change of Direction

The following strength/footwork drills improve lateral change of direction:

- Individual lunge movements (front, reverse, side, crossover, and drop-step)
- Lateral cone hops
- Hexagon drill
- Side-to-side box shuffle
- 30-60-90-second box drill

Tennis players should avoid static drills. Each drill used should have as its goal the promotion of developing perception, anticipation, and concentration that is transferable to the contents of match play. Many tennis coaches consider that players can do successfully and confidently in a match only what has been successfully repeated over and over again in training, according to German tennis coach Richard Schönborn.

Chu and Rolley

On-Court Movement Drills to Improve Lateral Change of Direction

Practice these on-court movement drills to improve lateral change of direction:

- 15-yard shuttle run
- Spider drill
- Diamond drill—five cones set up in a cross pattern, with the following motions run in any pattern going from cone to cone (change running pattern as each subsequent cone is reached): sprint, pivot carioca, pivot slide, pivot carioca, pivot slide, and backpedal
- Plyo groundies
- Forehand only

Keep in mind that you can see some improvement just by playing the game, but the greatest gains occur when the body is prepared physically to perform the on-court drills. The purpose of off-court preparation is to achieve better preparation so that you benefit more from performing the on-court running and playing drills.

Balance on Clay

There are many surfaces on which dynamic balance plays a role, but none more challenging than playing on clay. Learning how to adjust to clay is a separate technique that requires you to slide into ground strokes as you move from sideline to sideline. Not accomplishing this technique usually results in your taking three to four additional steps outside the court to recover after hitting a ground stroke.

Ideally, you should slide into the hit, then cross back over with the outside or supporting leg, and take recovery steps toward the center of the court.

If you are hitting an open-stance forehand, you should move toward the ball and then place the foot down flat and in a position that is parallel to the baseline. Do *not* place the toe down so that it acts to brake your sliding action. This will cause your C of G to move abruptly to the edge of the base of support you've established, even while sliding, and may result in an embarrassing stop as your body vaults over the braking foot.

As you slide in a stable position you should keep the body upright and your weight evenly distributed over the lead foot.

Of course, the key to developing an effective sliding action is to develop running speed before initiating the slide position. Moving timidly or slowly across the court will not allow you to develop enough momentum to assume and maintain the sliding position effectively.

Cedric Pioline demonstrates proper balance while playing on clay.

Slide Drill

Have a partner stand on the service line, in the center of the court. He or she should toss a tennis ball out wide and you should run and slide as you catch it. Use a crossover step to initiate recovery back to the center of the baseline. Repeat for five to six slides. After you've accomplished the slide technique, pick up the racket and try to hit the tennis ball using the same techniques.

Coordination and Footwork

Improvement of footwork is often a sign that you have achieved a higher level of coordination in the muscles of the lower extremities and upper torso. Coordination is defined as the ability to perform fine-motor skills, or tasks requiring postural control, and reciprocal motions such as walking, running, and performing functional activities. Balance is considered a coordination skill. However, the transition that must occur between acquiring a technique and

Chu and Rolley

implementing a technique often depends on on- and off-court training to make a particular skill automatic. An example is the initiation of the "first step." In order to make this movement an instinctive or automatic move on the court, you must practice it many times and in many different situations.

To accomplish any skill you must be exposed to learning, repetition, strengthening, and sport-specific practice. One of the strong points of tennis is that it is a sport deep in the art of drills. There are many drills to improve play at the net, to serve and volley, and for court coverage. Some of the most successful advice on executing these skills follows.

Split-Steps

As you move into higher levels of competition, you may find you are being passed a lot as you attempt to attack the net. The reason: you often are mistiming your split-step. Here's how to improve your timing:

"Focus on your opponent as you approach the net. When he is about to hit his shot, slow down and then, just before he makes contact, take a split-step. By accurately timing your split-step, you will be harder to pass and on your way to developing a winning net game"—Stan Smith, 2000 U.S. Olympic coach.

The First Step

The "first step" a tennis player takes to position himself to hit or return a ball is thought to be an essential ingredient of his success. Much ado is made about the importance of the first step, but not much appears in the literature about improving it. The concept of the first step extends far beyond the physical. If you understand the game you are playing, you understand the methods and means to force your opponent into a limited number of options upon attempting to return your serve, ground stroke, or volley. Based on your effort and the outcome, you then must "read" the options available to your opponent and anticipate what is coming next. This sense of anticipation is what differentiates good athletes from great ones and can determine the outcome of matches between great athletes. Whoever can anticipate the shots of his opponent best likely will become the most efficient at returning and forcing his opponent's shots into areas where the result will be in his favor. This is the most difficult area to teach the tennis player: oftentimes it is a matter of experience; more often it is a matter of coaching.

Thus the "first step" takes many forms. The basic choice of movement often will be determined by the circumstances. First and foremost, the first-step movement always is accomplished with a slight "countermovement" or rapid lowering of the C of G over the base of support. Leg strength plays a very important

Kiefer's first step is the key to the shot's success, because it involves anticipating the move of his opponent.

role in your ability to accomplish this. Basic strength drills followed by footwork and low-intensity plyometric exercises are the best ways to prepare for developing a powerful first step.

As an example of circumstances determining the type of first step taken, consider the running forehand shot of Pete Sampras. Sampras loves the opportunity to hit the running forehand. He feels it is a shot he has a lot of control over and it has become a powerful shot in his most potent arsenal. To initiate the running forehand, Sampras executes a crossover step. Therefore, his right foot pivots as his left leg takes a large crossover step. He emphasizes quickness in the initiation of the movement and length of his initial stride. In order to hit the running forehand, the crossover has to be fast and long. After hitting the ball, he then uses his right leg to plant and decelerate his body and start the push back toward the center of the court in order to recover.

Summary

This chapter has discussed moving from a split-step into various directions. These movements are mimicked by the moves in the "lunge series" of exercises.

The strength and ability of the legs to decelerate (descending) and accelerate (ascending) from the deeper positions will go a long way toward strengthening the thighs and hips in a manner specific to tennis.

Tennis is a game of many movement skills. You must have great footwork and yet also have touch and feel for the ball off the face of the racket. To improve your running skills on the court, you must not only isolate movement skills such as working on the first step, you also have to practice moving in drills that force combinations of movement patterns. Some of these can be accomplished both with and without tennis rackets (on-court).

In conclusion, tennis balance and movement drills can be both fun and challenging. They are most effective when applied to the sport during the preparation and training of the athlete at an early age. When the focus is only on the mechanics of hitting the ball, a golden opportunity to develop the complete athlete is lost. The window of opportunity is best accomplished while the athlete is preadolescent. Every year that movement training is delayed, the more difficult it is to establish the neuromuscular patterns necessary to move with the freedom and lack of conscious effort that make up the instincts of great athletes. Balance and footwork drills are built on a matrix of strength and power. These components of athletic fitness may be achieved both on and off court. They are integrally linked to the overall success and enjoyment of playing the game of tennis.

Chapter Six

Mastering the Kinetic Chain

W. Ben Kibler
Dennis Van der Meer

Coaching techniques for optimum tennis performance should be based on the biomechanical knowledge developed about efficient stroke production but also should be tailored to the individual preferences and abilities of the tennis player. Biomechanics research and coaches' observation and experience agree that there is no "one best form" for executing tennis strokes. However, research has demonstrated that there are several key positions and motions that appear to be common to all efficient stroke patterns. These "commonalities" can be used as tools of stroke analysis and as frameworks to construct techniques assuring that stroke production conforms to the optimal common points even though they may vary at other points.

Biomechanical Fundamentals

From both a player's and a coach's perspective, high-performance or effective tennis is concerned with how to "make the ball go" (make the shot successful)—

faster, harder, more efficiently, or with more endurance. The coach must analyze the individual player's abilities, reinforce effective stroking patterns, and correct or modify ineffective patterns that are "making the ball not go" (making the shot unsuccessful). A biomechanical framework to assist the coach in this effect is the kinetic chain, sometimes called the kinetic link or linked system.

The Kinetic Chain

The kinetic chain is a coordinated activation of the segments of the body (legs, trunk, shoulder, arm, hand) starting with the ground reaction force to the feet on the ground and ending with the acceleration of the racket through the ball. Its purpose is to place the end segment, the hand and racket, in the optimum position at the optimum velocity to best "make the ball go." Figure 6.1 shows the graphic representation of the kinetic chain segment activation. Efficient use of the segments creates a racket velocity that is much more than the sum of its parts.

Although the kinetic chains in tennis may be slightly different in the serve and the ground strokes, they have several points in common. First, the largest portions of kinetic energy or force generated in the stroke are developed in

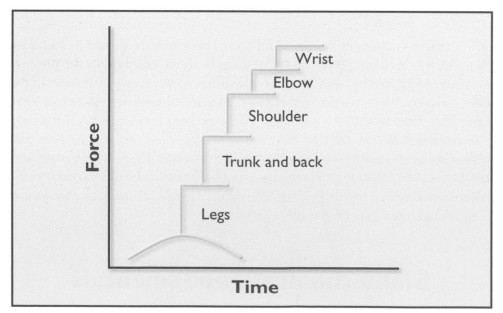

Figure 6.1
The kinetic chain for the tennis serve. Each segment produces force and acts as a stabilizing structure for the next segment's activity.

the legs and trunk. Fifty-one percent of the kinetic energy and 54 to 60 percent of total force are produced in this way (Kibler 1995; Schönborn 1999). Second, the kinetic chain is oriented to converting linear or straight-line momentum to angular or rotational momentum around a stable post leg (Schönborn 1999). Third, each segment has a cocking or stabilization phase and an acceleration phase (Kibler 1995). Fourth, large and rapid motions are required in the joints, especially the shoulder (Kibler 1993). Finally, segment dropout or kinetic chain breakage decreases the ultimate force or energy available to make the ball go, and it puts abnormally large strains on the surrounding segments (Kibler 1995). A 10 percent reduction in kinetic energy from the hip or trunk to the shoulder in the serve requires a 14 percent increase in shoulder rotation velocity or a 22 percent increase in shoulder mass to create the same kinetic energy at the hand and racket. There are several reasons for kinetic chain breakage, but the most common include muscle weakness, muscle inflexibility, joint injury, and poor mechanics of the strokes.

Limiting Factors and Personal Preferences

Players and coaches must be able to differentiate between "limiting factors"—biomechanically inefficient motions and positions—and "personal preferences." Limiting factors are detrimental to the production of the variables of ball control (direction, height, depth, spin, and speed) or may increase injury risk. The coach should analyze the limiting factors and be aware of early signs of injury. He then should be able to devise corrective strategies to overcome the limiting factors or be able to refer the athlete for consultation about the limiting factors. Personal preferences are those idiosyncrasies that account for individuality in style and may add a cosmetically pleasing flair to the game but do not have a major impact on "making the ball go."

The Serve

Here we discuss the biomechanical fundamentals and commonalities of the serve. Refer to the photos on pages 104-105 for an illustration of a serve.

Biomechanical Fundamentals

Efficient kinetic chain force production for the serve appears to require four common points in the sequence. First, the leg/hip segment requires some degree of knee flexion in cocking. Knee extension from flexion then provides the upward linear momentum, transferring the ground reaction force to the trunk (Elliott, Marshall, and Noffal 1995). The back leg provides most of the upward and forward push, whereas the front leg provides the stable post to allow rotational momentum. This creates a "pushing" movement from the ground to the racket. Second, the trunk and scapula must rotate and retract, to allow shoulder/arm positioning in cocking (Kibler 1998). This is the "full tank of energy," the stable position to allow rapid acceleration into the ball. Third, the shoulder must externally rotate and horizontally abduct to achieve cocking, and internally rotate in acceleration. Shoulder internal rotation from cocking to acceleration is the most important single biomechanical variable in the serving kinetic chain, having the highest velocity, occurring closest to the ball impact, and allowing maximum acceleration through the ball (Kibler 1995). Finally, the forearm must pronate to accelerate the racket through the hitting zone. This motion is coupled with shoulder internal rotation (Elliott, Marshall, and Noffal 1995; Schönborn 1999).

Serve: Commonalities That Make the Ball Go

Knee flexion in cocking, knee extension in acceleration

Trunk/scapula rotation to "full tank of energy" in cocking

Shoulder external (backward) rotation and internal (forward) rotation

Forearm pronation (outward wrist rotation)

Kinetic chain breakage usually occurs in the legs, back, or shoulder. Weak leg muscles, especially on the front leg, will decrease force production from the lower segments. In trying to maintain maximum serve velocity, the athlete changes from an efficient "push-through" movement from the legs to a "pull-through" movement using the trunk and arm muscles. Tight trunk muscles will decrease the ability to achieve maximum cocking. Without full cocking, the "full tank of energy" is not achieved, and maximum arm acceleration is limited.

Shoulder internal rotation frequently is decreased as a result of repetitive overloading of the muscles and ligaments on the back of the shoulder. Excessive tightness affects both shoulder rotation and the coupled forearm pronation, and it can lead to chronic soreness in the shoulder blade, shoulder, or elbow as an early sign of injury.

Serve: Problems When the Ball Doesn't Go

Weak leg muscles—"pull-through"

Tight trunk muscles—no "full tank of energy"

Shoulder internal rotation tightness

Commonalities for the Serve

In the serve, there are a number of commonalities that are prerequisite for the most efficient and effective execution of the stroke. These are the fundamentals that should be evident in every serve:

1. *A stable base.* The feet should be aligned, spread, and positioned sideways, allowing for knee flexion and the development of rotational momentum of both the lower and upper body.

2. *The simultaneous movement of both arms.* The tossing arm follows the line of the body rotation as the hitting arm goes into the cocking position (closed racket face). This closed racket position is best achieved with a proper service grip (continental). With the arms working together in this manner, you will be better able to achieve the desired trunk and shoulder rotation.

3. *The hitting phase.* The beginning of this phase is highlighted by the rotation of the hips, trunk, and hitting shoulder. This is followed by a deceleration of the right hip (blocking), which allows for the transfer of energy to the shoulder and arm. The shoulder internal rotation (leading elbow) influences the racket drop continuity and the acceleration of the elbow forward.

4. *The extension phase.* The racket begins its rapid ascent on edge. This permits optimal internal rotation of the shoulder and pronation of the forearm.

5. *Contact.* At this point, a complete extension of the hitting side is demonstrated. The pronation of the forearm and the outward rolling of the wrist continue through impact.

6. *Deceleration.* After the powerful action of hitting the ball and the ensuing extended follow-through, the player recovers balance.

Note: Any jumping that occurs is incidental and is a result of the upward thrust of the legs pushing against the ground.

Mary Pierce's serve.

Analysis for the Limiting Factors

Coaches and players should focus on only one of the anatomic areas that may be involved on any one serve. If the player is achieving the common position, no corrective measures are required. Potential limiting factors in the lower segments include no knee bend and no hip rotation in cocking or follow-through. Knee bending should be easy to check, but hip and trunk rotation loss may be harder to evaluate. Emphasis should be placed on watching back-leg-hip movement. If the hip does not rotate, or if the hip is pushing backward as the serve is hit, the pull-through movement is predominant.

Arm and shoulder rotation can be checked by watching for a "back-scratch" position, by the racket's being on edge, and by the outward rolling of the wrist after ball impact. Shoulder rotation can be evaluated by the back-scratch test.

Kibler and Van der Meer

Personal Preferences

The degree of knee bend, within normal limits, may have little effect on serve performance. No biomechanical effect has been demonstrated for foot-back versus foot-up position or both-arms-up versus arm-up/arm-down position of the ball toss.

Corrective Measures for the Limiting Factors on the Serve

1. When the hips and trunk do not rotate fully, do the following:
   a. Place the hands on the hips and rotate forward so that the toe of the right foot acts as a rudder while the weight is transferred onto the front foot.

b. Put the feet together while facing the net. Now the hips and trunk will rotate forward very readily.

c. As a final suggestion, face the net and place the right foot ahead of the left. Now it will be impossible not to have full rotation.

2. When full cocking is not achieved, do the following:

a. Be sure the cocked position has the racket face in a closed position like a "halo" rather than in a "waitress" position, that is, the side hitting the ball is facing toward your head.

b. In an extreme correction for someone who cannot master this "cocked" position, place the hitting side of the racket touching the back and then reach toward the sky, rotating the racket face to the extended contact point.

The Forehand

The kinetic chain as related to the forehand is discussed in the following section. Although similar to the serve, the forehand kinetic chain does have some different characteristics.

Biomechanical Fundamentals

The open-stance forehand allows more rapid rotational momentum and quicker response to a hit ball (Schönborn 1999). In contrast to the serve, most of the push-off and rotation force generation occurs through the same leg, the back leg. This requires strong hip muscles. This rotational momentum is transferred to the trunk to propel the arm. Maximum racket acceleration through ball impact is accomplished mainly by shoulder internal rotation, with hand motion, a combination of forearm pronation and wrist flexion, as a late contributing factor (Kibler 1995; Schönborn 1999).

Forehand: Commonalities That Make the Ball Go

Force generation and rotation off back leg

Trunk rotation allows shoulder internal rotation

Kinetic chain breakage involves weak hip muscles, poor shoulder internal rotation, or weak wrist muscles. Weak hip muscles cause inadequate back-leg "push-through," creating a "pull-through" by trunk or arm muscle use. If shoulder rotation is poor, forearm pronation and wrist flexion will be needed to accelerate the racket. Weak wrist flexion will cause the racket to lag behind and too far down in acceleration, with the contact point behind the center of gravity. These result in a pronounced "slapping" motion of the racket.

Forehand: Problems When the Ball Doesn't Go

Weak hip muscles—"pull-through"

Commonalities for the Forehand

In the forehand, a variety of actions fall into the realm of sound biomechanical execution. These adaptive technical actions result from the reception differences of each ball being hit—height, spin, speed, direction, and depth—combined with many possible sending intentions. Just the same, there are certain commonalities that form the basis of the modern forehand:

1. *Movement to the ball.* Though getting into position to hit the ball may require variations in footwork, ideally the last step should produce a relatively wide base.

2. *A stable base.* Having the feet well spread in the hitting stance allows for the center of gravity to move while staying within the base of support.

Kuerten's movement to the ball produces a wide base during the last step.

Add to this an appropriate knee bend and you are able to maintain balance for a longer period during the hitting phase. This wide, low stance provides the base of support that is needed to keep the upper body and head in balance.

3. *Grip/stance relationship.* Many of the most efficient and effective forehands in today's game are hit with a semi-western grip and from an open stance. This permits the contact point to be well forward of the center of gravity. For the right-handed player, the right leg acts as the drive leg and provides most of the push-off for the stroke. This stance facilitates rotation of the upper body, allowing for optimal prestretch.

4. *Preparation.* The backswing is initiated with a sequential backward rotation of the hips and shoulders (turn). This results in a coiling effect in which the shoulders rotate more than the hips and which increases the energy transferred from the legs. During the preparation, the nonhitting arm follows the line of rotation and is brought back parallel to the baseline.

5. *The hitting phase.* Preparation without timing is inefficient. This means that the backswing should flow into the stroke. As the racket is still moving backward, two things occur: the forward rotation of the right side begins, and there is a relaxed lowering of the arm. These two cause a prestretching of the wrist. The racket acceleration through the ball is a result of the force produced by the summation of rotations—hips, trunk, shoulders, arm, and wrist.

6. *Contact.* The contact point always should be ahead of the center of gravity, but it will vary according to the grip used.

7. *Follow-through.* This depends on the path of the racket before impact and the amount of rotation of the forearm and wrist. Most modern forehands finish with the hitting shoulder well in front and rotated over 200 degrees from the preparation phase. As well, the elbow is flexed and the racket wraps around the body.

Analysis for the Limiting Factors

Analysis of movement patterns should focus on how you move to the ball and how the last step creates a stable base and flows into hip and trunk rotation. The back leg should be firmly planted and the hip should not flex forward. If the trunk leans too far forward or too far to the side, "pull-through" compensation is being used. The elbow may be too far forward in acceleration, creating elbow pain.

A lack of shoulder internal rotation will alter the position of the elbow in follow-through. Normal shoulder rotation allows the arm and elbow to point toward the path of the ball. Weak rotation causes excessive arm pronation, with the arm and elbow pointing at an angle to the ball's path.

Weak wrist muscles result in the racket falling behind the body, creating extra stress on the wrist. Chronic wrist tendinitis may be a sign of this problem.

Personal Preferences

The full western grip is acceptable, but it probably is less useful as skills increase. You may vary in the "openness" of the legs in the stance. There is no biomechanical evidence that favors a short or a long backswing in preparation for the stroke.

Corrective Measures for the Limiting Factors on the Forehand

1. An acceptable range of grips is between the western and the eastern.
2. To correct improper balance, place an upside-down, turned cap on the top of your head. The cap must remain on your head throughout the stroke. This will ensure perfect trunk rotation position and body balance.
3. To obtain full forward rotation, a ball tossed from behind you toward the net will force you to turn forward, which will bring the hips and trunk forward.
4. Tip 3 also will encourage you to extend the follow-through so that the right shoulder comes through and faces the net, which has become a common feature on high-speed forehands.
5. To avoid weak wrists from drooping and being floppy, finish the stroke around the neck with the knuckles touching the left ear.

The Backhand

The biomechanical fundamentals and commonalities for the backhand are discussed here.

Biomechanical Fundamentals

The backhand stroke can be divided into one-handed and two-handed styles, and the two-handed style can be broken down further into nondominant-arm prime mover and dominant-arm prime mover patterns.

Anna Kournikova shows excellent trunk rotation in preparation for her two-handed backhand.

The one-handed backhand requires trunk rotation around the stable post of the lead leg and shoulder external rotation to accelerate the racket through ball impact.

The dominant-arm two-handed backhand is similar to the one-handed pattern, with reliance on the dominant leg for stability, and trunk rotation and dominant-shoulder external rotation for racket acceleration.

The nondominant-arm two-handed backhand is more similar to the forehand, with most of the acceleration contributed by nondominant-leg push-through, nondominant-shoulder internal rotation, and nondominant-wrist flexion.

Backhand: Commonalities That Make the Ball Go

Trunk rotation around front leg (one-handed and dominant-arm two-handed)

Shoulder external rotation (one-handed)

Trunk rotation from back leg (nondominant-arm two-handed)

Kinetic chain breakage in the one-handed backhand results from a lack of trunk rotation and weak posterior shoulder muscles. This results in decreased acceleration of the racket through the ball. The performance result is hitting

Kibler and Van der Meer

behind the body, and the injury result could be "tennis elbow" due to increased strain on the elbow and extra use of the wrist and elbow muscles to accelerate the racket.

The lack of trunk rotation is also a problem in the dominant-arm two-handed backhand, with consequent hitting behind the body. Tennis elbow is less likely because of the protective effect on the dominant elbow by the use of both hands.

The nondominant two-handed backhand is reliant on back-leg stability for force production and rotation, similar to the forehand. Kinetic chain breakage as a result of leg or hip weakness decreases the "push-through" movement and creates the "pull-through" movement. Also, the need to accelerate the racket causes extra wrist movement in cocking, leading to wrist overload and tendinitis in the nondominant wrist.

Backhand: Problems When the Ball Doesn't Go

Weak trunk rotation

Weak shoulder external rotation, with hitting behind the body and underspin

Weak back leg, with "push-through"

Commonalities for the Backhand

For the backhand, some of the commonalities of the forehand also exist such as the stable base. In the case of the one-handed backhand, we see the following:

1. *Stance.* A square stance is advocated although there is allowance for particular situations in which a closed or open stance may be preferable. The square stance facilitates torso and shoulder rotation (prestretch).

2. *The grip.* The eastern backhand grip permits a more stable wrist and an extended arm at impact and during the follow-through.

3. *The hitting phase.* The forward action of the racket is initiated by the trunk and external shoulder rotation. Because the hitting shoulder is positioned ahead of the body, the degree of hip rotation is limited. The angle between the shaft of the racket and the forearm is maintained throughout the hitting phase.

4. *Contact.* As a result of the grip and the position of the hitting shoulder, the contact point is well ahead of the body.

5. *Follow-through.* This is again a function of the path of the racket before impact and the degree to which the stroke is a rotating shoulder socket versus a rising shoulder socket.

In the case of the two-handed backhand, we see differences depending on the grip used. An eastern backhand grip with the right hand produces a dominant arm stroke. The left arm is more of a guide arm, but it has the effect of bringing the back shoulder and hips into a square position at contact. An eastern forehand grip with the right hand produces a nondominant arm stroke. In this stroke, we generally see a more aggressive rotation of the hips and shoulders.

In both the forehand and backhand ground strokes, in which you are hitting lifted strokes, the push against the ground (drive leg extension) combined with centrifugal force often leads you to leave the ground. This is not the case with underspin or slice shots.

Analysis for the Limiting Factors

In the one-handed backhand, analysis should focus on where the ball is hit and how much underspin is present. Hitting behind the body with lots of underspin is an indication of kinetic chain breakage. Similarly, leading with the elbow indicates too much reliance on the arm muscles to accelerate the racket.

In the two-handed backhand, also watch for the point of contact. Hitting behind the body indicates a limiting factor. Excessive wrist cocking in preparation, with the racket behind and down, indicates too much reliance on the wrist muscles. As in the serve, the final position of the hips indicates whether the back leg is supplying optimum force. If the hip is straight, the kinetic chain is working from the ground up. If the hip is going back, the "push-through" is working from the hips up.

Personal Preferences

Hand position on the two-handed backhand gives no specific advantage. Foot position in stance, either more open or more closed, does not result in kinetic chain changes.

Corrective Measures for the Limiting Factors on the Backhand

1. On the one-handed backhand, a substantial grip change to a full eastern backhand grip will help to stabilize the wrist.
2. Keeping the hips sideways longer will help to align the racket. Extending the left hand backward will inhibit an early hip turn toward the net.
3. On the two-handed backhand side, a very effective developmental tool is to play a left-handed forehand while choking the grip. This will help mold the early contact point, trunk and shoulder rotation, and racket stability. Now when you add the right hand to the full-length position of the racket, the two-handed stroke pattern already has been established.

Summary

Applying biomechanical principles to playing gives you a framework of analysis of the common points of effective tennis strokes. This analysis can be used to reinforce the good stroke patterns and devise corrective measures for biomechanically inefficient strokes.

Chapter Seven

The Interplay of Tactics and Technique

Richard Herbst
Patrick McEnroe

Our fundamental beliefs in tennis stem from coaching and playing on the professional tour. There is a reoccurring observation on the circuit: the game changes about every six months. Why?

Many of the major tournament winners over the years playing singles or doubles have helped redefine the game. Their individualized game styles—which dictate how they play the game tactically and then technically perform it—are unique. We recognize that there are some similar strategies, tactics, and technical commonalities, but each player's game has a signature about it, similar to an art form. After each match, the players, the artists, could almost sign this competitive art form.

We take a holistic view—you cannot separate tactics from technique. They are inextricably tied to the individual and his culture. For example, Pete Sampras has redefined how to strategically hold serve and at the same time has redefined how to technically serve; Andre Agassi has redefined how to strategically break

Pete Sampras has redefined how to strategically hold serve and how to technically serve.

serve and how to return serve. Both players have these very different signatures about their games. From where do these signatures come? We believe that culture, personality, genetics, playing, and coaching experiences all affect a player's vision of his game style and the development of his techniques for playing his game. Each has his own personal beliefs and perceptions of winning tennis matches.

The same observations are relevant to the game of doubles. The strategies, tactics, and techniques to play championship doubles also have been redefined by each of the great doubles teams of the open era. The dominant team of the 1990s, Mark Woodforde and Todd Woodbridge, redefined how to play doubles strategically and technically. They developed their own way of holding each other's serve and a system of breaking serve as a team. These two players created a doubles identity based on culture, personalities, friendship, genetics, coach-

Herbst and McEnroe

ing, playing experiences, and an agreed-on vision of how to play the game of doubles.

Keep It Simple

Top professional players keep it simple. How they win points, games, and matches is very repeatable—it is simple yet individualistic. Most of the top players have at least one or two repeatable weapons that they compete with. Champions will have weaknesses, but their game styles are built so well around their weapons that it is very difficult to exploit their weaknesses. The champion's game simply is using those weapons as often as possible throughout games, matches, and tournaments. Champions' opponents continually are reacting to them. The key by-product of playing this repetitive game style is confidence. And confidence is at the core of every successful athlete.

Develop Your Strengths

Develop your strengths and solidify your weaknesses. Players develop a signature game around one to three weapons that they really excel with from one area of the court. A player also is very competent playing from every other area in the court. For example, Lleyton Hewitt's game style is built around generating and ripping huge forehand winners or forcing errors with his forehand. Many times, his forehand produces a short ball and he still can finish off the point by going to the net and volleying. The reverse also holds. Pete Sampras loves to serve and volley and compete at the net. Yet, with his ground strokes he can hang with you from the baseline until he can go on the offensive. A player must have a weapon (e.g., Sampras' forehand) to break serve and generate approach shots that get him playing from his offensive area of the court. The all-court player has the ability to neutralize an opponent and to play offense and defense appropriately within points to generate his or her weapons.

Develop Personal Style

Always develop a personal game style. For starters, players need to understand how they *think* they win and lose points and games and how they *think* they

Lleyton Hewitt's huge forehand.

win and lose matches. Have your coach watch to see how you work on your concepts of winning. Your coach also can watch a couple of matches, looking again for patterns of play and to see if you actually win and lose points according to your concepts of winning and losing points. Look for a consistency among the three areas—the concepts, practices, and match play. How often do you actually repeat the patterns that you *think* you win points with? Then there are many other factors to consider: physical size, strength, quickness, endurance, genetics, personality, and culture. You also should consider softer issues, such as how you handle risk taking, making mistakes, losing, winning, and learning. And, the key factor—what is your personal vision of how you want to play the game?

Focus on Core Style

As a player you should focus on how you win now. Players lose sight of this all the time. Coaches on the professional tour constantly remind players of their

Herbst and McEnroe

identities and how they win. How players win and lose now is fundamentally how they will continue to win and lose points, games, sets, and matches throughout their tennis careers. What we are referring to here is a player's *core style*. His tennis game will continue to improve, develop, and perhaps gain dimension, but that core identity of who he is in terms of winning and losing has been confidently established as a personal definition of competition. There is a confident way that each of these players thinks that he wins and loses points, games, sets, and matches. This fundamental concept of winning started developing in the juniors. As players develop into top-level professionals, they just get better at these fundamental ways to win and lose.

There is evidence of this at the pro level. Year to year, the top pros play the big points repeatedly the same way. Under pressure, players, at whatever age or skill level, go back to how they were successful in the past—and especially in big matches. In fact, champions have figured out that winning or losing boils down to executing or not executing their games. This concept of how a player competes with her game—and especially, how she plays the key points in a match—needs to be addressed consistently and intelligently. When it is show

Players such as Martina Hingis are proactive in playing their games with a personal core style.

time, the important issue is this: Are you going to be proactive and play your game, or be reactive and wait for your opponent to play her game?

Take Ownership

Players must take ownership of their game. Ownership is a huge piece of the developmental puzzle. The coach can become a mirror for the player, to help each player develop his own ways to win points, games, sets, matches, and tournaments. Coaches sometimes use a questionnaire and an interviewing process to begin this task. This helps to separate a player's vision of how to win from a coach's or parent's vision of how this player should win. It puts the ownership of the game where it ultimately needs to be: on the player's shoulders. After all, who is playing? The coach then can use this information to design a program that starts with the coaching philosophy that a player's vision drives play and strategic development—and that generates technical adjustments, demands, and improvements.

You should know what you are going to practice on a certain day. Or, how are you going to play this opponent today? What are you going to pay attention to on the court today? How are you going to generate your strengths against this opponent? What are you going to do with your game today? And what do you want your coach to watch for? You need to take the lead role (ownership) in your game—in practice sessions, in lessons (you should be telling the tennis pro what *you* want to work on), and in match play.

A subconscious conflict is at work. The personal coach or parent has been driving the player's game from the beginning. It is important to reverse the roles, to return ownership to the player. In the long run it will be easier to win and harder to lose if you are designing your own game plan. When players know that after a match—or during a practice session—they will be held accountable for what they have told the coach to expect, the learning curve is awesome. Development and learning occur best when there is play and practice without ambiguity. Ownership is the critical component!

Practice in Matches

Professional tennis is a game of match play, head-to-head competition with a single-elimination format. Play lasts a week or, in some events, two weeks, and you must win four to seven consecutive matches to win a tournament. Each match is against a different player and playing style. Each match should build into the next one so that you peak in the final on Sunday.

This is how champions reinvent the game of tennis for themselves. Like all predators, they figure out how to win by playing hundreds of practice and tournament matches. For players to develop, they must play enough practice matches to learn how to win with their own game styles. The best kind of learning is based on firsthand experience. A player needs to play his game endlessly to find out what works (and what needs work) in a competitive setting. Ideally, out of this process of playing matches, a player learns how to trap an opponent into reacting to his game style. This is the key factor that determines who wins or loses a match.

So how does a top player learn his personal game style, learn to become a competitive match player, or string together enough matches to win a tournament? In my career when I was on the road or at home practicing, I worked on everything in practice matches or match situation drills. I did very little drilling. I played hundreds of practice sets and matches against anybody and everybody. Every weekend all summer I played every tournament I could get into.

—P.M

Recognize Unique Style

Each player's game is unique. Every pro plays the game similarly, yet very differently. Each game style has strategic cues that are unique to that professional player. A coach constantly asks questions about when or why a player chooses to rip the forehand or change direction with a shot. Players have to figure out these subtle changes for themselves within points, so they can use their weapons as often as possible. For example, a player has a great backhand and really likes to rip it crosscourt and set up the down-the-line winner. The coach asks him to figure out with each opponent where he has to serve to get a backhand for a second ball. Where should he hit his forehand to generate backhands? Where to hit his backhand to generate another backhand? How can he use the court to set up a backhand rip crosscourt or down the line? After a match, they review these issues. What worked on the serve to generate the backhand so the player could dominate the center of the court? Did the sharp crosscourt open up the down-the-line rip? How often did the player end up on the defensive? Did the wide slice serve to the ad court into the backhand create enough space to rip the return into the forehand side of the court, or does a kicker work better? These questions are basic for coaches, but to young players, they are huge issues that promote learning and developing their games. Players need to become active problem solvers with their games in a match.

Anke Huber has her own style of play, as does every professional player.

Adjust Your Game

Adjustment does not mean changing your game style. The difference between adjusting your game and changing your game is a huge issue. Adjustment means the tactical changes that you confidently can make to still generate enough opportunities to use your weapons. The key issue in adjusting is confidence. We do believe a player can make tactical changes confidently. Changing your game, however, is about a basic change of game style. For example, a baseliner who has a forehand weapon is losing and so decides midmatch to become a serve-and-volleyer and a net rusher. We do not believe that you really can change your game style confidently. It is unusual to change a game style and win. It would require a major mental shift and would undermine your confidence.

Herbst and McEnroe

When you change a game style, you are competing with your second-best game, a nonconfident game style, and usually the player who changes his or her game will lose faster. The key playing and coaching issue is that any tactical or strategic adjustments must not undermine a player's confidence. Remember that confidence depends on repeatability. Repeatability is built on the reliability of a shot (like a Sampras serve or Agassi return) or patterns of play (like Courier's inside-out forehand pattern or Steffi Graf's slice backhand to generate a forehand). Players should have several tactical sequences available within their games that produce repeatable opportunities to finish off points with their weapons.

Winning is very individual; it is about how often you can generate your weapons and play off them successfully. For example, Gustavo Kuerten wins lots of matches by setting up a repeatable finish, his backhand down the line. However, the real magic is his ability to adjust his overall game to set up that

Gustavo Kuerten sets up his backhand down the line as a finish.

finishing shot—getting to hit his backhand down the line regardless of whom he is playing. His tenacious commitment to this pattern, and an unbending attitude that "everyone is going to have to deal with my game," has taken him to the top of the game.

If your "A" game is not working, what do you do? First of all, try to play your "A" game better! For example, serve to your targets better, neutralize your opponent more effectively with your ground strokes, and make it count when you do get an opportunity to use your weapons. Second, if that does not work, make some tactical adjustments that get your weapons involved in the match. Changing your style is usually an illusion. For example, at the 1999 French Open, Agassi was following his ripping ground strokes to the net. This is really not that far from his A game; he still was dictating play off the ground, and he was competent enough to exploit the position advantages by getting to the net and volleying the ball. The surface demanded this modification to his A game. His game style was still about getting his opponent to react to him with his aggressive ground strokes.

Agassi's game is structured on taking time away from opponents, and at the French Open, that modification of taking the ball in the air did just that. The core of his game still was played from in front of the baseline, controlling the center of the court with punishing ground stokes. The surface and the opponent demanded that he finish more points in the air. He still had to generate the position advantages and short balls with his ground strokes to get in to the net. To say that he changed his game style is misleading. He adjusted his game to the demands of the surface and the match.

Neutralize Your Opponent

Find ways to neutralize an opponent. Most players think they are playing either offense or defense from the baseline. But there is a third dimension of play that is critical to the structuring of points—neutralizing. This quality of play is at the core of the professional game.

It begins with the service return, a way to offset the server's advantage. Then there is the ground-stroke trade-off. Once the serve is played back and the return of serve is played back, if neither player has a position advantage to capitalize on or a short ball to rip, it is time to trade shots. This is playing from the neutral position. The point is now like chess in motion. Each player is trying to get control of the point by controlling the center of the court. Each neutralizing ground stroke has to be deep enough, wide enough, or heavy enough, or with

Safin hits a neutralizing ground stroke to limit his opponent's options.

enough spin, or hit hard enough to limit your opponent's offensive options. These ground strokes should begin a sequence of shots (a confident pattern) to create a position advantage that you can capitalize on. These patterns should generate opportunities to rip your weapons or hit approach shots and get in to the net. This is one of the key ingredients to having your opponent react to you consistently in a match.

Play Your Game

The concept of scouting an opponent is confusing. It is good for players to watch how their opponents play. It generates knowledge that is invaluable. It allows players to watch how opponents generate their weapons and play big points. And it begins to focus players on how they are going to generate their weapons against this opponent.

But this is only a start. Once a match gets going, it's all about adjustments, and all that scouting you have done may be for nothing because your opponent

The Interplay of Tactics and Technique

also is going to be making adjustments during the match. Each match takes on a life of its own, and the active problem solver is usually the winner. This is why you should be grounded in confidence in yourself and your game. You need to learn that your game will work against any opponent if it is executed. Scouting should be used to generate a knowledge base so you can make sure at the critical stages of the match that your opponent is reacting to you and not the other way around.

We are not for one second suggesting that great players don't find a way to win every day. What we are saying is that they find a way to win every day within their own style of play. Winning then becomes trapping an opponent into reacting to a player's game more often than he reacts to the opponent's game.

Let Vision Drive Technique

Obviously, the fundamentals have to be there before a player's vision will develop into a successful pro-level game. There are universal fundamentals that have to be taught, but they shouldn't be the primary focus. Playing the game should be the focus. For example, if a player's vision of the game includes a love of the net and she is 13 and small, the coach would help find ways for that player to get in to the net. It's important to start the learning curve of how to win up there with this strategy. That style would demand a technical standard with respect to the quality of the ground strokes, approach shots, volleys, court positioning, and so forth. The decision to learn these skills stems from the player's vision. A player's vision improves technique. The vision of how a player wants to finish off the point creates the demands necessary for improving technique.

Broaden Your Experience

A player's education must have certain experiences. Players should be interacting and playing with the best practice competition available. You have to be able to hang with these players or you won't last as a practice partner. Also interact with other ranked players to soak up their perspectives and experiences.

Working with Pat McEnroe reinforced the very important concept of broad experience. Pat had defined himself in an unusual way. At tournaments he was working out and warming up for matches with players ranked between 50 and 100. I felt he had defined himself with these peers and created a performance reality. I suggested that he change his working environment at tournaments and in practice. His goal was to be ranked inside of 30 but in my opinion he lacked experience from that environment. At tournaments he started asking a different crowd of players to work out and warm up. We traveled around the country working out with many of the top-10 players to experience what it was like to practice with them. What were they doing that maybe we should be doing or not doing? Pat became a student of the top 30 in the world game. Those experiences clearly illustrated what it was going to take to get his ranking up into the 20s. Six months later, to his credit, he was ranked 28th. I know the experiences he had with this demanding group of players played a major role in this accomplishment.

—R.H.

Develop Professional Habits

Create a professional environment on and off the court whether you are at home or on the road. The great players who developed in the United States were playing like professionals in the junior ranks. Sampras, Agassi, Courier, Michael Chang, and Lindsay Davenport make up an impressive list of players who started developing their professional game styles in the juniors and have continued to develop in their professional careers.

I (Patrick) was lucky to have an older brother who was a top player and who introduced me to professional tennis. I believe that acting like a professional tennis player when I was an amateur was an important step in becoming a pro. John wanted me acting, eating, resting, training, practicing, and playing like a professional when I was a junior. He didn't believe that once you turn pro you suddenly start acting like one.

Accept Change

The professional game changes. Some say that you need to improve your game every six months or you are going to be out of a job. The rationale behind this statement is simple. What drives the improvements that we consistently see in this game are the players and our reactions to what other players are doing. Tennis is an ongoing "chesslike" game that requires ongoing problem solving. For example, recently we have been seeing open-stance backhands. This shot

Lindsay Davenport is an example of a player who developed her professional game style as a junior and has continued to develop that style as a pro.

was technically taboo just a few years ago. With players hitting the ball bigger, and with the demands of handling that pace and recovering for a second shot, the game demanded an adjustment in technique—the open-stance backhand. Today, all of the top players have the ability to hit an open-stance backhand offensively and defensively. It is just as it always has been—you keep developing and adjusting your game. This game drives the development of game styles, tactics, and the techniques to play one's game.

Conclusion

We believe that this game is about winning individually. The demands of performing at the professional level should become the ground rules for

Herbst and McEnroe

developing junior tennis players. No matter what game style a player has, it should be developed in concert with the pro game that constantly is evolving. We feel that a professional game style should be developed early in a player's career. That signature style should be congruent with the individual's culture, attributes, abilities, and a personal vision of how the game of tennis should be played.

Chapter Eight

Maintaining Technique Under Pressure

Jim Loehr
Tom Gullikson

In the 2000 Wimbledon final, Patrick Rafter was three points from taking a commanding two-set lead against Pete Sampras. Rafter won the first set in a tiebreaker and was serving at 4-1 in a second set breaker. Until now, his play had been solid. Given the 4-1 lead, it certainly appeared that Rafter would win the second set and, with a two-set advantage, probably capture the championship. Only three more points and the nearly insurmountable lead was his. Amazingly, Rafter committed three consecutive unforced errors and went on to lose the breaker and the match. He missed a relatively easy forehand volley, double-faulted, and then missed a point-blank forehand passing shot.

In an interview after the match, Rafter reported that for the first time in the entire tournament he got a bad case of nerves. He fully realized the importance of the moment and suddenly felt his muscles tighten up. His ability to execute even the most basic mechanics in this high-pressure situation was severely compromised. And every player who has seriously competed painfully understands what can happen when nerves and mechanics collide.

Understanding Choking

Tennis players commonly refer to what happened to Rafter as "choking." Fundamentally, choking is a physiological event tied to the perception of threat. Primitive fear mechanisms are activated via a relay race of powerful hormones. The cascade begins with the hypothalamus, on to the pituitary, and finishes at the adrenal glands. The end result is an excess of powerful hormones such as cortisol that leave tennis players feeling nervous, tight, tentative, unfocused, and awkward. Heart rate and blood pressure increase and breathing typically becomes shallow and irregular (the origin of the word "choking" comes from the common experience that athletes have of "choking for air" when the adrenal glands produce excessive cortisol in response to threat).

Patrick Rafter's inability to execute his mechanics under pressure was, by his own admission, clearly due to excessive nerves. But there are many other highly disruptive potential influences that can undermine a tennis player's ability to execute proper mechanics under pressure. These include such things as temper and anger, low blood sugar (poor nutrition), dehydration, insufficient sleep, fatigue due to poor fitness, low self-confidence, poor concentration, low motivation and effort (tanking), and poor or faulty biomechanics. Failure in any of these can seriously derail a tennis player's ability to execute under competitive pressure.

A Multidimensional Model

The ability to perform under pressure is all too often reviewed solely as a mental competency. In reality, performing to the full limits of one's capacity in competition represents a multidimensional set of complementary skills that are evidenced in the form of acquired positive habits. Figure 8.1 depicts the authors' view (from Loehr's 30 years as a sport psychologist and Gullikson's 24 years of coaching and playing at the highest level in tennis).

The competencies that serve mechanical precision under pressure are hierarchical. Each competency is evidenced in highly specific positive habits (rituals) supportive of that specific competency. The most important *physical* competencies are sound biomechanics, efficient movement, flexibility, sound nutrition and hydration, and physical fitness. The most important *emotional* competencies are self-awareness, self-regulation (arousal control), mistake management, breath control, and positive body language. The most important *mental* competencies are concentration, goal setting, visualization, mental preparation, time

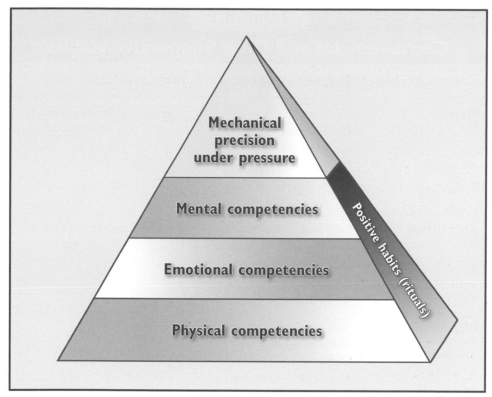

Figure 8.1
The hierarchy of competencies that serve mechanical precision under pressure.

management, and positive self-talk. The competencies, corresponding supportive habits, and most important time considerations are summarized in table 8.1.

Physical Competencies

Mechanical precision in competition begins physically. Failure to perform under pressure often is linked to one or more physical deficiencies. Let's examine each of the physical habits supportive of performance under pressure.

Sound Biomechanics

Coaches and players often are quick to attribute repeated stroke breakdowns under pressure to mental problems. However, in all likelihood a second serve that constantly fails when the pressure builds in competition reveals biomechanical, not mental, weaknesses. Solid biomechanics allow players to continue to play effectively in spite of problems with mild nerves or fatigue. If every time a player gets nervous or tired his serve or forehand collapses, in all

Table 8.1

Competencies and Their Supportive Habits

Competencies	Supportive habits	Most important time
Mental	Concentration Goal setting Visualization Mental preparation Time management Self-talk	During and between points
Emotional	Self-awareness Self-regulation Mistake management Breath control Body language	Between points
Physical	Sound biomechanics Efficient movement Flexibility Nutrition and hydration Fitness	Between matches

probability it's not his head that needs fixing, but rather the faulty stroke. This is precisely why the same strokes repeatedly break down with players. The strokes with the most fragile biomechanics fail first. And repeated failures over time result in additional problems in the confidence area that further erode the player's ability to execute under pressure. What is now a mental and emotional problem, however, began as a biomechanical deficiency.

Efficient Movement

Precision mechanics and precision balance are nearly synonymous. Inefficient movement patterns compromise players' ability to get to the ball in balance. Under the pressure of competition, inefficient habits of movement can be particularly problematic in terms of balance. The result is tight, restricted muscles and the failure to selectively recruit those muscles prerequisite to mechanical efficiency. The sequence is depicted in figure 8.2.

Players often report that under pressure, their feet stop moving resulting in a dramatic loss of biomechanical control. Reports of rubbery legs or loss of feeling in the legs or feet are common in high-stress situations. Combining problems of nerves with faulty movement patterns—such as the failure to split-step or the center of gravity being too high when moving to the ball—leads to repeated mechanical breakdowns.

Loehr and Gullikson

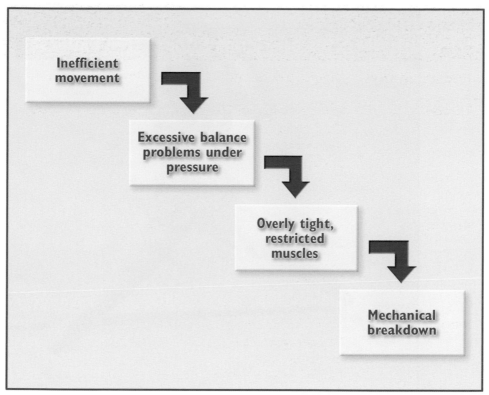

Figure 8.2
The process that leads to mechanical breakdown.

Flexibility

Inflexibility exacerbates mechanical problems under pressure. Sympathetic nervous-system arousal associated with fear and threat typically causes muscles to constrict and tighten. From an evolutionary perspective, you simply are bracing yourself for an anticipated life-threatening attack. This instinctive defensive reaction plays havoc with a range of motion, fine-motor skill control, and balance, all core elements of mechanical precision. The authors' experience clearly has been that inflexible players are more prone to problems of choking than flexible players. This is particularly evident in players who are very strong (have large muscle mass) but have failed to do proper stretching. Most players understand the importance of flexibility in injury prevention but fail to connect inflexibility with mechanical problems under pressure.

Nutrition

From a nutritional perspective, the most critical consideration during match play is the stabilization of blood sugar. Both depletion of stored muscle glycogen as well as low free-floating blood sugar (glucose) seriously can impede biomechanical execution. Neurons require minimum levels of glucose and oxygen

Maintaining Technique Under Pressure

Serena Williams displays flexibility as well as strength.

to maintain normal functioning. When blood sugar levels fall below a certain point, problems with concentration, focus, decision making, intensity control, and irritability are common. Each of these problems in turn negatively affects mechanical precision. Carbohydrate supplementation may be required for high-intensity matches lasting more than 90 minutes. Players often poorly understand the sequence depicted in figure 8.3. They rarely connect lapses in concentration to the issue of low blood sugar.

Hydration

Dehydration is also a destabilizing factor biomechanically. The connection between mechanical precision and the consumption of water is simply too far removed for many players. But hydration puts the body into a life-or-death survival mode. Maintaining proper body temperature becomes the number one priority in the physiology. Nearly every system in the body is affected by the alarm mobilization. Considering this, a breakdown in mechanics is not surprising.

Fitness

The fitter the athlete, the better the chance he or she will hold up mechanically under pressure. Insufficient aerobic or anaerobic capacity as well as strength

Loehr and Gullikson

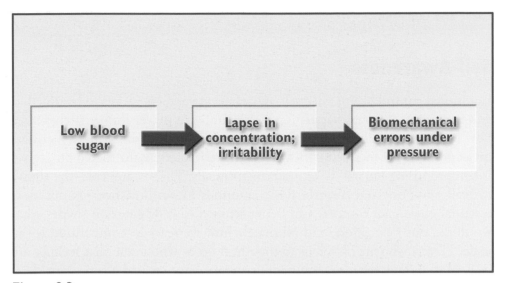

Figure 8.3
Low blood sugar can lead to lack of concentration and biomechanical errors.

deficiencies can completely disrupt stroke accuracy and precision in long or highly demanding competitive situations. Leg strength and endurance are particularly critical. Leg fatigue typically translates into players' failure to stay down on balls, reduces explosiveness to the ball, and compromises overall speed—any of which can have devastating effects on mechanical precision.

Muscular fatigue requires the body to make compensatory movements to adjust. Strokes and supporting footwork clearly change as muscular fatigue sets in. From an observer's perspective, it may appear that the player is struggling with excessive nerves (choking). Many of the typical signs of choking are apparent—awkward movement, slow reaction time, incomplete or abbreviated strokes, and so forth. The real culprit, however, is not fear but fatigue!

Inadequate aerobic capacity can erode biomechanics in the same way muscle fatigue does. Clearly the two are related, but players with an insufficient aerobic base fail to recover adequately in the 20 seconds between points and are forced to play with elevated heart rates. Executing a stroke at a heart rate of 180 versus 140 is far more challenging. It is very tempting for players and coaches to reflexively attribute a performance drop to problems with nerves, but in reality, the underlying causative factor may well be poor aerobic fitness.

Emotional Competencies

Once the physical competencies are in place, the foundation is set for mobilizing the right emotional response. Mechanical precision requires emotional precision. Let's examine specific emotional competencies required for that objective.

Self-Awareness

Emotional control begins with self-awareness. Awareness means to be tuned in and conscious of what's happening. For example, a player immediately senses how the increase in tension in the muscles of her hands and arms at a critical break point or her increasing frustration and irritability as the match progresses is compromising her ability to perform optimally. That awareness—the ability to read emotions and connect those emotions to performance—is the most essential emotional competence. Being attuned to how emotion shapes what we think, our perception, and ultimately how we react in competition is the issue. Players who are oblivious to their feelings or who argue that feelings are irrelevant and unrelated to competitive success have created a substantial barrier to mechanical precision under pressure.

Self-Regulation

At the heart of self-regulation is the ability to control arousal. Staying positive and keeping disruptive emotions in check are fundamental to biomechanical execution. Summoning the right intensity at the right moment, and finding the appropriate balance between too little and too much arousal, occurs only with considerable trial and error. No two players require the same precise intensity. Everyone is unique. Fiery competitors such as Jimmy Connors and Thomas Muster have entirely different arousal requirements than more laid-back players such as Todd Martin and Pete Sampras. Optimal arousal levels for the same players can even vary from match to match. No two competitors are alike, and conditions are different every time a player steps on a court. Without the ability to skillfully regulate arousal, mechanical precision under pressure is simply not possible.

Mistake Management

Closely linked to self-regulation is the ability to manage mistakes. Staying positive and unflappable in the face of repeated mistakes represents quite a challenge for most players. Occasional mistakes and mechanical breakdowns are inevitable in tennis. Errors, be they forced or unforced, are realities that never will go completely away. Mistakes can trigger a diversity of disruptive emotions, such as anger, rage, fear, negativity, and tanking. Mistakes can completely undermine confidence, focus, and self-control. Players must become highly disciplined in how they respond emotionally to mistakes. Learning how to constructively walk away from mistakes is linked directly to the accuracy and precision of stroke production.

Lleyton Hewitt emits an appearance of confidence and positive attitude.

Breath Control

The rhythm of one's breath both during and between points clearly affects bio-mechanics. Breathing in or breath holding during a stroke causes muscles to tighten, affecting racket acceleration and fine-motor control. Breathing is a window to the physiology and represents a powerful tool for regulating sympathetic and parasympathetic arousal during play. Top players such as Monica Seles have learned to synchronize their out-breaths with stroke execution. They breathe out as they swing through the ball and breathe in while the ball is in the air. Because exhaling stimulates muscle relaxation, strokes tend to be more fluid and smooth when contact point and out-breaths are coordinated. For some players, this takes the form of grunting.

Between points, rhythmic, diaphragmatic breathing (belly breathing) facilitates recovery, both physiological and psychological. Diaphragmatic breathing lowers heart rate and blood pressure, improves mental clarity, and reduces the intensity of disruptive emotions such as anger and fear.

Body Language

Body language between points and mechanical precision during points may appear completely unrelated. The connection is emotional. A positive body

13

Maintaining Technique Under Pressure

language *between points* facilitates the flow of positive emotions *during points*—confidence, poise, optimism, and enjoyment. Looking sad, frustrated, disappointed, angry, fatigued, or defeated on the outside simply reinforces the underlying physiology. Negative emotional states can completely undermine stroke production. Top players eventually come to understand how mechanical precision during points and body-language precision between points are linked via emotions. Players such as Andre Agassi, Patrick Rafter, and Martina Hingis project a strong image of confidence and high energy regardless of how they might be feeling on the inside.

Mental Competencies

Once the physical and emotional competencies are in place, the stage is set for performing mentally. Performing mentally is supported by six separate but related competencies.

Concentration

Your focus of attention during competitive play clearly affects mechanics. Ironically, the more you focus on mechanics between and during points, the less likely you are to execute properly under pressure. The "paralysis by analysis" syndrome is all too familiar to players. Temporal focus also is important in competition. Focusing on the past such as missed opportunities or bad line calls or focusing on the future such as thinking about what people will say if you lose can completely derail stroke production. The specific competency required here is the ability to maintain a present focus, to essentially focus on only one point at a time. A present moment-to-moment focus during points facilitates a highly instinctive style of play. Players consistently report they perform best when stroke production is essentially on automatic pilot. Mentally focusing on watching the ball or "fast feet" facilitates the desired automatic effect.

Goal Setting

The types of goals players set both before and during matches can powerfully influence mechanics. Outcome goals such as winning the tournament or making a particular ranking can substantially increase feelings of pressure during play. Increasing first-serve percentages by 10 percent or attacking short balls and coming to the net can be an example of performance or process goals. These help to focus players' attention on relevant aspects of play without typically causing feelings of pressure and fear to significantly increase. Performance goals are under the athlete's sphere of direct control, and outcome goals are not. The bottom line is that the types of goals players set have arousal consequences during play, and arousal affects mechanics.

Visualization

Players consistently report that visualizing the serve or serve return before the start of the point facilitates execution. Using images to mentally rehearse complex biomechanical movements typically does not lead to the "paralysis by analysis" syndrome. The re-creation of experience through images stimulates an entirely different area of the brain from logical, analytical thought. Stimulation of the nondominant hemisphere of the brain, which is what happens in visualization, facilitates instinctive and automatic play.

Using visualization to correct mistakes during play can have a very positive effect on mechanical precision. Simply "feeling" the correct stroke or mentally and physically rehearsing the specific correction before the next point builds confidence and positive response expectancy.

Mental Preparation

Players execute mechanically under pressure better when they feel mentally prepared. Following highly specific routines of sleeping, eating, practicing, dressing, and time alone mobilizes you to adapt constructively to the competitive stress you are about to experience. Solid mental preparation reduces the risk that excessive nervousness will interfere seriously with stroke production and movement. Clear prematch strategies and tactical game plans permit you to be less analytical in your thinking during matches, thereby helping you to remain instinctive and spontaneous in your play. Proper mental preparation clearly facilitates confidence and positive belief, both directly linked to mechanical precision under pressure.

Time Management

When players feel rushed for time, strokes begin to fail. Most players perform best when they feel that time slows down. They have plenty of time to get to the ball, set up properly, and execute the shot. The skillful use of time before and during match play enhances the feeling of time slowing down. Something as simple as arriving later than normal to an important match can fast-forward the sense of time. All players have a unique tempo that's best for them. Steffi Graf is different from Monica Seles and Andre Agassi from Pete Sampras. The important issue is to develop the sense that you are controlling time and not time

Gullikson's Top Ten List: Maintain Mechanical Precision Under Pressure

1. *Take your time before big points; focus on your breathing to help your recovery.*

2. *Use visualization before serving or returning to help you "see" how you want the point to develop.*

3. *Plan your play and play your plan. Have a crystal clear idea of exactly how you want to play in pressure situations.*

4. *Maintain present focus. Concentrate on playing one point at a time to the best of your ability.*

5. *Focus on attacking the ball with your feet. Good footwork and positioning translate into precise shot making.*

6. *Maintain light grip pressure on your racket. This will help keep your arm muscles relaxed and will allow you to achieve good racket head speed with little effort.*

7. *Focus on seeing the ball come off your opponent's racket, which will help facilitate early preparation.*

8. *Think tactically, not technically, in a match situation. Trust and believe in the strokes you bring to the match court on any given day.*

9. *Always have a strong, positive self-belief in your abilities to cope with difficult situations in any given match situation.*

10. *Present a strong image on the court. Positive, energetic body language will tell your opponent you are confident and ready to battle.*

controlling you during play. Adhering to highly specific between-point rituals is particularly important. These would include such things as the pace of your walk, bouncing the ball a certain number of times before serving, toweling off, deep breathing, and eyes on the strings.

Self-Talk

When players are executing well under pressure, they invariably report a distinctive sense of internal quiet. That annoying critical voice inside their heads starts to fade. A familiar sense of stillness descends. The louder the voice and the more negative and critical it is, the more disruptive to mechanics. Positive and encouraging self-talk serves to enhance personal control of the stress response for many players, and the opposite is true in the case of negative self-talk. Berating yourself, and constantly finding fault with what you do and how you do it, increases negative arousal and can severely compromise your

Keeping your eyes on the strings can be a between-point ritual.

mechanical precision in high-stress situations. The general rule regarding self-talk in competitions is simply this: say as little as possible and whatever is said, make it positive and encouraging.

Conclusion

Mechanical breakdowns in competition can be fully understood only in the context of a complex matrix of related physical, emotional, and mental competencies. Mechanically performing under pressure requires much more than simply mastering mental skills. It's tempting to label the collapse of a serve or forehand in high-stress competition as simply a mental choke. In reality, the culprit may well be the result of several interactive deficiencies that exist mentally, physically, and emotionally. Only through a fully integrated mind/body training model can players and coaches effectively address the issue of mechanical precision under pressure.

Part Two

Perfecting Your Strokes

It's been said many times before. Practice does not make perfect. Practice makes permanent. Only perfect practice makes perfect. For that reason this collection of authors has been assembled to ensure that the information you receive is not only the "perfect" information for your game, but that this information and the people offering it have stood the test of time. These authors are well schooled in the basic sciences and the instruction you received in part I. These experts have also been "there," at the top of the game. Many have played and coached at the Grand Slam tournaments. Others have served their countries as Davis Cup captains and as Olympic coaches.

This part of *World-Class Tennis Technique* is in an orderly progression of how to learn tennis technique. The ground strokes are written in extraordinary fashion, with the forehand chapter coauthored by the ITF's director of coaching education, Dr. Miguel Crespo, and Jose Higueras, one of the top clay courters of his era and, since retirement from the pro tour, one of the top coaches in all of tennis. The backhand chapter is coauthored by two legends in tennis, Vic Braden and Jack Kramer. Kramer is said to have had one of the best backhands ever to hit a tennis ball. The volley and overhead, specialty shot, and serve and return chapters are coauthored by top national coaches Frank van Fraayenhoven, Paul Dent, and Nick Saviano. They are accompanied by Davis Cup captains Michiel Schapers, Patrice Hagelauer, and one of the world's foremost tennis educators, Australian Dr. Bruce Elliott. And finally, what would a tennis technique book be without a chapter teaching you how to evaluate your own game? This self-analysis chapter was coauthored by biomechanical researcher Dr. Duane Knudson and tennis legend Pam Shriver, who has developed an awesome player/analyst perspective on the game as a television commentator for major tennis events.

So you will learn your tennis techniques from the very best; not only from the people who have been among the best players but also from some of the world's most respected tennis coaches and educators. Good luck on your adventure to becoming the very best player you can be.

Chapter Nine

Forehands

Miguel Crespo
Jose Higueras

The great Bill Tilden stated: "There are two general rules of body position. . . . (1) Await a stroke facing the net, with the body parallel to it. (2) Play every stroke with the body at right angles (sideways) to the net. . . . For all forehand shots the left foot should be advanced toward the right-hand sideline of the player, thus bringing him sideways automatically."

This does not seem to be the way top players play the forehand nowadays, however. Tennis has changed dramatically during the past 30 years. Today's champions seem to be stronger, faster, and fitter; they are mentally more aggressive than ever; the new rackets help players to hit harder; and most tournaments are played on surfaces that produce high and consistent bounces.

Tactically speaking, tennis has become a more aggressive game. Most players attack in almost all phases of the game and need to develop an explosive and dynamic playing style with several powerful weapons. The player's ability to consistently hit the ball with immense power is a distinguishing feature of the modern game when compared to that of several decades ago.

In fact, the players' search to add more power and speed to their games and combat the subsequent time constraints has led to a veritable technical evolution in each of the tennis strokes. This evolution is more evident in the forehand stroke than perhaps any other.

Characteristics of the Modern Forehand

The forehand shot is one of the cornerstones of tennis stroke production and clearly one of the most important strokes in tennis. In the modern game, the forehand is the shot that dominates the game of most advanced players during the baseline rallies. It assists them in placing their opponent under time and space constraints and allows them to dictate the point from the outset. In light of this, it is the intention of this chapter to present the specific characteristics of the modern forehand technique.

The development of the modern forehand has seen a forehand stroke that relied on linear movement as its primary source of power, to be modified such that rotation is now the key.

Historically, players delivered their forehand strokes with essentially an arm movement combined with the slight transfer of body weight forward. Gradually more body segments have been introduced into stroke production. In an effort to hit with topspin to add more variety and control to the forehand shot, players such as Rod Laver and Manuel Santana displayed the first real signs of the modern forehand shot.

But it was Bjorn Borg who revolutionized the game with what was then considered an unconventional forehand. The great Swedish champion, together with players such as Guillermo Vilas and Harold Solomon, based his game on sound and consistent play from the baseline. The forehand hit with heavy topspin, to attain better clearance over the net, thus increasing safety and consistency of the shot, was the key stroke for all of them.

The technical characteristics of this type of forehand provided the foundation for the modern-day production of the forehand stroke. They include

- an open-stance position,
- a western or semi-western grip,
- a low position of the racket at the end of the backswing,
- a delayed swing of the racket,
- shoulders positioned facing the net,
- a hitting area located forward, and
- a very powerful forearm action.

Although these players used the topspin forehand for different tactical reasons than those of the modern day (power and speed), the need for height over the net and depth close to the baseline has imposed the topspin forehand as the most-used ground stroke in modern tennis.

This major technical progression has almost deemed the slice forehand shot obsolete (only used on grass and for defensive shots, low balls, or approaching the net), and the flat forehand also is used less often.

Research further shows that the main reasons that players are hitting with an open stance are the following:

- There is a lack of preparation time for the forehand stroke because of the speeding up of the game.
- The use of modern rackets allows for more powerful strokes even with occasional, abbreviated preparatory movements.
- The playing surfaces produce higher and more consistent bounces in general, which allow players to hit harder.

Let's examine more closely the differences between the so-called "traditional" forehand and the "modern" technique.

Differences Between the Square- and Open-Stance Forehand

There are a number of aspects that differentiate the "traditional" forehand from the "modern" one. However, one of the most relevant is the stance of the player during the stroke. In the traditional forehand, both feet are aligned perpendicular to the net resulting in the label of "square" stance. Conversely, the modern forehand has been referred to as the "open" stance because both feet are aligned parallel to the net.

However, there are other ways of positioning your feet to produce the forehand stroke. We can consider the "closed" stance, in which the front foot is crossed in front of the back, and also the "semi-open" stance in which the closer foot to the hitting zone is slightly behind the other foot.

Even though the closed stance was the one taught in the early days, there is a general consensus in the literature that this type of forehand is less effective when playing regular strokes and is used only in emergency situations such as

- when you are hitting on the run,
- when you are playing a defensive forehand, or
- when you are coming to the net if the ball bounces well in front of you.

Closed-stance forehands are typically used in emergency situations such as hitting on the run.

Some experts also have expressed concern over the closed-stance forehand blocking the entire hip area, which potentially can lead to injuries being sustained in the hip as well as in the lower back. Obviously with this type of forehand the transfer of momentum forward is almost nonexistent, which makes it very difficult to use if you want to hit with power.

In many cases the "semi-open" stance has the same advantages as the open stance. But in this semi-open position with the leg closer to the hitting zone, you are able to transfer the body weight forward more effectively. This is the typical stance of players hitting from the baseline with more offensive mentalities.

The main features of the traditional (square-stance) and the modern (open-stance) forehand strokes as obtained by biomechanical studies are compared in table 9.1.

A recent study also has shown that the motions of the trunk, arm, and racket are surprisingly very similar in both the open- and closed-stance forehands. Research additionally has shown that the activation of the abdominal and back muscles does not differ from one type of forehand to another. Thus, there is no scientific evidence that the open-stance forehand creates larger loading on the trunk and upper extremity.

Crespo and Higueras

Table 9.1

Traditional vs. Modern Forehand Stroke

Aspect	Traditional	Modern
Recommended grip	Eastern	Semi-western or western
Stance position	Square	Open
Initial footwork	Step forward	Slight step to the sideline
Backswing of the racket	Straight (racket rotated to perpendicular; 90 degrees to the baseline)	Looped (racket often rotated to 135 degrees from the baseline)
Hip and shoulders	Try to remain more square	Tend to face the net earlier
Forward racket swing	Pivoting from the shoulder	Multisegment
Joint actions	Similar joint actions used to generate power in the forward swing in both variations of the forehand	
Impact zone	More accurate racket path in the horizontal zone	Reduction in the window of time during which the ball can be hit successfully
Position of the knees	Bent through contact	Extended at contact
Risk of injury	Similar with both types	
Court coverage	Slower	Faster
Follow-through	More in front	More over the shoulder
Position of feet	In contact with the ground	In the air
Footwork	Takes longer to execute	Allows the player to hit on the run

Angular and Linear Momentum

Universally acknowledged as a very important component of successful fore-hand stroke production is the coordination and summation of forces generated by each segment of the forehand's linked system.

Contextually, momentum is the product of the mass and velocity of a body part. We can further distinguish two types of momentum: linear and angular. In the forehand, both types of momentum are generated from ground reaction forces.

Linear momentum is the quantity of linear motion that a body possesses. It is very important for the production of a sound topspin forehand. Angular momentum—equally if not more important for sound stroke production—is the quantity of angular motion that a body possesses. It is produced from a sequence of body rotations occurring at the different segments of the linked system starting from the ground up (legs, hips, trunk, and upper limb).

Evidently the different stances used for the forehand utilize linear and angu-lar momentum to varying degrees.

The closed-stance forehand generates

- considerable linear momentum as you step forward toward the ball; and
- some angular momentum from the rotation of the legs, hips, and trunk.

In the open-stance forehand, there is

- little or no transfer of linear momentum because the step is taken side-ways; and
- a significant amount of angular momentum generated by the rotations of the different body segments (legs, hips, trunk, and upper arm).

However, you can produce more linear momentum by stepping toward the sideline with the back foot such that it is almost parallel with the baseline. A second step toward the ball with the front limb creates a semi-open stance that allows full rotation of the hips and shoulders as well as the transference of body weight forward.

Irrespective of stance, it is important that you coordinate the development of linear (extension of the knees) and angular (rotation of the hips, trunk, and upper limb) momentum to produce the most effective forehand.

Learning to Hit the Forehand

Since all the top players use the modern open-stance forehand, should all players learn this type of shot? There are differences of opinion about which forehand is best to learn.

Several experts have stressed the importance of not copying or imitating techniques of advanced players. Why? Reasons for this can be the following:

- In some cases top players develop "individual movements" in their strokes (e.g., John McEnroe's stance for the serve, Boris Becker's grip and follow-through in the serve, Chris Evert's left arm position for the forehand). These movements are considered personal interpretations of technique and do not contribute substantially to the success of the shot; thus they are unnecessary for other players.

- In other cases, top players perform their strokes with great success not because of their technique but because of their physical abilities. Other players with different physical attributes may be unable to achieve the same result.

- Players and coaches should look at the technical commonalities of these champions (balance, use of body rotation, generation of power, etc.) and not at the different stroke techniques they use.

Although from a biomechanical perspective these experts state that the square-stance forehand has small technical advantages compared to the open stance when trying to learn the shot, we prefer using a more holistic teaching method. This strategy implies a more global approach in which the players are introduced to the game and not taught to adopt a specific stance for any shot—provided they respect the basic biomechanical principles for stroke production at beginner levels.

For competitive match play at advanced levels, we recommend the use of the semi-open or open-stance forehand, mainly because of

- the various court coverage advantages,
- the ease in negotiating the return of serve according to the obvious time constraints, and
- the fact that it allows players to more effectively hide the intention of their shots.

Conclusion

Coaches should try to help their players learn all types of forehands using many different variations or stances. By doing this, players will be able to benefit from the advantages of each technique.

The square-stance forehand can be used to good effect when emphasizing the transfer of the body weight forward. At the top level, this usually is done when the ball bounces short and is at a comfortable distance for the player to step in.

However, the open-stance forehand has to be used when the player is under time pressure, when the ball goes directly into the body, or when it goes too much to the side.

Stroke Production: Technical, Tactical, and Physical Considerations

"In looking at the area of advanced stroke techniques, we have to appreciate that there are many variations of good technique. For example, if you ask which players in the world have a great forehand, you will hear many different answers . . . Agassi, Moya, Sampras, Davenport, Seles, etc. There is no one correct answer as to which forehand is the best. Without dispute all of these forehand strokes are extremely effective. In looking at correct stroke techniques at the advanced level, the coach needs to be much more concerned with the biomechanical effectiveness rather than the conformity or the cosmetics of the stroke" (International Tennis Federation, 1998).

Correct technique is situational because it must adapt to the specific characteristics and purpose of each shot. Players also develop their own styles or personal interpretations of technique for hitting their forehands with power, precision, and control. Regardless of this style, however, all the best players respect the fundamental biomechanical principles applicable to the production of the modern forehand stroke.

Grips

The disparities in the technique of the forehand are reflected by the variation of grips used to hit this stroke. The grip serves to orient the racket at impact while also allowing for hand mobility and the firmness required to give strength to the shot and to avoid torque at impact.

The grip you use for your forehand is determined to some extent by the surface on which you start to play, which in turn defines your playing style. For example, clay- or slow-surface specialists tend to use "closed" grips such as the western and semi-western, whereas all-round players and serve-volleyers may prefer to hit their forehands with the eastern forehand grip.

The following grips are being used to play forehands in today's modern game.

Eastern Grip

The eastern grip is the most classical forehand grip. Although top players rarely use it, there are some players such as Tim Henman who do. With this grip, the palm of the playing hand is placed on the side of the handle. Players using the eastern forehand grip tend to use more horizontal flexion and abduction about the shoulder and more flexion at the wrist. With the contact point being lower and farther from the body than for the semi-western or western grip, this grip encourages shots played flat or with slight topspin.

Advantages of the eastern grip include the following:

- It allows for a natural wrist position.
- It keeps the lower arm musculature relaxed.
- It makes it possible for players to adapt their strokes to the net game with more ease than with the other extreme grips.

It is important to note, however, that certain players using these less-extreme grips can lose efficiency on clay due to the height of the bounce, the lack of power, and the reduced amount of topspin imparted to the forehand.

Semi-Western Grip

The semi-western grip is the most popular forehand grip and is used by players such as Andre Agassi and Lindsay Davenport. It produces two important features: a laying back of the wrist, and a closing of the racket face on both the backswing and forward swing. The playing hand is placed well behind the handle, which ensures maximum transfer of force and spin into the shot.

The natural contact point is higher and closer to the body but more in front than for the eastern grip. It is normally well above the waist, usually just under shoulder height. Shots usually are played with a stance between semi-open and fully open. This grip is preferred because it allows players to impart topspin to the ball better, to take it earlier, and to hit on the rise.

Some of the disadvantages associated with the semi-western grip include difficulty when dealing with low-bouncing balls and with the net game.

Western Grip

The western grip is used by players such as Tommy Haas and Conchita Martinez. It is the one used by pure baseline players and clay-court specialists. This grip produces a more pronounced laying back of the wrist and a more closed racket face during the swing than the semi-western forehand. It places the playing hand below the handle and allows a lot of wrist mobility while maintaining racket orientation at impact.

The natural contact point is higher, closer to the body, yet more in front than for the semi-western grip. Players using this type of grip usually play their forehand with a full open stance.

The western grip is preferred because it allows the player to more easily generate topspin (e.g., players such as Alberto Berasategui and Anke Huber). It is

Note the closed racket face in the follow-through on Lindsay Davenport's semi-western grip.

particularly effective when you're playing high balls (above shoulder), as it helps give the ball more topspin and a safer and shorter trajectory. Some players such as Berasategui can even play forehand and backhand with the same side of the racket, such is the extreme nature of their forehand grips. These very extreme grips allow for the application of even more topspin to the ball.

The use of the western grip has the following disadvantages:

- Difficulty in hitting low-bouncing balls and fast wide balls.
- Difficulty adapting to the more conventional volley grips.
- These extreme grips often cause a backward thrust that prevents any forward weight transfer.

However, these disadvantages can be negotiated with good footwork and a quick change of grip toward the continental for the net game if need be.

Crespo and Higueras

Conclusion

There are differences of opinion about which grip is best to use for the forehand. Clearly the most popular grip among top players is the semi-western forehand grip. It also is recommended as the grip that players should use to play the modern forehand as it provides for the best transfer forward of both power and spin. We agree with this and further view the semi-western grip as the preferred grip with the eastern and western grips being the two varieties.

Stroke Mechanics

Defining the type of movement of the forehand is difficult and historically has been plagued with controversy. However, recent biomechanics research has shown that the forehand is a whole-body action. When hitting the forehand, the body summates the velocities of different segments. This summation starts when the lower limb pushes against the ground and generates a reaction force from it. This force then builds sequentially as all contributory body parts rotate toward impact.

From a stroke-production point of view, the forehand can be divided into the following: preparation, backswing, forward swing, impact, and follow-through. To facilitate the discussion of the mechanical attributes of the modern forehand, photographic sequences of Martina Hingis (see pages 158-159) will be referred to throughout.

Preparation

The forehand shot begins with the preparation stance. This ready position or "athletic" position has several common features for almost all players:

- The feet wide apart
- The knees slightly bent
- The weight moved forward toward the balls of the feet
- The waist marginally flexed
- The racket positioned in front of the body and held by both hands
- The trunk leaning forward
- The shoulders parallel to the net
- The head still

While the stance adopted by a player will be specific to the individual and therefore may differ slightly from the one described here, it's important that the ready position adopted allow you to sprint to the ball as quickly as possible and provide a comfortable stance between strokes. One feature of the ready position

Martina Hingis' forehand.

that will facilitate this movement toward the ball is the split-step. When you've determined the direction of the movement, a split-step in which the knees flex and accelerate the body downward can be used to facilitate the storage of elastic energy in the thigh muscles (which contract to brace the movement downward). This energy then is to be used to assist your explosion toward the ball.

It is also important to note that an excessive flexion of the knees and the hips will increase stability but will detract from your ability to optimize the storage of elastic energy and quickly react to the oncoming ball.

Maintaining good balance before, during, and after the strokes is one of the most important aspects for producing a successful forehand. The key aspects involved in maintaining balance for the forehand shot are as follows:

- The position of the head (the organs of balance are situated in the ears)
- The position of the upper body (where the center of gravity lies)
- The position of the legs (by its contribution to the base of support)

Although slightly more advanced in her preparations, Hingis has adopted a ready position similar to those outlined here. The racket is held out in front and her weight is beginning to shift in the intended direction of her run. More noticeably, despite Hingis' readying herself for a run wide to the forehand, it is clear that she has excellent posture and balance.

Crespo and Higueras

Backswing

Hingis has her right knee flexed, elastic energy has been stored, and she is ready to drive off this leg toward the ball. The slight flexing of the knee brings the center of gravity closer to the base of support and thus improves balance. In some forehands, it is the knee of the leg closest to the ball that is bent more and gets down low; this is a common feature of the modern forehand stroke.

During the backswing of a modern open-stance forehand, players essentially use their bodies in two ways to provide for greater balance. That is, they adopt a wide base of support with a low and solid stance, and they place their free or nonplaying arm out in front to counter the motion of the racket arm.

You can achieve the wide base by separating both legs slightly wider than the distance between the shoulders. The stance is kept solid by taking a side step with the foot closer to the ball. It may be more advisable to take a larger step with that foot in order to keep the trunk inside the base of support.

The free arm, initially used to help take the racket back (and assist shoulder and trunk rotation), helps you maintain balance by remaining out in front (as if pointing at the ball) and at almost the same height as the playing hand. Hingis does this to good effect. The free arm then moves in the opposite direction to counter the motion of the racket arm. By doing this, you keep the center of gravity inside the base of support and remain balanced.

Another characteristic of stroke production that emphasizes the variation that exists between forehand techniques is the method of racket preparation during the backswing. Players generally use two methods for the modern topspin forehand: leading with the elbow, and a conventional or "single-unit" forehand.

Leading with the elbow is characterized by

- moving the elbow back in synchrony with the shoulder turn,
- the tip of the racket pointing to the oncoming ball,
- the racket face being closed as the elbow is raised, and
- then the forearm and racket pivoting about the elbow such that the racket is rotated up to a position above the elbow and shoulder.

This type of swing, as performed by Lindsay Davenport, is considered an individual feature of several advanced players, because it facilitates the optimization of their arm speed. However, this kind of swing has to be performed by players who can put the racket in the proper hitting zone at the correct time to avoid hitting the ball late.

In the conventional or "single-unit" forehand, the racket is moved back in synchrony with the shoulder turn and the movement implies a rotation of the whole racket arm about the shoulder. With this swing it is easier to have the racket head ready to hit.

The player's physical attributes can provide further information on the type of backswing he uses. That is, we can distinguish between the backswing produced by

- the more fluid or free-flowing players such as Pete Sampras and Lindsay Davenport, who get their power by rotating their shoulders and lengthening their backswing; and
- the more compact players such as Agassi and Hingis, who have a reduced swinging radius and rely more on the development of angular momentum during their rotations toward the ball.

Irrespective of the type of backswing used, however, almost all modern players use a looped (circular) preparation that helps to produce a more fluent stroke and allows the racket to accelerate over a larger distance. The forehand of Hingis is no exception. Studies on the difference between the circular and the straight backswing for the forehand have concluded that the circular swing averages higher racket-head velocities at impact.

The position of the racket at the completion of the backswing is similar for the two styles with research indicating that the racket is rotated approximately 45 degrees past a line perpendicular to the baseline (i.e., 45 degrees beyond a position where the racket would point to the back fence). A backswing that is either too short or too long is not very economical and can cause a loss of power during the stroke.

We advocate that the multisegment forehand, which has been shown to have a more compact arm motion during the backswing relating to less shoulder abduction and more elbow flexion, be used in combination with a small-looped backswing. The small-looped backswing

- provides for increased racket velocity,
- facilitates the generation of linear and angular momentum, and
- doesn't affect the timing and control of the stroke.

The styles of different players illustrate the multisegmental nature of the forehand stroke and the varied looped backswings that elite players use. It is evident that the backswings of both Hingis and Lindsay Davenport are characterized by a more exaggerated loop, while Tommy Haas, when preparing to hit a stationary forehand, has a lower take-back. Make further note of the different types of racket preparations: Davenport (elbow-leading) versus Haas (single-unit).

With most of the power needed for the modern forehand generated from the ground and the larger body parts, some authors have asserted that the rotation of the body is the single most important component in the modern tennis technique.

Elastic Energy

In an effort to optimize the rotary potential of the forehand, it is important that players make use of the stretch-shorten cycle. This is a sequence of eccentric (lengthening of the muscle) and concentric (shortening of the muscle) movements that facilitate the production of muscular force.

More specifically, as alluded to earlier, when the muscle is stretched, energy is stored in it. When it is shortened, the energy is released. With reference to the forehand shot, the backswing is considered the stretching phase, whereas the forward swing is considered the releasing phase. However, there are several aspects that should be taken into account:

- If there is a long pause or delay between the two phases, the energy will dissipate. The longer the delay, the more energy is lost. That is why it is important to execute a more or less "continuous motion" and to avoid backswings that are commenced too early.
- The greater the velocity of the stretch, the greater the storage of elastic energy.

The rotations of both the hips and shoulders, important features of the backswing, are used to facilitate the storage of this energy in the large muscles of the legs, hips, shoulders, and back. "Loading" the musculature in this way provides for the vigorous rotation of the trunk and upper limb during the forward swing to impact. Research has further shown that the rotation of the shoulders during the backswing is rather more pronounced than is commonly thought. That is, from a position parallel to the net in the ready position, the shoulders are rotated to a position past a line drawn perpendicular to the back fence. This means that the popular perception that the shoulders should be rotated to this perpendicular position is not correct.

In summary, at the completion of the backswing,

- the knees are slightly flexed,
- the hips are well turned,
- the shoulders are rotated to a position past a line drawn perpendicular to the back fence,
- the racket arm is not fully extended,
- the hand is hyperextended at the wrist joint,
- the forearm and the racket are not aligned, and
- the racket is rotated approximately 45 degrees past a line perpendicular to the baseline.

The hyperextended wrist joint and the nonalignment of racket and arm are particularly evident in the Hingis forehand shown in the photos on pages 158 and 159. Although she is on the run and has not rotated her shoulders as far as some players do, it is clear that the planting of her right foot and leg will provide her with a pivot around which the trunk and shoulders can later rotate. Also take note of the position of the left arm. Hingis has used her left arm to good effect to assist with the shoulder turn and then help maintain balance.

In conclusion, there can be several different types and shapes of backswings (small-loop, leading with the elbow, big-loop, etc.), but all of them should be adapted to your characteristics, the type of incoming ball, and the type of shot that you want to hit. This is no matter if you are more muscular or free-flowing; if the ball is high or low, fast or slow; and if the shot is going to be played flat or with topspin.

Forward Swing

The motions described earlier, which are performed during the backswing phase, generate force against the ground. The ground then pushes back with an equal and opposite force. From a biomechanical perspective, the player is applying the principle of opposing forces or "action-reaction."

Previous tennis literature indicated that there was a continuous acceleration from the backswing through to contact with the ball. However, research has highlighted that a slight pause at the end of the backswing does occur during the production of the forehand stroke. Experts agree that this pause does not have a detrimental effect as long as it does not exceed 200 milliseconds. If the pause is any longer, the player will lose the accumulated energy.

The forward swing is initiated after the rotation of the trunk away from the ball reaches its maximum.

The thrust of the right leg starts the swing by projecting the right hip forward. This action is further complemented by the rotation of the hips toward the ball. This release of the hips triggers the uncoiling of the upper body (trunk rotation), which in turn produces a lagging of the arm and racket. The lag is further exaggerated by the drive of the lower limb. The musculature of the shoulder and chest subsequently is placed on stretch to store energy that will be used during the rotation of the arm and racket toward the ball. This arm and racket "lag" is particularly evident during the forehand played by Tommy Haas.

Given the multisegmented nature of the modern forehand's forward swing, the sequence of movements involved can be summarized as follows:

- Forward thrust of the right leg
- Rotation of the hips
- Trunk rotation (uncoiling of upper body)
- Elbow extension
- Horizontal flexion or abduction of the upper arm
- Internal rotation of the upper arm
- Ulnar flexion or palmar flexion of the hand

Of considerable importance is that these movements be sequentially coordinated to generate optimal racket velocity. That is not to say that each movement in the sequence ceases to give way to the next. Rather there will be a "staircase" effect in which acceleration and deceleration of each movement (link) produce a summation of forces to assist in developing the racket speed for impact.

Of further interest is that some movements may not even directly contribute to the development of racket velocity but play an important role in aligning the racket for impact. Similarly, segmental involvement also may vary slightly depending on the type of shot to be played and the magnitude of topspin to be applied to the ball. However, research has shown that the velocity of the racket head in the multisegment forehand is produced primarily by the horizontal flexion/abduction and internal rotation of the upper arm and the linear movement of the shoulder.

Good balance during the stroke demands that the head be upright and still. The head and the upper body should be a unit. As the hips and shoulders tend to open up and face the net relatively early in the open-stance forehand, there is a tendency for players to turn the head approaching impact. This should be avoided. When looking at top players we can notice that their heads barely move throughout the forehand. Even when drawn wide, as is the case with Hingis, or required to propel themselves forward, elite players maintain excellent dynamic balance. Also note that in order to maintain control over the racket head at impact and to hit through the ball's line of flight, the arm remains at a comfortable distance from the trunk during the forward swing.

Impact Point

The impact point is the most critical and important phase of every stroke because the alignment of the racket at impact determines the direction of the ball.

At this point, you need to obtain maximum speed toward impact. In order to do so, you have to increase hyperextension of the wrist, which causes considerable delay in the racket-head transfer. It is the last link in the chain. This delay is obtained by a looseness of the wrist in the moment before impact.

Research has shown that the linear velocities of the different body segments increase as these segments approach the point of impact. Much of the increase in racket velocity occurs because of this increase in linear velocity. This is produced because the segments of the linked system (elbow, wrist, and racket tip) are farther away from the shoulder, which is the axis of rotation for the forehand.

You can achieve complete efficiency in hitting the modern forehand by doing the following:

- *Hitting in front of your body, with your center of gravity positioned just behind an imaginary line extending from the hitting hand.* This allows you to effectively transfer all the forces generated from the linked system to the racket to achieve maximum velocity.

- *Maintaining a firm grip.* Though not an important factor in determining the velocity of the ball in central impacts, a firm grip helps to reduce any racket rotation induced by any off-center impacts.

Studies have shown that players change the angle of the racket and the contact zone to vary the direction of the ball. The larger wrist angle at impact allows the ball to be hit further in front for the crosscourt forehand than for the down-the-line stroke. Researchers have further shown that the racket should have a more horizontal trajectory near the impact zone to minimize the timing errors that can be associated with a steep vertical racket trajectory.

On the other hand, the racket face at impact for a topspin forehand should be almost vertical or slightly closed if a player wants to produce topspin effectively.

At impact, balance is crucial. The free arm plays a key role in keeping its position on the side of the trunk and prevents the upper body from rotating too much. When under pressure, it is very important to maintain balance throughout the shot. In these situations it is not always possible to transfer the body weight forward. You should, however, adopt a firm rear-foot stance to avoid moving backward during the stroke. This is also one of the reasons for frequent jumps in defensive situations.

Nowadays, most of the top players hit with their feet off the ground. The timing of when players leave the ground is sometimes misunderstood:

- Research has shown that some players do not leave the ground until the instant of impact. This means that the jumping action, itself, does not contribute to the power of their strokes. Rather it provides for a higher contact point or is merely a secondary characteristic of force development (i.e., not a conscious jump).

- Players do not leave the ground well before or after hitting the ball, because jumping too early would mean that the summation of forces would cease and there would be insufficient transfer of momentum to the upper limb.

- The fact that top players leave the ground at the very last instant before impact, when the energy they have created is in their smaller body parts (upper body) and not in the larger ones (lower body), ensures that the loss of energy is minimal and that they can hit with good dynamic balance.

The photographs of Hingis emphasize the importance of excellent balance and posture, irrespective of the type of forehand shot to be hit. Further, we believe that coaches should not teach players to consciously jump when hitting, because it may occur naturally during the course of developing a powerful forehand.

Follow-Through

The last part of the forehand shot, the follow-through, is also very important. Reasons for this include the following:

- It makes the racket follow the path of the ball. By doing this, you can maintain the balance even after the impact point.

- It makes it possible to continue the acceleration through impact. It is necessary to achieve maximum velocity and to impart the correct amount of topspin to the ball. If you avoid the follow-through or make it too short, you will have to slow down the racket before impact to do so.

- If it is complete, it may reduce the possibility of injury by allowing normal racket deceleration. Hitting with no follow-through causes the muscles of the arm to produce fast eccentric contractions that may cause injuries.

- If it is correct, it generally means that the whole stroke has been produced in an acceptable way. Coaches may focus on the follow-through as one of the means of evaluating the quality of the stroke.

In the traditional forehand, the racket finished pointing toward the net. However, in the modern forehand, the follow-through is more varied and depends on a number of different factors, namely the following.

- Your style and the type of shot you play.
- Your grip. The semi-western grips tend to promote a full follow-through that wraps around the neck or higher. But the western grip, favoring more exaggerated forearm and wrist action, is often a source of a shorter and lower follow-through.
- The tactical intention of your shot. This is perhaps the biggest determining factor. A full follow-through is the result of powerful, relatively flat shots or topspin shots hit late. A short follow-through (such as Hingis') is indicative of a more violent spin. The best follow-through in the modern forehand, however, is the one that drives out and toward the target allowing you to finish with the weight forward and arm relaxed.

During the follow-through there is a gradual deceleration of the body segments. At the same time, if the shot has enough linear momentum, the rear leg moves forward to a position level with the foot in front to prepare the movement for the next shot. At the end of the follow-through, balance also is critically important.

Other Key Elements of the Successful Forehand

There are several key characteristics of a good forehand, including proper footwork and the production of spin, as we discuss in this section.

Footwork

Footwork has become an instrumental aspect of today's game. The ability to get to the ball as quickly as possible and maintain balance for the next stroke is crucial for a successful forehand. A forehand played with an open stance is favorable in this light.

After hitting with an open stance you have to be able to perform the correct footwork to recover the position. This is achieved by pushing off with the leg

Dominique Van Roost's follow-through wraps around her neck.

closer to the shot to return (a recovery step). Then you will have to use shuffle and crossover steps to recover the exact position for the next shot.

However, in certain circumstances (e.g., approaching the net), an open-stance forehand is difficult to execute and you must manipulate your feet and body position to lose as little power and time as possible. Quite often, you will be forced to play this type of ball with a closed stance. Thus in an effort to optimize recovery when playing with this stance, the following options are available:

- Extending the front knee and rotating the trunk, landing onto the rear foot
- Extending the front knee and jump landing onto the front foot
- Bringing the back leg forward during the follow-through to put it to the side

The footwork when running around the backhand has several special features:

- You have to use short side steps to run laterally and slightly backward to the backhand side.
- It is then important to move diagonally toward the ball if possible, planting the back foot in preparation to push off with power.
- After the shot, you have to move forward in the direction of the shot to follow the path of the ball.

And finally, when hitting on the run, the most important aspect is to keep balance by moving the opposing limbs in synchrony and driving the arms during the run.

Production of Spin

The production of topspin is one of the key factors of the modern forehand. When you try to combine power with control, topspin is the most effective means of increasing the margin for error over the net and inside the court. The magnitude of topspin imparted to the ball is determined by the gradient of the racket's low-to-high trajectory during the forward swing to impact and the orientation and velocity of the racket head at impact.

More specifically, players tend to align the racket and ball and then, when the impact is assured, they increase the trajectory of the racket to impart an off-center force to the ball. At impact, both for topspin and slice shots, the racket is almost vertical to the ground. However, research also has shown that a racket slightly closed by 5 degrees is capable of producing larger levels of topspin at a given racket trajectory than does a vertical racket orientation.

When the racket moves vertically to produce topspin, you sacrifice some horizontal racket speed and the shot occasionally can lack pace. This has prompted some players to hit their forehands with less topspin, preferring to flatten out their shots, especially when the ball is well above the net. This provides for a flat forehand played from high to low that speeds up the game and gives their opponents less time to react.

Modern Forehand in Relation to Surfaces of Play

The modern forehand has become a lethal weapon on all surfaces. However, it seems to be more effective on slow ones such as clay and hard courts. Almost all the best clay-court specialists in the world—players from Spain, Argentina, Brazil, and several European countries—have developed a sound and devastating baseline game style built around a powerful forehand.

For some coaches working with these players, it is the forehand and not the serve or the return that is the most important shot for a clay-court baseline specialist. The slower speed of the game on clay courts allows these players to have more time to get to the ball; thus they are able to hit their forehands from all areas of the court.

The combination of the slow court together with the improvement of the player's footwork has created the possibility of playing the forehand from the backhand side, the so-called inside-out forehand.

This variation of the modern forehand has made a big difference in terms of the attacking possibilities from the baseline. This shot can be played to the weaker side of the opponent (usually the backhand corner) both with a very deep trajectory and a very short angle to move the opponent and open the court. Another variation is the inside-out forehand played to the forehand of the opponent (if a right-hander). This is the typical wrong-foot tactical pattern against players with very good forehands.

Clay courts produce a higher bounce of the ball, thus allowing players to hit the ball more on the rise. It also makes players use western or semi-western grips and higher backswings in an effort to produce a more effective forehand shot. On these surfaces, players hitting their forehands with eastern or continental grips will have more problems when playing high balls.

On fast surfaces such as indoor carpet or grass, the modern forehand also is used prolifically; however, the speed of the game makes it more difficult to play continuous inside-out forehands. When they are played, they tend to be hit with less topspin.

When you have no intention of going to the net it may be more advisable to use an open-stance forehand. In this case you do not require linear momentum to come in (a feature of the closed-stance forehand), and you still will be capable of producing a powerful forehand stroke from the baseline with the open stance.

Modern Technique in Relation to Tactics

Control and power seem to be opposite qualities in the game of tennis. However, they now are invading the game—starting with the forehand.

The forehand is one of the cornerstones of the tennis-stroke arsenal of today's champions. Most, if not all, players are building their game around a powerful and penetrating forehand together with excellent footwork and balance. This stroke is an open skill because the players should adjust their motion to the characteristics of the incoming ball. During the game, the intention of the shot—the tactics—is what counts, no matter the level of play.

From the point of view of the tactical use of the court, the forehand no longer is confined to the right-hand side of the court as it was in the past. That is, coaches tended to discourage hitting inside-out or runaround forehands because it left the other side of the court very open. Nowadays, however, players hit winning forehands from everywhere on the court because their physical attributes (great speed and effective footwork) allow them to be perfectly placed. The players tend to impose their tactical patterns by using the court in a geometrically efficient way. To do this, the inside-out forehand is one of the most-used shots because it provides players with the opportunity to use their best strokes in all situations.

Today's players, whether male or female, have a mentality for offense that is reflected in the way they hit the ball. These players are capable of firing off devastating forehands. In all its variations—down the line, crosscourt, angled, inside-out, short or deep—the forehand is a permanent threat to the opponent.

In addition to using the inside-out forehand in high, short, and sliced balls, top players tend to put pressure on their opponents by reducing the time of the rally. By hitting the ball well in front and, if possible, by hitting the forehand early and inside the court, these players take advantage of all weak balls in all parts of the court.

Another clear tactical advantage of the inside-out forehand is that it does not provide too many cues to help the opponent anticipate the shot. The fact that the player moves around the backhand and "hides" the shot with his forward movement toward the ball makes it very difficult for the opponent to deduce where the ball will go.

No matter on which surface they play, the players try to win the point in two or three points. Great champions have automated their personal tactical patterns, which allow them to dominate their opponents in crucial situations. Thus, each shot has its specific tactical intention. Weak shots should be punished. Players should try to find the opportunity to take advantage of short or weak shots from the opponent by coming in, and using their best shot (usually the forehand), hitting it in front and early to be aggressive.

On the other hand, we can notice that all top players have learned to take the ball early and on the rise to counterattack heavy topspin shots. That is why the best players use flatter forehands and avoid hitting with excessive topspin.

Summary

In this chapter we have presented the principles that define the most efficient forehands. These guidelines should be flexible enough to adapt to everyone's style and personality. The present technique that the top players use is oriented mostly toward power even if it is sometimes detrimental to precision. We should not forget that today's technical principles are no longer the same as yesterday's and that we should expect a continuous evolution of this stroke in the ensuing years.

We conclude by saying that a champion is the player who is able to adapt to all situations and to use technique to continuously experiment and invent unique movements in any new situation to deliver an increasingly efficient forehand.

Note: The authors would like to thank the contribution of Machar Reid.

Chapter Ten

Backhands

Vic Braden

Jack Kramer

Historically, the backhand has been defined as the stroke that causes the back of one's hand to be facing the opponent when striking the ball. For a right-handed player, that would mean a ball is approaching to the left side of the body and vice versa for a left-handed player. But the emergence and popularity of the two-handed backhand have forced some reconsideration of that definition. Because the position of the hands on the racket varies so greatly for a two-handed backhand, the more simple explanation is that a backhand is the shot that approaches to the left side of a right-hander and to the right side of a left-hander.

History

For more than a hundred years, the backhand was hit primarily with only one hand gripping the racket. But in recent years, the number of two-handed backhand hitters appears to have outnumbered the one-handed backhand players. In the 1930s and 1940s, Australian Vivian McGrath was sporting a two-handed backhand. Ironically, it was a two-handed forehand of Pancho Segura in the 1950s and 1960s that began to capture the attention of many players. His control of the ball was nothing short of amazing and he held his own against the taller and stronger professional players. However, it was the success of Chris Evert in the 1970s and 1980s that created the two-handed backhand explosion. Segura primarily played before a few thousand spectators and Evert played before millions on international television. Once the women saw Evert holding a Wimbledon trophy, it almost closed the door on future one-handed female backhand hitters. On the men's side, it was Bjorn Borg and Jimmy Connors who set the pace for two-handed male players. The myth that a two-handed male backhand player could not win on the Wimbledon grass courts was dispelled by Borg, who won the coveted prize five times. None other than Pete Sampras has stated that the Russian phenom Marat Safin will be the two-handed backhand hitter to watch as the dominant player in the early years of the 21st century. Sampras may be right, as he lost the United States Open finals in September 2000 to Safin in three straight sets.

In the 1990s, Pete Sampras and Steffi Graf proved that the one-handed backhand was not being discarded totally as they primarily dominated that decade. A few of the great one-handed backhand hitters beginning in the 1940s through the 1990s were Don Budge, Pauline Betz, Maureen Connolly, Lew Hoad, Ken Rosewall, Margaret Court, Rod Laver, Ivan Lendl, and Martina Navratilova.

If a two-handed backhand appeared to be such a great shot, then why not play with two hands on both sides? Frew McMillan of South Africa started that trend, and American Gene Mayer and Yugoslavian sensation (and now American citizen) Monica Seles followed closely behind. In 2000, American Jan-Michael Gambill led the U.S. two-handed forehand and backhand player contingent.

Backhand Swing Pattern

If you wanted to develop a swing pattern that would hold up in amateur and professional play, it would have the following four characteristics: (1) The racket would be traveling forward and upward at an approximate 30-degree angle, using the court as a horizontal baseline; (2) the racket face would be near vertical to the court as it impacted the ball; (3) the racket face would be pointed toward the intended target at the impact point with the ball; and (4) the racket would be traveling fast enough to hit a 50-mph shot. The result of this swing against typical players would be a shot that would travel five feet over the net, possess a slight topspin, and land very close to an opponent's baseline. Obviously, there would have to be some minor variations based on the speed, incoming angle, and spin of an opponent's shot.

In Hewitt's backswing, the racket face is near vertical to the court at impact.

Many of today's players, sporting new and improved rackets, are hitting shots with greater speed using only a 10- to 20-degree forward-and-upward swing pattern. This forward-and-upward swing produces a ball that has almost no rotation and requires exceptional timing.

Follow-Through

Though the follow-through plays an important role, its function often is quite different from that expressed in popular tennis magazines. As the ball is in contact with the strings approximately 4 milliseconds, research has shown that the ball has left the racket before the central nervous system and brain realize the ball has been struck. In addition, it normally takes the brain more than 100 milliseconds to send messages down to the muscles to respond to any racket-ball impact information. Thus, when you feel the ball, it's already too late to influence a shot with a standard or unique follow-through.

Then what is the role of the follow-through? There are two primary functions. The first is to keep the racket face going properly toward the target as long as you comfortably can afford, because it acts as a safety valve for players swinging too early. In other words, it provides a longer safety zone in case you have swung too early on the shot. If you are too late, the follow-through has no value for guiding a poorly timed shot.

The secondary function is to release tension on the muscles used during the swing. In a long follow-through, the arm muscles that were stretched during the swing are now allowed to relax while the swing slowly comes to a halt. In addition, the muscles that contract and accelerate the arm during the swing need time to decelerate during the follow-through phase of the swing.

In modern tennis, there is a tendency for the student to be taught how to wrap the follow-through around the neck as a way of increasing racket-head speed before impacting the ball. Unfortunately, most of the swing around the neck is completed long after the ball has left the racket face. The majority of follow-through patterns that end up around the neck often achieve their fastest speed more than a foot after the impact point. The majority of speed generated by this type of follow-through seems to be achieved by abruptly slowing down the upper arm and transferring some energy to the forearm. This swing pattern produces a more severe arc and necessitates more accurate timing on the hitter's part. The longer follow-through will allow for a greater safety zone in the impact area, but it also appears to be a somewhat stiffer motion for the hitter. The muscle has no memory, so you must work hard to develop a motor program for the desired swing pattern, and it's normally more effective when you have carefully thought through the strengths and weaknesses of each swing pattern.

Footwork

The tennis-playing public prefers to identify body positions during the swing as possessing an "open" or "closed" stance. The closed stance, used primarily by one-handed players, places the player's side that houses the dominant hitting arm facing the net. The player's back foot normally begins pushing the body forward while positioned parallel to the net. The open stance features a prehitting body coil while the toes of both feet point toward the net or the net post. The open stance also is referred to as the stance used when the player's navel is facing the net before beginning the body coil on the backswing.

In all cases, correct footwork allows one to coil and uncoil properly by achieving a balanced position. To learn the amazing role of proper contact with the ground, imagine standing on a giant "lazy Susan" or turntable and trying to swing properly. The lazy Susan would spin in the direction opposite your body, and you would not be able to transfer energy up the linked system. At the Coto Research Center in Southern California, coaches and students were asked to jump from a trampoline and then try to coil their bodies to hit a ground stroke. It was extremely difficult for both coaches and students to achieve 50 percent of the normal ball speed.

Body Coil

Biomechanical studies show that there are rather distinct differences between the body coiling of one-handed and two-handed backhand hitters. In the one-handed backhand, it was easier to distinguish four body segments (legs, hips, upper body, and arm) moving in sequence from the ground up until the ball was impacted. This system of each segment contributing energy to the next segment above it is called the "linked system." In the two-handed backhand, it was easier to detect differences between the legs and upper body in a two-segment effort. The hitting arms were moving more "in sync" with the upper body rather than trailing as a separate third link. In other words, the racket swing path would be dictated primarily by the upper body. But there were exceptions. For example, there were two-handed backhand hitters who simply did not rely on their upper bodies to control the flight pattern and would make last-second adjustments with their forearms to complete the swing.

In all cases, as described in the footwork section, the hitters had to rely on achieving the body coil and uncoiling by using the ground as the stabilizer. This facilitates a proper coil and uncoiling of each link. It is impossible to coil and uncoil correctly without proper contact with the ground. Thus footwork, discussed earlier in this chapter, becomes a major issue.

Perception Versus Reality

One of the big stars in 1999 and 2000 was Andre Agassi. One of the most commonly heard comments about Agassi was his excessive wrist motion on both the forehand and backhand strokes. In many clubs around the world, players are taught the Agassi "windshield wiper" strokes. To some, it appears on television that Agassi strokes the ball while moving his wrist and racket in a manner similar to a car's windshield wiper. Yet, in a three-dimensional biomechanical study on Agassi's forehand and backhand, his wrists were fixed at the impact point and there were no so-called "wristy movements." Agassi normally hits his backhand with a closed stance, with a great effort to get his front foot moving forward toward the net. Both arms on the backhand stroke extend in a fairly straight line toward the target as far as he can reach before he releases the arms and racket to move around the neck. This misinterpretation of Agassi's stroking pattern is a typical scenario unless one can study strokes shot with high-speed cameras and played back in slow motion.

Grips

There are two types of grips most commonly associated with the one- and two-handed backhands: the eastern and the continental. The eastern grip on the one-handed backhand places the palm of the hitting hand on top of the grip at approximately a 45-degree angle to the racket handle. This requires an eastern-grip forehand hitter to change grips when switching from a forehand to a backhand, and vice versa. The continental grip places the palm on the top right bevel for a right-hander and the top left bevel for a left-hander. This grip normally is used for both forehand and backhand ground strokes and volleys, thus requiring no grip changes in the heat of the battle. Many argue that there is insufficient time to change grips. Studies have shown, however, that a player can learn to switch grips faster than he can move his feet a single step. The hands are simply faster than the feet. There were some situations in which players had difficulty performing two separate tasks (stepping while changing grips) simultaneously.

Each person would be wise to experiment with both grips and note the position of the wrist to achieve a vertical racket when impacting the ball. The advantage of the continental grip is that it places the racket face in a ready position

Richard Krajicek's one-handed backhand.

for an undershin backhand, but it forces the wrist into a vulnerable position to strike the ball with topspin. In today's professional tennis, the undershin backhand shot is used far less than a flat or topspin shot. For intermediate and senior tennis, the undershin shot is used more often.

The two-handed backhand players normally prefer to have the left hand on top of the right hand when the ball is to the left side of a right-handed hitter, and vice versa for left-handers. However, some players use two-handed strokes for both forehands and backhands. In rare cases, they do not change hand positions when switching from forehand to backhand and thus end up hitting in what baseball players call the cross-handed batters. That is, the left hand is positioned below the right hand when a right-hander is hitting from the left side. Some left-handers hit cross-handed on the right side and we have seen the reverse versions with hand positions. In the end, it's the nature of the racket's flight pattern and the position of the racket face when striking the ball that count. The unique grips are mentioned here because the style of tennis stroking underwent rather radical changes in the last five years of the 20th century.

One-Handed Versus Two-Handed Backhand

The terms "offensive player" and "defensive player" have taken on new meaning in modern tennis. In former years, a player who preferred to play around

the baseline throughout the match was considered a defensive, or counter-punching, competitor. The player who loved to attack the net at every opportunity was considered to have an offensive style. The big change is that professional players now are hitting so hard that they have become offensive players from the baseline. The older interpretation of offensive and defensive players still appears to be applicable to the general population.

To illustrate how the professional game has changed from the baseline, we offer a 1998 five-set match at the U.S. Open between Carlos Moya and Michael Chang. Both players are noted as two of the best baseline players in the history of tennis. Moya defeated Chang 3-6, 1-6, 7-5, 6-4, 6-3. Counting the serve that was put into play until the last hit, the average number of hits per point were as follows: 4.30, 4.28, 4.86, 4.55, 4.77. Thus, not in a single set did the average number of hits per point reach a total of five shots. Another example of the changes in the game was Marat Safin's straight-set win over Pete Sampras in

Yevgeny Kafelnikov's two-handed backhand.

the 2000 U.S. Open Finals while using a devastating two-handed backhand. The average number of hits per point for this match was even less.

One problem appearing on today's junior competitive scene is that players often are sacrificing accuracy for more speed. Thus, the number of errors is increasing as well as the number of outright winners. The winners in today's international junior competition are those players who can mix speed while reducing the number of errors. This is being accomplished by more and more players who are converting to increased topspin in favor of "flat-only" shots.

There seem to be three major theories for new players to consider when caught in this decision-making process. Net-rushing professionals seem to prefer a one-handed approach because they can move through the approach shot without having to set up for a two-handed shot. Pete Sampras and Patrick Rafter both won the U.S. Open with this approach. They feel they have more options

and can reach the net sooner by using a one-handed backhand. Professional and amateur baseline players prefer to have more time to prepare for the backhand. In both professional and amateur tennis, the two-handed backhand for this type of player appears to be the choice of the majority.

The one-handed players have to understand that they will occasionally get passed at the net. Their major concern is to win the majority of points as a result of their attacking style. The amateur baseliner prefers to have the opponent make the mistakes while countering the attacker from the baseline.

A third consideration is that some individuals appear to have no problem coiling their body in preparation for the two-handed backhand, whereas other players prefer to use more forearm action. The players using more forearm action normally will take longer to learn the two-handed backhand.

Learning Tips

Motor-learning specialists have provided wonderful insights for helping players make major positive changes in their tennis strokes. The backhand for the one-handed player requires a greater role for the legs in lifting the center of gravity upward to follow the direction of the racket swing pattern. However, coaches often teach students to stay down as they stroke the ball. A body that is falling while the racket arm is rising often produces a shot into the net. When you have two separate, and opposite, vectors for body and racket-arm movements, the normal direction of the ball is somewhere between those two lines and often goes into the net. When a dot was placed on Agassi's center of gravity on each film frame, the result was a miniature stroke pattern that matched the flight pattern of his racket.

The objective in learning the backhand is to see the value of the legs in generating a lifting body motion that would be in sync with the hitting arm. The most common error is for the coach, or ball machine, to be hitting balls that travel too fast for you to achieve the proper sensations through the central nervous system.

Having the balls hit or pitched very slowly and holding the racket still while the body lifts the racket to the impact point is a million-dollar lesson. You quickly can see that the legs and body can act in sync and the ball no longer heads for the net. To illustrate this, in 1999, John McEnroe's center of gravity was traced on both his topspin and underspin shots, and his center of gravity was lifting on both strokes. Feeling the sensation that your legs actually can control the ball flight often is a brand-new sensation for many. The critical factor, however, is the very slow ball toss while you are rather close to the net.

After each successful series of leg lifts and ball control, you then should move back a few steps and lengthen the stroke. Finally, you will be back at the baseline and taking a full stroke with an appropriate body lift.

It is important to learn to lift without throwing your head up to the sky. You can practice lifting while maintaining a very quiet head. When you lift your head in a rather rapid motion, your body usually follows that motion and you don't achieve the desired stroke. There is a basic tenet in motor learning and biomechanics called the "speed/error" ratio. The faster and more violently you swing, the greater the number of errors. The key seems to be to hit the same old "boring winner."

Chapter Eleven

Volleys and Overheads

Frank van Fraayenhoven
Michiel Schapers

Your game type in tennis determines how often you will go to the net, in which game situation you will go to the net, what kind of shot you will use to go to the net, and how many shots you will have to play when you are at the net.

Your game type is predominantly based on your personality. Important personality aspects are the willingness to take risks and the desire to seek adventure. Players who like spectacular situations at the net, but do not like to lose points because of their own mistakes, tend to go to the net only when it pays off or if any other solution seems to be without a chance for success.

In this chapter we will look at the different parts of approaching the net as well as net play itself from the perspective of four different game types:

1. The net rusher
2. The hard hitter
3. The all-court player
4. The defensive baseliner

Those four game types can be used as a rough way to divide all players into categories. Some players will feel they do not fit in one box but would prefer to be placed in a combination of two boxes. This is fine, and they will be able to combine information out of those two game types.

Why do players go to the net?

- Shorter points
- More pressure on the opponent
- Easier to hit winners
- Weak backcourt skills
- Unable to retreat after a short ball

Why don't players want to go to the net?

- Don't feel safe
- Too slow on reacting or anticipating
- Weak volleys
- Weak defense (afraid of lobs)
- Strong baseline game

In addition, you should consider the court surface before going to the net often. Far too often coaches advise a player to go to the net just based on technical prerequisites.

Approach Shots

Approach shots are the link between the backcourt and the net position. You can't reach the net position, "all the way" from the baseline, at once. You will need to play one more shot in between. This can be (a) a "traditional" approach shot such as a forehand or backhand drive, (b) an approach volley (often a low volley) when playing serve-volley, or (c) a drive volley when closing in on a high defensive shot from the opponent.

You can see these three methods on all court surfaces, but when studying more closely you'll find several differences. Those differences are decisive for the effectiveness of the player who applies approaches.

The most important prerequisite of approach shots is the pressure they put on the opponent. This pressure can be a result of the speed, the "skidding," or the depth of the ball—or a combination of those factors. The baseliner, who has to deal with this pressure, often will have a tendency to try to gain time and in so doing will lose balance and, as a result, control and/or power. Coaches and players as well should pay more attention to the quality of the approach. Far too many people from both categories concentrate on safety or consistency or just depth, but the essence of the approach can be seen after the bounce. What happens after the bounce should "threaten" or "hurt" the opponent.

In modern tennis a lot of players use extreme grips and heavy topspin on both sides and especially on the forehand side. The disadvantage of those extreme (western) grips lies in the high bounce that enables the opponent to hit from shoulder height almost downward to play the passing shot. Racket-face control means more than just the way to hold the racket. Of course there is a direct relation between the grip and the position of the racket face, but the flexibility of the joints in the arm and wrist can allow the racket face to move effectively through the path of the ball in order to hit an effective approach shot.

Looking more closely at the ingredients of approaches, we will follow these next steps:

- When to approach
- From where to approach
- Where to aim the approach
- How to hit the approach
- Where to go after the approach

When to Approach

A net rusher will try to approach in almost every situation. Balls that allow the net rusher to hit one meter in front of the baseline will be perceived as a possibility to follow the ball to the net. The net rusher will follow his serve almost every time and will play a first volley around the service line. He also will try to approach after a return: if possible on a return of a first serve, but certainly on the return of a second serve. During baseline play the net rusher could come in with an approach shot or a drive volley.

The hard hitter generally is not fond of the net. However, since she delivers a lot of pressure with strong drives, she will have several opportunities to finish the point by closing in on defensive shots hit by the opponent. Very often the shot she will use is meant to be an outright winner and less intended to be followed by a volley.

The all-court player feels at home at the net but is not as eager to go there as the net rusher. The all-court player will wait for the appropriate moment to close in or even sneak in. His approach shot is a real buildup shot and he expects to play a volley afterward.

The defensive baseliner does not like to go to the net and will try to move back to the baseline even after going forward to hit a relatively short ball. This player will stay at the net only when he or she realizes there is no time to retreat.

From Where to Approach

As explained earlier, the game type determines mostly from where the player would like to move to the net. The contact point for the approaching player is the crucial factor. Many coaches talk about the bounce of the ball, but we advise you to focus on the anticipated contact point to decide whether to move to the net. After the bounce, the ball can behave very differently, depending on the speed, spin, angle of projection, and court surface. The height of the contact point in combination with the distance to the net will determine whether a player decides to go for a winner, hit an approach, or stay back at the baseline and wait for another chance.

Where to Aim the Approach

An approach shot that is supposed to be followed by a volley generally has one good area to aim for: down the line and deep. This enables the approaching player to cover the net optimally. In junior tennis many players "get away with" crosscourt approach shots because of weak backhands or underdeveloped court coverage and footwork. As it becomes a habit for juniors to play crosscourt approaches, they will be in trouble when reaching the age of approximately 16, and especially on slower courts. Therefore, it is better for juniors to get in the habit of playing down the line with the approach shot and to hit crosscourt only for either a winning shot or to "keep the opponent honest."

Approach shots (as well as return approaches on second serves) sometimes are placed down the middle of the court. The advantage of this strategy, often used by net rushers, is that it offers the opponent fewer angles for passing shots and it will draw errors from players who are tempted to force the issue and try to get an angle anyway. This specific approach down the middle can be used best against fast-moving defensive baseliners who like to play against net players. By hitting right "into" the baseliner's body instead of away from him, you eliminate the speed factor by pinpointing him in an awkward position and thus offering him fewer possibilities for using his strengths (angled passing shots and lobs).

How to Hit the Approach Shot

In modern tennis we can find a lot of players using their most comfortable grip for their approach shots. Those players will hit with a lot of speed and with medium spin. For this stroke, the thrust of their legs is, as with all strokes, very important. Depending on the height of the contact point, we can see players jump, run, or stand during the shot. Proper balance is critical, and dynamic balance (i.e., moving through the ball) is optimal for a quick close into the net. In all cases of footwork, the coil—and uncoil—action is important. The uncoiling is initiated by the thrust of the hind leg. The sideways position of the trunk enables the arm to swing forward freely as a result of the uncoiling action. The low-to-high movement of the racket face allows good acceleration in both the horizontal and the vertical plane. Players who use too much speed for this approach will not give themselves enough time to take a good net position. Excessive spin, on the other hand, gives the opponent the opportunity to use a high contact point for the passing shot.

Players with a more moderate grip will be able to hit more flat, or they will hit the more classic, and still very useful, slice approach shot. For this shot the player again will need the thrust of the legs. The sideways position is as important as it was for the spin approach. In this case, however, the racket face starts aligned with the contact point or a little higher. The racket face is slightly open—only a few degrees, depending on the trajectory of the ball before the contact point. If the racket starts too high, there will be a tendency to "chop" the ball and this will make it hard to control the shot. The racket speed for this slice approach is lower than for the topspin approach and the bounce will be much lower. A perfect approach will skid away and make it difficult for the opponent to get the racket under the contact point.

The approach volley has the same possibilities as the approach shot. One extra feature is closing in on an opponent's defensive shot and thus taking away the time the opponent needs to recover to the bisector. With the opponent not reaching the bisector you have the opportunity to wrong-foot him, which creates even more of an emergency situation on his side.

In modern tennis we have seen the development of topspin drive volleys that are hit with enormous ball speed. Again, we should realize the difference between an approach volley with the intention of closing into the net to finish the point with a volley, and the drive volley that is meant to finish the point at once. The aggressiveness could be similar but the direction will be different in most cases. The setup volley is expected to be followed by another volley, and we believe it's important not to hit too much topspin (just as with the approach drive). Therefore, the racket should not be too far below the contact point and it should come through the ball enough to impart the speed necessary to put pressure on the opponent.

Don't forget to pay attention to the nonhitting arm. In both the approach drive and the approach volley the speed is higher than it used to be. For the high racket speed the hitting arm needs to accelerate strongly, and the trunk

Lindsay Davenport's slice approach shot.

delivers (based on the legs) an angular impulse for that purpose. The nonhitting arm works as a catalyst, which means it can support or hinder the angular movement or stay neutral. Some players have a tendency to exaggerate the movement of the other arm in order to gain as much energy as possible. This exaggerated movement may be the cause of less control or of a tendency to hit mostly crosscourt. The nonhitting arm can hinder the angular movement if the arm stays across the chest. The other arm not only affects the acceleration of the trunk but also is involved in the balancing process during forward running. This double task of the other arm requires fine coordination and should be a specific point of attention for players and coaches during the early learning stages in the development of the approach shot.

Where to Go After the Approach

There are two dimensions to court positioning when going to the net: (1) the position in relation to the middle of the court, and (2) the distance to the net.

The position in relation to the middle of the court is in principle similar to positioning in the backcourt. You should try to bisect the angle the opponent can use for her passing shots (see figure 11.1). The visual difference lies in the

van Fraayenhoven and Schapers

fact that the path of the ball being hit from the backhand corner (of a right-handed player) runs through the right side of the service box on the opposite side of the court and the left side of the backcourt.

The distance to the net originates from the dilemma of predominantly covering the lob or the passing shot. If you want to be sure to cover every lob, you will not be standing too close to the net. The net position that is mostly taught on the beginner level makes you highly vulnerable for lobs. The most comfortable position to cover lobs is at the service line. However, this position makes you extremely vulnerable against passing shots. Altogether this means there is no solid, let alone absolute or definite, position that will make you feel safe against both the lob and the passing shot.

The very first question the player has to answer is whether the opponent is going to lob or to pass. As soon as you know he is not going to lob, you can close in a few steps more. Closing in to the net means that you are better able to cover the angle and play a good volley. Answering the "lob-or-pass" question requires good anticipation skills for the approaching player.

An essential point in relation to this positioning is the split-step. The split-step is a very natural part of footwork for someone who does not know whether to go to the right or to the left. A goalkeeper in soccer at the moment of a

Davenport's topspin approach shot.

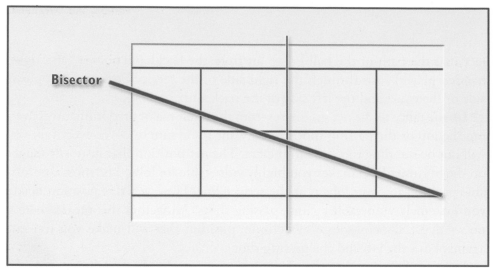

Figure 11.1
Bisect the angle your opponent can use for passing shots.

penalty kick is a good example of that. The feet are apart in order to make it possible to thrust the center of gravity to either side. A net player who tries to cover only passing shots will position her feet more or less at the same distance to the net. In this way it is possible to cover a maximum width in relation to the angle the opponent has for her passing shots. However, a player who also is concerned about a lob will use a kind of "turned" split-step, that is, approximately a 45-degree turn, in order to be able to thrust the center of gravity backward in case of a lob. Players who are concerned only about lobs or short balls will position themselves more like crabs. Putting players in these kinds of situations automatically will develop this essential part of footwork for net players.

Volleys

After an approach shot the player will hit either a volley or an overhead. A volley is the answer to the passing shot. Since the definition of a volley is restricted to "a ball that does not bounce in your court," we can study a wide range of different volleys. The main intention of a net player is to finish the point by hitting a winning volley. This is easiest at shoulder height and when close to the net. Most opponents, however, will try anything not to "feed" you these kinds of balls. Opponents will try to hit the ball away from you and as low as possible. This has many consequences for the shot intention and therefore also for the movement (technique) of the volley. One other specific volley problem is the body shot.

192

In this chapter we will discuss these volley variations: the high volley, the low volley, the wide volley, and the body shot.

High Volley

Typically, high volleys get the most attention when you are learning how to play tennis. The most common position for this shot concerns a distance of fewer than six meters from the net (i.e., within the service box). The closer to the net you are, the more possibilities you will have. The angle for putting away the volley is maximum from shoulder height and really close to the net. The key elements of this volley are (1) early preparation, (2) a turned body position, (3) a moderate to short backswing, (4) pushing off (thrusting) with the legs, (5) a contact point in front of the body, (6) a short follow-through, and (7) quick recovery.

A crucial point for effective execution of this accelerated volley is the "turning point" in the energy chain. By this we intend to look at the moment the preparation phase changes into the hitting phase of the stroke. The turning of the hips and shoulders in conjunction with the racket being at the end of the backswing makes it possible to start the thrust from the legs. The legs will accelerate the trunk both linearly and angularly. The angular movement of the hips will accelerate the shoulder and they will "pass on" the energy to the hitting arm. The movement of the hitting arm is compact. Depending on the actual height and distance to the body, the dominance of one part of the arm may differ from the other. All parts of the arm are more or less involved, but the wrist should never be loose. On a slower-passing shot the backswing for the volley could be longer, and on a fast-passing shot it will be shorter. Especially in emergency situations, players appear to have problems adapting the turning point in the stroke to the reduced time. This often results in volleys lacking control, ball speed, or both. In the low-to-high and inside-to-outside energy chain we then can spot deficiency in several ways:

- *The legs start thrusting while the shoulders still are turning*. This results in only linear energy for the hips and almost no angular energy. The player will have to compensate with the arm and often will lose control, speed, or both.

- *The player starts swinging forward while the trunk still is turning*. This results in slow racket-head velocity and mostly in a late contact point.

The best places to aim for with the high volley are the spots in front of the service line and angled in a way that the opponent is drawn far out of the court in his (hopefully unsuccessful) attempt to reach the ball. Angled volleys open up the court for the opponent and should be practiced as much as possible from

Tim Henman's high backhand volley.

shoulder height. Far too often players practice hitting more or less to each other, which is understandable from a social point of view. Playing angled volleys does not mean aiming for the lines! It is important to keep a margin of error, in order to make sure that "less precise" shots still will land in the court.

Low Volley

Low volleys make it more difficult to hit direct winners. Very often the player will have to play another setup volley to ensure that the net position still will be safe after the first one. This is actually a second approach volley, but now from a closer distance of the net. As an approach volley it is best to hit the ball deep and down the line or deep and down the middle. Close to the net the low volley can be played as a stop volley or a drop volley. The drop volley (with underspin) and the stop volley (more or less without spin) both can be played straightforward and crosscourt, depending on the position of the opponent and the angle of the passing shot.

In the execution of the low volley we like to point out one specific point: the hind leg on the low forehand volley. The hind leg works as an elevator for the hip and thus for the shoulder. For a right-handed player, the right hip

van Fraayenhoven and Schapers

and shoulder can descend only when the right knee bends and comes close to the ground. The essence of bending this knee is to try to create a shoulder-height volley on a low contact point. As long as the shoulder gets under the contact point, the player can almost continue to volley just as with a high volley. As soon as the contact point gets below shoulder height, the player will have a tendency to open up the racket face too much or drop the racket, resulting in a slower and less-threatening volley that often "sits up" after the bounce. With a low shoulder it still is possible to hit a solid or heavy volley off this low contact point. However, the low shoulder should not occur because of bending the spine or at the hips. This would affect the thrust from the legs (mostly the hind leg) and therefore the initiation of the hip, shoulder, and racket.

Wide Volley

Wide volleys still can be more or less "ideal" volleys but only if the footwork gets you to the right spot in time. We like to speak about "eager feet," which means feet that are willing to go to the best spot as soon as possible. But even with eager feet, a good passing shot down the line cannot be reached without

Richard Krajicek's wide volley.

stretching the arm. Those wide volleys or stretched-arm volleys are very important to practice. The forward thrust of the legs is minimized and this means the hitting arm has to compensate in order to control or accelerate the volley. In this case the movement from the shoulder has to be dominant and you should emphasize the through-the-ball movement of the racket in order to control the ball. For an angled volley from this position, the wrist has to be the dominant link, and this is one of the only situations in tennis in which the top of the racket will be significantly ahead of the wrist.

This far-away volley asks for specific legwork. We advise players to try to move the center of gravity along a straight line. This is only possible with strong legs. Naturally players have a tendency to thrust with the legs and come slightly upward. At the moment the next leg takes over to thrust, you will first see a slight descending of the center of gravity and then again this upward movement. From the side, the center of gravity seems to take a "bumpy road" and thus loses some time. A player trying to move along a more or less horizontal line needs to combine the thrust of one leg with an eccentric contraction of the other leg. Only in this way can the center of gravity travel in a straight line.

The same principle goes for the recovery footwork coming from the side of the court. If your volley is returned by the opponent, you can't afford to waste any time or distance. Therefore, the center of gravity should stay as low as it is and you should try to make as few steps as possible to the outside of the court to

van Fraayenhoven and Schapers

first decelerate the center of gravity and then accelerate in the direction of the bisector. Wasting time in this situation can be seen in the case when the center of gravity does not stay at the same level but first goes down and then comes up again. Weak leg muscles are primarily the cause of this problem. Wasting distance can be seen when a player needs too many steps to the side to slow down. You can see this problem quite often with players bending at the hips in their effort to accelerate to the side of the court. It occurs in both jumping and sprinting.

Body Shot

The body shots are another specific situation for a net player. A slow ball in the direction of the body gives the net player enough time to move to the side and play a "normal" forehand or backhand volley. On a faster body shot you need very fast footwork and appropriate body preparation to be able to move around the contact point. The combination of "stepping out" to the side with the left foot and "turning away" with the right (around the left hip that is moving to the side because of the left foot) gives the best possibility of creating enough room for the hitting arm to play a good volley. Also, the hind leg may have time to thrust forward for extra energy in this volley. With even higher ball speed the emergency increases. The thrusting action from the hind leg certainly will disappear and very often the player can use only one side step. Players then naturally prefer to play a backhand volley. The anatomy of the hitting arm in combination with the position of the hitting shoulder and the length of the racket shaft force the player to choose a backhand volley when confronted with a body shot. It is a well-known fact that the "Achilles heel" of a net player is a shot directed at the shoulder of the hitting arm. It is very difficult to keep racket-face control during your attempt to play this kind of volley.

The ultimate time pressure with body shots leaves you no other solution than trying to block the ball to prevent yourself from getting bruised. A firm wrist and good racket-head orientation are the key points in this situation.

In volley practice we see too many players volley in more or less static situations and when they are moving, the movement is mostly one-dimensional (i.e., left-right). The procedure then is as follows: ready position, step (and stand still), hit, and recover. This is not bad for a basic volley, but we advise you to practice as soon as possible with aspects of coming in, covering sideways, and solving the problem of (moderate) body shots. This dynamic volley practice also counts for low volleys. The specific timing of split-steps in combination with the sequential dynamic balance needs to be practiced as soon and as much as possible. The importance of this preparation can be seen with players playing good low volleys in static half-court position and after that playing in a serve-and-volley situation. Most players lose a lot of quality in that seemingly similar situation because of moving through the split-step and low volley. Only players who still are practicing this dynamic situation can keep their levels of play up. This principle counts for coaches as well as for players and that is why players are advised to practice volleys as much as possible in dynamic situations.

Grips

Grips for net play have been discussed for many decades. First of all, you need to decide if you have enough time to try to change grips.

Changing grips for forehand—or backhand—volleys is not possible under extreme pressure. In the case of a body shot or a volley rally at close distance, there is no time to change grips. However, since changing grips can take less than a half-second and can be combined with and take place during the preparation of the volley, it is possible to change grips for volleys. A prerequisite for this is the support of the racket head by the "other hand" in combination with not squeezing the handle with the hand of the hitting arm. Grip firmness or the tightness of the grip should vary during all strokes and is essential during the net game. A more or less loose grip during the ready position enables the hand to position itself quickly in the desired setting.

Why should a player want to change grips? Of course, it is not the absolute position of the hand that bothers us—we are looking for racket-face control! Gripping the racket means lengthening the arm by positioning the projection of the two bones of the forearm on the handle of the racket. Those two bones—the radius and the ulna—are projected on the handle by means of the knuckle of the index finger and the heel of the hand, respectively. By positioning these two points of reference anywhere on the octagonal-shaped handle and then closing the hand, we determine the margin for the angles between the forearm and the racket in three dimensions. Observations of those angles can be made from the front, from the side, and from above. We are talking about a margin for angles because of the amount of movement in the wrist and forearm. However, because the wrist is strongest in the so-called neutral position, either combined with dorsal flexion or not, we do have preferences for certain angles between the forearm and the shaft of the racket when observed from the side. This position of the racket face in relation to the wrist enables you to hit the ball sideways and in front of the body and ensures a good transfer of power. A slightly open racket face (such as with a continental grip) is appropriate for low volleys but is not ideal for high volleys, while a slightly closed racket face (as with a semi-western grip) is OK for a high volley but has disadvantages on low volleys.

The problem with a one-grip volley originates from the angle we can observe from above. Only with a strong wrist and a firm grip is it possible to volley with one grip for forehand and backhand volleys. Most players prefer to reposition the heel of the hand slightly along or even across the top bevel of the grip. By doing this, the position of the racket head changes in relation to the wrist and the forearm turns slightly and brings the wrist into a more resilient position with regard to absorbing the shock at impact. Altogether, we advise a margin for grips for effective net play. This margin includes continental grips and grips in between the eastern and the semi-western. The semi-western grip itself is not an appropriate grip for all-round net play. It will be used only by players applying mostly drive volleys and will not be seen with good doubles players or net rushers in singles. Volley grips depend on or will be determined by forearm strength, available time, reaction time, support of the other hand, grip looseness during the ready position, preparation, height of the contact point, footwork, and shot intention. Some grips will exclude possibilities and others will enable possibilities. One absolute best grip cannot be determined, and a player with a lack of power in the wrist should be advised to feel comfortable with "flexible" grips.

Overheads

Every lob should be "punished" with an overhead smash. Allowing the lob to bounce in the backcourt while moving away from the net in most cases means the opponent can take the initiative. This section explains the different situations for overheads. The easy overhead can be played against an almost neutral lob—that is, a lob of moderate height and depth—giving you ample time to prepare, position yourself, and hit. In the execution of this stroke you can find many similarities with the serve. The possibilities for projection, however, are very different from the serve. When it is hit from about half-court with a contact point at an average height of somewhere between 2.5 meters and 3 meters, you easily can clear the net and direct the ball to anywhere in the court. Where the serve is limited to a distinct vertical and horizontal angle, the overhead has one of the biggest margins for error. The ball can be hit both deep to the backhand side and angled to the forehand side, or the other way around, and that means

Lisa Raymond's overhead.

you have many choices for the put-away. For this easy overhead the preparation movement can be long or short. There is enough time for a full backswing as in most serves. A short preparation movement, in which the racket starts moving upward while the trunk turns sideways, is also good and will continue to be effective under time pressure as well. An essential checkpoint within the execution of the short preparation is the arm and racket position at "stop," just before the racket starts moving down the loop swing. At this "stop," the upper arm should be almost horizontal but certainly as an extension of the shoulder line. The forearm should be vertical and the racket should point at the highest point of the lob while the racket face is on its side. From this position the racket is loaded with potential energy, which can be released in the dropping movement to the lowest point in the loop swing. This energy will be amplified through the movement of the trunk, resulting in a high-speed racket movement on its way to the contact point.

A deep loop swing will give a large path for acceleration of the racket. The secret of a good loop swing behind the back is the timing of the acceleration of

the elbow in relation to the position of the racket on its way to the lowest point in the loop swing. If the elbow is held back until the racket is at the lowest point, you will see a full stop in the movement. If the elbow moves outward and forward too early, the racket has not reached enough speed and the elbow eliminates the full dropping movement. Only when the elbow (on the basis of a preliminary movement of legs, hips, and trunk) moves forward and upward at the moment the racket has enough speed, and almost reaches the lowest point in the loop, does the player get maximum acceleration.

The contact point for the overhead is very similar to the serve's contact point. When the nonhitting arm drops just before the upward movement of the racket, the shoulder line (shoulder axis) comes closer to a vertical position than to a horizontal position. The upper arm stretches out to the ball, but it is more or less an extension of the shoulder line and is not in a position similar to holding an object above your head with two hands. The emphasis therefore should be more on turning over the shoulder axis than on raising the arm as high as possible.

The rotational movement in the forearm (pronation) should not be seen as a movement by itself. This pronation is necessary to "neutralize" the supinated position of the forearm as a result of the vigorous acceleration of the racket head during the loop swing. Not pronating would lead to a severe slice shot probably hit wide. Maybe you would even hit the ball on the frame of the racket. The pronounced "wrist snap," which is very noticeable on action photos, appears to be more a result of the prestretch in the muscles of the forearm (caused by the impact with the ball) than an intended movement. In emergency situations the wrist action can be more deliberate.

The follow-through in the easy overhead could resemble the end of the serve. However, different playing directions do have their influence on the "hitting zone" and the follow-through. The more difficult overheads are played in situations of better lobs. We will discuss deep lobs; lobs to the sides of the court; and low, fast lobs.

Deep Lobs

Deep lobs, both offensive and defensive, will test predominantly the footwork skills of the net player. The first step is decisive for the eventual result. Stepping out and in the direction of the baseline with the leg on the same side as the hitting arm (i.e., right leg for right-handed player) is essential. The body should turn at the same time while the eyes stay focused on the ball. The other arm can be used as a "compass" and enhances shoulder-turn and shoulder-axis turnover. With this quick and effective preparation, you can get into a position in which you can hit another relatively easy overhead using the characteristics as described.

But even with a quick start and proper footwork, you may have to solve the problem of this lob heading to bounce behind you. In that case a jump can save you. This jump overhead has some specific differences in comparison to the easy overhead as described. First of all: the jump. After the side steps or cross-over steps, the hind leg should thrust forcefully to change the direction of movement of the center of gravity from backward to (mostly) upward. Right after you jump, the nonhitting arm will start to come down, supporting the turnover of the shoulder axis and thereby accelerating the hitting arm.

The timing of this complex movement is crucial. If the contact point still is behind your head, there has to be a profound wrist movement to compensate for the position of the racket face. Without this wrist movement—which primarily is not meant for acceleration—the racket would be open or still on its side causing miss-hits or direct errors. After the more or less vertical jump, you normally can observe a scissorslike movement of the legs. This movement is essential for balance and Newton's law about action equaling reaction. As a result, you almost always will land on the opposite leg from the leg that pushed off for the jump. In case the center of gravity still is moving backward at the moment of impact, you should try to make as few steps as possible after landing. Every step backward puts you farther away from the net, and this step has to be covered again on the way back to the net.

The follow-through for this jumping overhead is much shorter than the one in an easy situation.

Lobs to the Side of Court

Lobs to the side require specific footwork combined with trunk control. Overheads hit while you are moving to the forehand side often give more problems for the net player than when moving to the backhand side. The steps to the side affect the position of the hips. And as we know from the field of biomechanics, the hips initiate the trunk rotation. Especially under time pressure, those steps can harm the coordination pattern of hips and shoulders and thus decrease the racket-face control. To develop a feeling for this specific body coordination, players are advised to work on these less-familiar overheads covering the lobs to both sides.

Low, Fast Lobs

Low, fast lobs create extreme time pressure, and only excellent anticipation of the path of the ball can save you. These low and fast lobs are impossible to run down and the only escape is to jump vertically and vigorously with both legs. Of course, the racket needs to take the shortest possible preparation and the hit will be very compact and explosive. Only in this way can you cover those offensive lobs.

Fast lobs over the backhand side will force you to hit a backhand overhead (backhand smash). This stroke cannot be compared to the average overhead, not even in easy situations. That is why every player will try to move around the backhand smash. On fast lobs, however, this is impossible. During practice you

Executing a backhand overhead in an emergency situation.

need to develop a feel for the specific timing of the awkward "backward" wrist action at the moment the arm is almost stretched. In this way the racket can gain enough speed to hit with reasonable power. The second key point to be aware of is the "turning point" of the shoulder turn. A hitting shoulder still moving backward as a part of the preparation will absorb most of the energy needed to accelerate the upper arm. A quick turn, followed by a forceful stop in the trunk, will provide enough resistance to accelerate the arm.

We hope that this chapter provided you, as a player or as a coach, with information and motivation to work on specific areas of net play. Working on this gives a lot of excitement, a good workout, and lots of fun!

Chapter Twelve

Serves and Returns

Bruce Elliott
Nick Saviano

Τhe serve and the return of serve are the two most important strokes in the game of tennis. The success of players such as Pete Sampras, Richard Krajicek, Mark Philippoussis, Greg Rusedski, Venus Williams, and Lindsay Davenport is at least in part because of their powerful serves. Although court surface plays a role in reducing the effectiveness of these serves, Andre Agassi, Gustavo Kuerten, Martina Hingis, and Monica Seles, just to name a few, have developed the service return such that this stroke now can be considered a "weapon."

This chapter presents the latest research on both strokes with dramatic photographic sequences used to illustrate the mechanics of the best in the world, so you can apply their techniques to your game.

Serve

There is no single technique used in the tennis serve, a point that clearly is illustrated by viewing the top professionals. However, there are certain

Figure 12.1 Pete Sampras' serve.

fundamentals in technique that must be incorporated into the action of a powerful serve. Photographic sequences of Pete Sampras are included here to illustrate key features of the service action. Critical mechanical features integral to a successful service action are discussed with reference to these photographic sequences. The general structure used in this discussion may be applied to the power serve along with the slice and kick serves.

Preliminary Movements Tips

1. Sampras is in the starting position just after finishing his pre-serve ritual of bouncing the ball, in figure 12.1a. At this stage he is deciding where to serve and how to set up the point.

   • There is relaxation in the facial muscles, which usually indicates there is relaxation throughout the body. This is important for maintaining good timing and maximizing power and injury prevention.

Elliott and Saviano

- The weight is more on the back foot as he starts the tossing action.
- The front toe is pointed at an angle to the baseline to allow the rotation of hips and shoulders. Sampras will turn the toe even more as he begins to rotate. Virtually all of the outstanding servers will start with the toe either pointed to the side or angled to the baseline. They then turn the toe (normally pivoted about the heel of the foot) as they rotate their shoulders and hips. If this does not happen it makes it difficult to get adequate rotation and may place stress on the front knee.

Research has shown that initial weight distribution is an individual characteristic. However, regardless of where the weight initially is positioned, it always will move forward for impact such that it is forward of the front toe, regardless of type of action.

2. Different starting positions are a function of individual style.

Ball Toss and Leg Drive Tips

1. The ball should be "pushed" into the air using the "straightforward and up" technique, as in the pictures shown, or using the "rotary style."

   - Notice how the ball is held in the fingers (figure 12.1b). The palm is facing directly toward the sky as the arm goes up. Both of these factors help to limit spin on the ball and enhance overall control of the toss.
   - The tossing arm goes up the side of the body, assisting trunk rotation. Sampras rotates very effectively.
   - The weight starts to move forward as the arm moves upward.
   - Notice the rotation in the hips and shoulders.

An analysis of players at the Atlanta Olympics showed that the toss should be positioned such that it was in front and marginally to the left of the front foot at impact (Chow et al. 1999). Individual player preference and type of serve will alter this location between marginally to the left and marginally to the right of the front foot.

2. Some players start this phase of the action more quickly than Sampras. They may already start to bring the racket head up whereas Sampras still has his racket pointed toward the ground. These are personal differences in service rhythm, timing, and style.

   - The racket face should stay perpendicular (closed) to the ground during this part of the swing, which keeps the shoulder muscles relaxed. A common mistake is to open the racket face in the backswing, which often causes the elbow to be too low when accelerating upward.
   - He has full extension of the tossing arm with the shoulders tilted and weight leaning forward.

3. Sampras has significant knee flexion (see figure 12.1c). In addition, he has good rotation of the hips and shoulders. Note that Sampras is serving in the deuce court. The positioning of the elbow, where the upper arm is aligned with the shoulders, is consistent with an optimal throwing position.

4. Sampras uses the foot-back technique to drive upward and forward. This movement of the back foot, as we describe, is a matter of style.

Research has shown that players may use a foot-up or foot-back technique. The foot-up style produces greater vertical force, which results in a higher impact position and a better up-and-out hitting trajectory compared with the foot-back style. Larger horizontal force is produced by the foot-back style, which may be more conducive to rapid movement to the net (Elliott and Wood 1983). Players may choose either style or any foot positioning between these two extremes.

Force produced during the "leg drive" should be such that the body is driven off the ground for impact (Elliott, Marsh, and Blanksby 1986). This leg drive together with trunk rotations "drives" the racket away from and behind the lower back.

Backswing Tips

Sampras now has adopted the "power position" of the service action (figure 12.1d). He stores elastic energy in the major shoulder muscle groups (good leg drive and trunk rotation) before exploding up after the ball. If players can attain a good power position, this is an excellent platform for an effective serve.

- Notice Sampras' head is up as he starts his vertical and slightly forward explosion.
- As the legs thrust upward, the racket is forced down behind the back, which will help generate more power in the serve.
- The racket face is relatively perpendicular to the ground, which permits a long acceleration path to the ball.
- Notice that the racket head is away from the shoulders, which is critical for maximizing the distance the racket moves to impact (it also places the appropriate muscles "on stretch"). This is contrary to the old "scratch the back" theory of having the racket close to the shoulders.

Research has shown that leg drive and trunk rotations produce a forced external (away from the direction of the serve) rotation of the upper arm. To stop this movement, the internal rotators are stretched, which stores elastic energy ready for the acceleration phase of the service action (Bahamonde 1997).

This storage of energy has been shown to produce approximately 15 to 20 percent of additional hand speed during the forward swing if there is no, or minimal, pause between the backward and then forward movements (Elliott, Baxter, and Besier 1999).

It is about this position that the shoulder and elbow joints are placed under their greatest load (Noffal and Elliott 1998). Training of the muscles, particularly about the shoulder girdle, is therefore of paramount importance to produce powerful serves that do not place undue stress on the body. The major muscles of shoulder-joint internal rotation are latissimus dorsi, pectoralis major, and subscapularis.

Swing to Impact Tips

1. The key to an effective serve is rhythm. That is, a sequence of movements produces racket speed (see the sequence listed in the upcoming mechanical factors section), impact height, and racket trajectory.

   - The contact point is slightly to the right of the head (notice the position of the head and shoulder alignment). See figure 12.1e. Remember that the ball generally is impacted in line with the front foot for all types of first and second serves. The actual contact point often will vary depending on service style and type of serve being hit.
   - The upward drive from the legs has propelled Sampras off the ground as he gets close to full extension (professional players do not intentionally jump from the ground).
   - Note that the alignment of the shoulders is closer to the vertical than to the horizontal.

Research has shown that speed of rotation of the hitting arm and the impact height were two key differences between advanced and intermediate players (Bartlett, Piller, and Miller 1995). A rhythmical action is the key to an effective serve.

The sequence that generally builds from the court up is as follows:

- Leg drive
- Trunk rotation (produces approximately 10 to 20 percent of racket speed at impact)
- Upper-arm elevation
- Forearm extension, upper-arm internal rotation (produces approximately 40 percent of racket speed at impact), and forearm pronation
- Hand flexion (produces approximately 30 percent of racket speed at impact)

Recent research has supported a commonly held view by coaches on the role of trunk rotation in the serve (Bahamonde 2000). Trunk rotations in the three planes are observed in the period before impact.

- Minor levels of rotation about the long axis of the body help drive the racket backward.
- Shoulder-over-shoulder rotation (cartwheel action) produces momentum and prepares the body for impact.
- Forward rotation (somersault action) allows the player to produce momentum that is shifted from the trunk, to the arm, and finally to the racket.

- The left arm is pulled down and tucked in close to stomach and chest. This helps slow the trunk down, which in turn creates more "whip" at the top of the action and transfers momentum from the large trunk muscles to the smaller arm and racket.

The approximate 100-degree angle between the upper arm and the trunk reduces the loading on the shoulder (Noffal and Elliott 1998) and permits internal rotation to be of maximum benefit in enhancing racket speed (approximately 40 percent of racket speed at impact) (Elliott, Marshall, and Noffal 1995).

Players who keep their shoulders relatively parallel to the court at impact must lower the impact position to gain maximum benefit from the large internal rotators of the trunk and shoulder. The technique used by Sampras is to angle the shoulders to the court for impact. The ball is positioned approximately in line with the front foot such that the hitting arm and racket are not in a straight line, thus gaining height but not eliminating the effect of internal rotation before impact.

2. An up-and-out hitting action is essential for serving consistency.

High-speed film and video have shown that elite players impact the ball after it has begun to drop (2.5 to 20.0 centimeters). Brody (1987) reported that it was desirable to hit the ball a few centimeters below its maximum height. It follows that to facilitate this, the ball should be pushed only marginally above the outstretched position of the extended racket.

There is a strong association between the height of impact and success. If serving at 145 km/h, increasing the height of impact from approximately 2.16 meters to approximately 2.68 meters will double your chance of success (Brody 1987).

3. In the slice serve, the level of forearm pronation (rotation of the forearm) is reduced before impact (racket face angled) to impart an off-center impact to the ball. Impacting the ball at 2 o'clock imparts a combination of sidespin and topspin to the ball and so is an effective way of producing a slice serve.

Follow-Through Tips

1. There will be a continuation of internal rotation of the upper arm and pronation of the forearm during the early phase of the follow-through.

   - These two mentioned actions are important in reducing the stress on the shoulder and elbow regions of the body. The internal rotation is a continuation of the powerful action needed to develop high racket speed, and the pronation is the alignment of the racket for impact.

- It probably is better to position the trunk and impact positions correctly and just permit the actions discussed here to occur naturally.

2. The vertical explosion and shoulder-over-shoulder trunk action, combined with a ball toss that is out in front of the body, propel Sampras into the court such that he lands on his left foot (front foot). See figure 12.1f. Data on male and female touring professionals have shown that approximately 95 percent of players land on their front foot (i.e., left for a right-hander). This is irrespective of the service action used.

- Sampras will land on his front foot with excellent balance, which enables him to explode forward to the net.
- The left-foot landing is indicative of maximal vertical momentum being derived from the serve, while the "kickback" of the other leg provides the reaction force necessary to provide dynamic balance in this phase of the action.

Return of Serve

The return of serve, like the game, has changed dramatically over the past 20 years. Much of the evolution of the forehand return of serve has been dictated by the speed of the serve in the modern game. Tactically, the forehand return always has been used as a means of attacking the serve, particularly the second serve. This basic strategy has not changed. However, backhand returns have improved so much that the forehand return, by comparison, is often not as intimidating as it once was.

Forehand Return

The evolution of the forehand return has, in part, paralleled changes to technique used for the forehand drive, and as stated earlier, it has been dictated by the reduction in time to prepare for the stroke. A more open stance, greater emphasis on rotation, and the use of the individual segments of the arm are now all part of service-return techniques. To illustrate this stroke, we have chosen Andre Agassi, generally regarded as having the best return of serve in the world.

Preliminary Movements Tips

1. Agassi is in the process of landing from his split-step. His upper body is leaning slightly forward. See figure 12.2a.

   - The split-step is used to store energy in the thigh muscles so that movement to the ball may be enhanced. Once the decision to move is made, the knees flex and the body is accelerated toward the court. It is the contraction of the thigh muscles that stops this downward movement and stores elastic energy ready for use in the drive to the ball.
   - He has a wide stance with a relatively low body position.
   - He is using a forehand grip.

2. Note that, based on where he is standing, Agassi is returning a first serve. Research has shown that superior service returns are associated with movement into the split-step just before service impact (Hennemann and Keller 1983).

Backswing Tips

1. Agassi has started his unit turn and his initial racket preparation. See figure 12.2b.

   - His right foot has turned out, in the direction he is about to move.
   - As he is turning his upper body, his left arm comes across the body, which facilitates the shoulder turn and helps in the storage of energy in the shoulder and back muscles. This arm movement is a key to early preparation.

2. Agassi is getting into the "fully loaded" position, in which he is storing energy in his large muscle groups (legs, hips, back, and shoulders). See figure 12.2c.

   - His quick move into this position produces an abbreviated backswing compared with that used in the ground stroke. Much of the post-impact ball speed is "taken" from the speed of the incoming ball.

Research studies have shown that continuous time-to-contact information is critical to success. Abernethy (1990) emphasized the need to concentrate through the critical time periods about impact (160 to 180 milliseconds before and 80 milliseconds after impact). Cueing that takes into consideration both pre- and post-impact information is therefore important in the service return (and therefore should be practiced).

Figure 12.2 Andre Agassi's forehand return.

Groppel (1992) revealed a common sequence that elite performers follow in initiating movement during the service return:

- Early preparation (based largely on personal preference)
- Unweighting (see the preceding on storage of elastic energy)
- A unit turn
- The movement of feet

3. Agassi has excellent upper-body posture. Note the open stance, the pronounced shoulder turn, and the low center of gravity. Preliminary research has shown that the shoulder joint is loaded in a similar way for open and semi-open forehands (Bahamonde and Knudson 1998).

Backswing to Impact Tips

1. Agassi retains excellent posture and balance (figure 12.2d).
2. The short backswing is completed and he has positioned himself to optimize ball impact with reference to the body.

   - Note that Agassi has one of the most compact backswings in the game. The fact that he gets a great "body coil" in the preparation phase enables him to generate power with such a short backswing.

Figure 12.2 *(continued)*

- He displays excellent dynamic balance even though he is off the ground or has minimal contact with the ground close to impact.
- Notice how he has exploded up and into the shot from his back leg while at the same time vigorously rotating the trunk (figure 12.2e). This propels him off the ground and transfers his weight forward into the court.

3. He has his head focused on the point of contact.
4. Note how little the head has moved through impact.

Follow-Through Tips

1. Tremendous rotation and racket movement are evident. Notice how significantly Agassi's body has uncoiled and how quickly the racket arm has rotated, resulting in a follow-through finishing to the side of the body, in figure 12.2f.
2. The racket continues to wrap around the body as he finishes the stroke. From this point, the player immediately will go into the recovery stage and prepare for the next shot.
3. He continues to maintain excellent dynamic balance.

Figure 12.3 Serena Williams' backhand return.

Space limits full discussion of the one-handed backhand return, although in general terms it almost can be viewed as a mirror image of the forehand return. Although this stroke often is hit with an open stance in returning a power serve, where time permits, a semi-open stance generally is adopted.

Two-Handed Backhand Return

One of the most significant changes in the game over the past 20 years has been the emergence and evolution of the two-handed backhand. Each generation has seen players with aggressive backhand returns. Jimmy Connors took the meaning of an aggressive return to a new level, such that today outstanding two-handed backhand returns are the rule instead of the exception. We selected 1999 U.S. Open champion Serena Williams to illustrate this stroke.

Preparation Tips

1. Williams has just landed from her split-step and has recognized that the ball is going to her backhand (see figure 12.3a).
2. Notice the excellent posture in which the back and shoulders are relatively straight.

3. The wide stance and deep knee bend allow her to generate energy from the ground for a quick first step.

Mechanics dictate that the reduced distance of impact to the body for the two-handed technique may help you develop higher racket speed and quicker movement in positioning the racket for impact.

The reduction in body segments used independently in hitting a two-handed backhand (i.e., different segments move together) makes preparation for impact easier than with the one-handed stroke (i.e., segments move one after the other).

Backswing Tips

1. Williams steps out with the outside leg as opposed to stepping across (figure 12.3b).
2. She has made a quick turn of the shoulders, which initiates the racket preparation.

   - The quick movement of the front shoulder combined with the open-stance preparation creates a "loading" about the front shoulder region. This is one of the secrets to success on the return. From this position she can deal with a powerful serve as well as generate an explosive return.
   - Notice how the left leg is flexed, ready to assist the drive to the ball.

Backswing to Impact Tips

1. Williams has taken a full yet compact backswing (figure 12.3c).
2. She has a western backhand grip with her left hand, which permits impact to occur at a variety of heights. The more eastern grip used by Williams with the right may not permit her to contact the ball as far in front as would a more continental grip (figure 12.3d).

Previous research has shown that the majority of high-performance players use a western grip with the bottom hand and a continental or eastern forehand grip with the top hand. Variation in the grips used by players appears to have some influence on the segmental interaction of the two arms. Players who adopted a more western grip with the bottom hand incorporated the elbows and wrists more in stroke production. Conversely, players who used the eastern grip were characterized by elbows that were more extended during the stroke.

Follow-Through Tips

1. Williams has been pulled out wide by the serve, yet she is extending the racket head through the hitting zone (figure 12.3e).

2. The Williams finish: Williams is showing her athleticism by maintaining her dynamic balance as she adjusts to a difficult serve that has pulled her into the alley.

Conclusion

An understanding of the mechanical features critical to success permits the player or coach to decide which aspects of performance to modify, and which to leave alone. This chapter has provided a theoretical framework for your play, which, when linked to your individual flair, will increase your chances of success.

Chapter Thirteen

Specialty Shots

Paul Dent
Patrice Hagelauer

Tennis is combative in nature and as such provides a constantly changing playing environment for its participants. It is a game that often requires an acceleration phase, followed immediately by a deceleration phase, just before performing a fine hand-eye coordination skill and then instantly accelerating once again to continue the cycle. Moreover, all of these phases must be performed in relation to a moving ball.

All shots are specialty shots, but some are just more special than others! Every shot requires balance, timing, appropriate racket control through the hitting zone, and an early and accurate judgment of the ball and movement, but the levels or degree of which is placed on a continuum. Specialty shots simply place these factors on the edge of their capability.

Specialty shots usually are played by those players who commonly are known as "talented." Conversely though, the fewer specialty shots you have to play, the more talented you are likely to be! The description of being "talented" at tennis usually is associated with "tennis-speak" words such as good hands, feel, touch, fast hands, soft hands, good timing, improvisation, absorbs pace well, relaxed, fluid hitter, and stroke player.

Talented sportsmen and sportswomen make their chosen sport look easy. There is a feeling or look indicating that they have a lot of time to execute. These players buy themselves time through early recognition and interpretation of the situation, which allows them to position themselves and prepare their bodies and rackets in advance. Talented players absorb pace effectively because they have good receiving skills (through early and accurate spatial and temporal awareness) rather than necessarily an aesthetically pleasing sending look/hitting picture/style! We feel that a greater "talent" for tennis is having the ability to defend rather than to attack. Defensive situations place skills such as movement, balance, timing, and touch toward the limit of a player's capability. Players in the world who fit this description are Tim Henman, Martina Hingis, Nathalie Tauziat, Carlos Moya, Marcelo Rios, Pete Sampras, Andre Agassi, Fabrice Santoro, Nicolas Lapentti, Natasha Zvereva, and Gustavo Kuerten, to name a few.

Specialty shots usually have a precision rather than a power objective, so their technique should be to aid control, and this is usually fine control.

Talented players such as Martina Hingis show great balance in defensive situations.

Visible Versus Invisible Technique

For the purpose of this book we will break this section down into visible and invisible technique.

Visible (Cosmetic) Technique

The visible technique is the type of technique it's "nice to have." Orthodox, traditional teaching actions—for example, amplitude and path of racket preparation, follow-through, grips, footwork stance—encourage the specific movements of body parts, such as a knee bend and shoulder turn. This technical teaching tends to focus on and challenge the sending (action) part of the skill.

Invisible Technique

The invisible technique is the type of technique you "need to have." Invisible technique is primarily coordination, but contained within that all-encompassing attribute are subskills such as movement, balance, timing, touch, and relaxation. This technical teaching notion has a bias toward emphasizing the receiving aspect of the stroke cycle.

Invisible Technique and Court Surface

The improvement of a player's ability to play specialty shots would involve the teaching and learning of invisible technique. The notion of a specialty shot is that it occurs less frequently than the game's fundamental shots, for example, forehand and backhand ground strokes, serves, and volleys. As such, these would be shots that are not taught in a formal, systematic way with the emphasis of teaching visible technique, because specialty shots do not tend to look the same. We almost accept that two consecutive drop shots by a player can be different from one another, as can topspin lobs.

We do not believe that the Spanish and South American coaches spend endless hours formally teaching their young, developing junior players to hit drop shots. It is the court surface on which they predominantly practice and compete that encourages them to "play around" with the ball. The characteristics of a clay court promote the learning of invisible technique in that players discover that to play effectively on the surface they need to take into consideration the characteristics of the court. This generally is achieved by moving the opponent off the court both wide and deep and attempting to knock him off balance to either elicit an unforced error or to force a weak shot (usually short with little pace) from which to then attack. To achieve the desired tactics, the player then learns to hit drop shots and short, angled ground strokes—crosscourt, aggressive, semi-moon balls landing three-quarters court—to push the opponent outside the singles sideline and backward.

Conversely, however, players have to be able to defend against these shots. So clay-court players also learn to play a sharper angle than the one they have just received—high, defensive recovery shots with topspin when they are out of position—and play a drop shot from a drop shot or steer it past the advancing player. This last situation then gives rise to another specialty shot, the lob volley, as the first person to drop-shot who then moves toward the net plays a lob volley over the opponent. If, as people say, "repetition is the mother of learning," then players who practice and compete on clay courts certainly gain enough practice on specialty shots.

The majority of these shots require a significant amount of coordination, involving movement, balance, touch, relaxation, timing, and awareness of the use of different body parts in hitting—for example, the legs, hips, elbow, and hand.

Marat Safin returns a drop shot with another drop shot.

The more experienced and knowledgeable the coach, the more tolerant he invariably is of technique per se, because he has learned that visible technique is "nice to have," but with invisible technique, there is a "need to have." This is not to say that there is no place for teaching visible technique, as it can impinge on invisible technique, but there is a shift of emphasis in teaching toward helping players develop invisible technical skills and receive the ball.

Movement

If you can't move to the ball in time, you can't utilize the sound technique (visible) you may have! Players, however, often are stroke conscious rather than ball conscious.

An essential ingredient of speed and agility is to begin to think of the body as a series of small, coiled springs rather like watch springs, which, when activated, sequentially result in the whole of the athlete's body contributing to propelling the person in the desired direction.

Moving efficiently on a tennis court requires that you can change direction and pace/speed smoothly and, above all, quickly. To do this, it is important to use the shoulders and head effectively and not to assume that it is just the legs that determine the quantity and quality of movement. So your upper body and lower body need to work together.

Split-Step

Top players make a split-step just as the opponent is starting the forward swing. It is a movement that in effect puts the body "in neutral" but at the same time primes it in readiness for explosive movement in any direction.

To perform the split-step efficiently, your feet should be about shoulder-width apart with your legs slightly flexed (approximately 40 to 50 degrees) and your upper body leaning slightly forward, resulting in your weight being distributed through the balls of your feet. Drop your body quickly and very slightly by bending your knees so that you feel for a split second as though you no longer can feel the ground under your feet. This maneuver is termed "unweighting." You will have come across this term if you have ever been skiing and the instructor asks you to move up slightly followed immediately by "sinking" through bending your knees to lower your hips. The effects of unweighting are demonstrated most effectively when you sink quickly by bending your knees when standing on a bathroom scale. You will see that the scale momentarily indicates that there is less weight (force) above it. As soon as you stop bending your knees and begin to return to a more upright position by actually pushing into the scale, the weight exerted on the scale will be greater than your actual weight.

This extra force applied through the scale is the result of a synchronized coordination of the whole body in pushing rapidly against the ground. These ground reaction forces are necessary to decelerate the body from one direction and accelerate the body in another direction.

First Movement

Far too often when working on movement, there is too much emphasis on what the feet should be doing and not enough attention on using the upper body. There should be a coordinated team effort between the legs and the upper body.

When working on the volley, top coaches will tell players to "volley first, then step" rather than "step then volley." What they are expressing by saying this is that they want the player to initiate the first movement with the upper body and not the legs! Using the upper body to lean toward the action just before the legs add their contribution also is seen in the way that players move to ground strokes.

So in order to move well, players need to efficiently coordinate their upper and lower body. Players who appear to have stiff trunks invariably move slowly on a tennis court because they find it difficult to change direction easily and stop and start smoothly.

Body Angle

A body angle in which the shoulders are forward of the hips will encourage weight transfer from back to front, in other words, linear momentum. This often will result in more control and more power. The "lean into the ball" tends to level out the path of the racket as it approaches and as it leaves the impact point, resulting in a longer, more stable hitting zone. This linear motion of the racket and body also encourages much more of the force of the racket head to be applied in the intended direction of the shot.

If you do not move well, you will find that you are having to improvise a lot of the time. And so you're playing with your hands rather than your feet and body. Players who move well make good shapes. Their bodies seem almost pliable, rather like plasticine.

First Step

The first step is vital in tennis because there is very little time over which speed can be built up, so a fast, explosive start is essential. A fast, short, stabbing-type

This player shows good coordination between the upper and lower body when volleying.

contact with the ground will give you a greater feeling of explosion. The more force you can apply with your feet to the court surface over a short space of time, the more explosive your first step will be. This will allow you to move into position to the ball early, which then will provide you with the opportunity to glide to the ball, aiding dynamic balance during impact with it.

Balance

Balance is influenced by the following factors:

- The height of the center of gravity—the lower it is, the more stable the object.
- The width of the base of support—the wider the base, the more stable the object.

- The distance of the center of gravity from the edge of the base of support—if the center of gravity is equidistant from each base support, then this is where an object will be most stable.

When players want to be stable, they lower the center of gravity, by assuming a wider stance (the base of support is roughly that area between the two feet). This increases the base of support and drops the hips into a lower position.

The closer to the edge of the base of support the center of gravity moves, the more unstable the object. To move, you need to first unbalance yourself by shifting your center of gravity toward the edge of the base of support, rather like a child when first learning to walk! Players who move particularly well have mastered the art of using the upper body to help initiate motion by "leaning" into the direction of where they want to move. By moving your upper body first, you in effect lean out over the edge of the base of support; that is, your feet thus shift the body's center of gravity in that direction and make your body more susceptible to losing balance, but in a controlled manner, in the direction you wish to move.

Tennis is a sport of almost continuous motion with one of its major strategies being to knock the opponent off balance. With its necessity for improvisation, agility, and control of the ball when moving and changing direction at speed, tennis requires a great degree of dynamic (moving) balance rather than static balance.

Balance can be subdivided into three main areas:

- *The head.* It should ideally remain in front, straight, and still.
- *The trunk.* It should remain straight and the shoulders should be level.
- *The stance.* The legs should work to ensure a solid hitting platform through a wide base, that is, stance and a lowered center of gravity.

For the upper body (head and shoulders) to remain in control when your opponent is attempting to knock you off balance or take time away from you, you need to be relaxed and calm just before, during, and immediately after impact.

This will ensure that your head does not move unnecessarily and that the shoulders are relatively straight. Both of these will ensure that the contact point is correct and the trajectory of the racket head through the hitting zone is optimum for the tactical objective of that particular shot.

In extreme situations of time and space, it is important to keep your head in front. In these situations, there is a tendency to lean back as you often have to move back to provide yourself with more time to play the shot. Good players ensure that they keep their heads in front even when receiving a fast ball or when having to move wide or backward.

Most "natural athletes" move and hit with a relaxed jaw, neck, and shoulders rather like a cheetah when chasing its prey. The cheetah does not appear to be grimacing with unnecessary muscle tension through "trying too hard."

So players need to be careful with what happens when they're asked to "try harder." They tend to increase their muscle tension, which reduces the efficiency of the ability of their body parts to join together and add onto each other to produce power. Control also is compromised as the body's increased tension, particularly in the neck, face, and shoulders, tends to cause it to produce jerky rather than smooth, fluid movements.

Timing

Timing is the synchronization of not only your stroke in order to center the ball at the proper impact point, for whatever shot you are playing, but also the smooth coordination of the different segments of your body. That is the "timing" of the coordination chain, so that control and power can be achieved efficiently.

To achieve this, it helps if the body is relaxed. Appropriately timed shots depend on "quality coordination" of body parts, an awareness of which parts of the coordination chain to use in different situations on the court, and knowing how much or how little of each one to use.

A player who has good timing

- is very consistent;
- has excellent ball control, particularly when redirecting the ball;
- can put pace on the ball without apparent effort; and
- rarely misses hits.

Rhythm

Associated with timing is the concept of rhythm. Rhythm is the smooth, progressive timing of the swing. Professional players have a smooth preparation with the racket head accelerating just before impact. With pro players there is a significant change in the speed of the stroke just before impact. This ensures that they establish a consistent optimal contact point.

Contact Point and Hitting Zone

What do we mean when we use the phrase "hit through the ball"? Hitting through the ball implies that the racket head has continued out through the front of the ball after impacting the back of the ball, giving a sensation of nearly all the force of the racket head being sent through the ball in a path that moves directly toward the intended target.

Most top coaches in the world will tell you that the most important part of the stroke is the impact point. This product of proper timing is a common feature within the multitude of individual stroke techniques of the best players in the world.

Arnaud Clement demonstrates good control of the racket face immediately following impact.

In successfully executing specialty shots, the control of the racket face/angle on impact and the plane of the hitting zone—that is, the area about 10 to 20 centimeters before and after impact—are paramount. So the hitting zone is the size of the "window of opportunity" when the angle of the racket head is optimum for the shot being played.

Factors Affecting Hitting Zone

- Head movement and positioning. Head movement often is related to relaxation or composure on the hit.
- Timing of rotation of body parts—for example, trunk and hips.
- Footwork positioning to the ball.
- Contact point.
- Positioning of the hips and trunk in relation to the height of the actual impact.
- Grip. Western grips offer only a short hitting zone, whereas semi-western and eastern grips offer a longer hitting zone.

Note: Supporting the shot with the body will help stabilize the hitting zone.

Touch and Feel

"Touch and feel" is about knowing how much force to apply. Tennis, first and foremost, is a control game. The concepts of "feel" and "touch" underlie control. The ability to make fine changes in the racket trajectory, its angle, and the amount and direction of its force is common in all so-called talented players. Players who execute specialty shots with consistent success have a fine sensitivity regarding the application of force and its timing. They appear to have an uncanny understanding and appreciation of gravity, which allows them to play lobs and floated backhand slice shots that consistently land close to the baseline.

Absorbing the Impact

The best way to understand absorbing and redirecting the ball's speed is by thinking of it as withdrawing the contact surface from the oncoming projectile (ball). To have "soft hands," as the term suggests, a player needs to have soft muscle tension, that is, be relaxed. "Soft hands" is a phrase associated with players who have excellent ball control. It is as though the ball were on a piece of string.

Rick Leach exhibits "soft hands" hitting a drop volley.

For example, these players can execute drop volleys in which they are able to reduce and control an oncoming ball speed of, say, 70 mph into one that is traveling less than 5 mph. The general opinion appears to be that this skill of absorbing and redirecting a ball's speed has to do with having "good hands." However, when "talented" players play a drop volley, they instinctively let the ball come in to them, ensuring that the contact point is closer to the body so that they can use the body to cushion the impact. So it is not so much that these players have soft hands but rather that they have a soft, malleable body.

To best withstand a punch by an opponent, a martial-arts expert would move with the punch rather than to try to resist the force. Pete Sampras does something similar when he uses his body to cushion the impact on an inside-out backhand volley.

Camouflage and Disguise

A related aspect of quality and speed of coordination is the ability to change the nature of the stroke at the last second. As soon as we emphasize perception, it is a consequence that players then have to learn disguise.

Dent and Hagelauer

Players whose movements and strokes "flow" invariably disguise very well. The word "flow" gives the impression of being a liquid rather than a solid; that is, it is flexible with no locked parts. This implies that those players who are very coordinated are able to unlock the body through an awareness of its different segments.

The ability to disguise is particularly important if the player has little touch or feel for the ball. Conversely, the more touch and feel a player has, the less need there is for disguise.

Disguise requires fine control (sensitivity) of the racket face immediately before and on contact. Because disguise is a last-second skill, it demands fast, manipulative hand speed. Fast, manipulative hands enable the path of the racket to the ball to be changed significantly in a very short space of time and also allow a fast, smooth grip change just before impact.

Disguise requires the use of small body segments to initiate the last-second adaptation and large body parts to provide the cover or camouflage. From this statement it therefore is obvious that a player needs control of all the body segments to disguise and then execute the shot effectively.

Relaxation Versus Tension

To deliver power, the body needs to utilize as many of its segments as possible. To "unlock" the different parts, muscle tension needs to be low, so the player has to be relaxed. The fewer body segments involved in an action, the more precision, thus there is less to go wrong. So an increase in muscle tension is needed to "lock together" body segments.

Tension should be viewed on a continuum from low to high. Skillful players change the tension in the body depending on the situation they are in, the shot they have to hit, and the stage within the stroke itself. Many unskilled players tend to "choke up" on the grip during the racket preparation, developing too much tension in the arm and inhibiting its ability to accelerate. Skilled players remain relaxed throughout the preparation and forward swing, only increasing the tension of the muscles in their arm just before impacting the ball. Then they reduce the tension to encourage a longer follow-through, which provides a greater distance over which the racket head can decelerate. In certain situations when the player is short of time, such as when being attacked with power, her tactical objective is one of control. The player will need to increase the tension in her legs, trunk, and arm to lock her body together more and to stabilize her racket head and body to withstand the collision with the ball. This awareness and control of tension also is required when volleying. Certain volleys—for example, those hitting balls traveling relatively slowly above net height—need to be "punched" away, whereas below-net-height volleys need to be "feathered." The coaching phrase "punch" implies greater muscle tension than the instruction of "feathered."

Relaxation in tennis is vital, as from it comes explosion. Unfortunately, however, it is far easier to conjure up tension on demand than relaxation.

Players who are able to play a range of specialty shots with ease are invariably those who are smooth, relaxed hitters. This major component of effective technique is not commonly taught. It is an aspect of invisible technique and as such often is neglected. Being relaxed and composed during the hit enables you to produce a smooth stroke so that the racket path moves efficiently for the desired shot. Relaxation reduces the chances of any unnecessary movement of body segments and increases the chance of each part moving sequentially and rhythmically.

There is a close relationship between muscle tension and relaxation. The more relaxed the player, the lower the muscle tension. To efficiently use the coordination chain, the body needs to be relaxed. Martina Hingis supposedly was taught to move and hit with relaxed shoulders from a very early age.

Drop Shot

Before we examine the technique of the drop shot, let's take a look at its tactical objective: to make the opponent have to move a long way forward. To achieve this, the ball needs to

1. land short in the court,
2. ideally move away from the opponent on landing or at least not move toward the opponent to any significant degree,
3. be contacted just on or before the top of the bounce, and
4. have disguise.

Technical Execution

In order to achieve the drop shot's tactical objective as discussed, the following must be done:

- To achieve requirement 1 (as listed), the racket-head speed should be slow.

- To achieve requirement 2, the ball should have underspin or sidespin, or a combination of the two, and the angle of approach to the court surface should be very steep, ideally vertical.

The stroke production of the racket is similar to that of a volley in that it is hit with an abbreviated backswing, has a grip (i.e., continental) that encourages an open racket face, and creates a short hitting plane that moves from high to low through the ball.

To do this, the racket head should contact the ball in a downward action with a slightly open racket face. The grip change toward more of a continental often occurs at the last second to position the hand around the grip so that it can manipulate the shape of the racket head more easily and open up the racket face more effectively. If you played the drop shot with a semi-western or western grip, you would have to use your hand and forearm dramatically to change the existing angle of the racket face caused by those grips to the one that is required to execute a drop shot effectively.

Players who execute the drop shot effectively are very sensitive and aware of how much force to apply with the racket onto the ball and the direction/plane of that force. Talented players also reduce the muscle tension in their forearm and hand on impact to further help absorb the pace of the oncoming ball and to open up the racket face more.

Spin

Each type of spin has its own characteristics, which are determined by

- the angle of the racket face (hitting plane) at impact,
- the angle of bypass of the racket swing (racket path), and
- the speed of the racket head on impact.

When playing a drop shot, it is invariably the surprise element that wins most of the points rather than the actual placement of the ball. So drop shots are most effective when disguised and played at the right time, ensuring that element of surprise.

The success of the drop shot, therefore, depends as much on perceptual qualities as technical qualities. The racket preparation for the drop shot should be that of a normal forehand or backhand drive with modification occurring at the last second.

The drop shot, if played appropriately, can be a very destructive tactical weapon. It usually is played when the opponent is out of position, deep behind the baseline. It particularly is useful against players who do not move forward well or who do not feel comfortable playing from the net. The drop shot is used as a rhythm wrecker to upset the rhythmical pattern in which many players like to play. It is a particularly effective shot on courts (e.g., clay, grass) that tend to have a certain amount of give in them and, as such, absorb the drop shot's pace.

The drop shot also is effective because of the ball spinning in the opposite direction than it was traveling in when it bounced, which produces more friction between the ball and the court surface. The ball therefore "grips" the court surface, causing it to "sit up" and rebound at a sharper angle than a flat shot hit with the same initial speed and approach angle. This friction also absorbs more of the ball speed than on a topspin or flat shot with the same initial speed.

The drop shot is a particularly useful accompaniment to a player whose tactical game style is based around an all-court attacking forehand. With the use of the drop shot, even though it sometimes is unsuccessful, the seed of uncertainty is placed in the mind of the opponent every time the player "sets up" to hit a big forehand. This slight uncertainty is enough to slow down the opponent's response time when the power forehand actually is played. So the player's attacking forehand becomes a more effective weapon because of the uncertainty given to the opponent by the possible option of the drop shot.

Nicolas Kiefer's opponent has hit a drop shot, leaving him with few options for the next shot.

Drop Volley

The drop volley has a precision, control objective in that it has to send the ball only a very short distance. The technique therefore should meet this tactical need by using fewer body parts in the hitting action and moving the racket head over a short distance.

This stroke uses a similar racket preparation to an orthodox volley, with the racket head being prepared using the hand and forearm. In the preparation for volleys, which require slightly more power, the forearm is used more in readiness for a "hit" feeling on impact. The fine control element of the drop volley, however, necessitates a technique in which the racket head moves very little before and after impact. This is achieved when the racket head's preparatory distance is controlled only by movement at the wrist segment rather than the elbow and shoulder segments.

You cushion or absorb the impact with the body in the same way you would use it if you had to catch a raw egg. As your hands are just about to touch the

Tim Henman's drop volley.

egg, they would be moved away from the egg in the same direction and similar speed as it was falling. This is achieved by bringing your hands into your body as your body is lowered, by bending your knees, and by lowering your shoulders and curling over with your trunk.

Pete Sampras does something similar when he uses his body to cushion the impact on an inside-out backhand volley when serving and volleying to the advantage court and redirecting the crosscourt return to a short angle in the deuce court.

Lob Volley

The lob volley occurs infrequently, particularly in singles, where it is used in a situation in which both players are at the net. It usually is executed in doubles

Anna Kournikova's lob volley.

or in singles after a drop shot has been played and the advancing player then plays the opponent's response to the drop shot as a lob volley.

Important characteristics of the lob volley are the angle of release of the ball and its force. In the singles situation mentioned here, the player may have to add some extra pace to the oncoming ball. The skill in this, and most of the other specialty shots, is having a sensitivity regarding the path of approach of the racket head, its speed, and its angle on impact. Players with good touch have an acute awareness of force and the necessary angle at which the ball needs to "exit" (move away from) the racket after impact.

Lob as a Specialty Shot

This category of shots includes the lob as a defensive shot or as an offensive (sometimes referred to as attacking) shot.

Defensive Lob

Defensive lobs invariably are hit in situations in which the player has a 30 percent or less chance of winning the point. They usually occur when the opponent has forced a player to play his shot from outside the singles sideline and

Marat Safin's defensive lob.

then approach to the other side. So defensive lobs usually are played in response to a shortage of time. The main tactical objective of a defensive lob initially is to provide time for recovery and then ideally to force the opponent to have to smash from deep in the court. To achieve this, these types of lobs usually are hit "sky high."

The stroke production of an underspin, high-defensive lob is similar to that of a forehand or backhand slice. However, owing to the extra height needed on the shot, the racket face is much more open and the racket path (angle of bypass) moves through a more upward plane.

If the ball received is traveling fast, then the backswing should be much shorter. It is important, however, to maintain a slight follow-through feeling if possible, as this often ensures more depth on the lob.

A defensive lob with the opponent at the back of the court is seen a lot on the clay courts of Europe, especially in the junior game. Players use it to neutralize a baseline attack by the opponent that has taken them out of or toward the edge of the playing area.

If the player is not at full stretch, the lob can be played with a small amount of topspin, which on bouncing will significantly move the opponent away from the attacking area of the court. This shot requires dynamic balance as it is hit on the run, and it requires good timing because of the short hitting zone of a topspin lob.

Attacking Lob

The topspin lob is the type of lob used most frequently as an attacking shot. This is because the topspin helps to bring the ball down, allowing the player to hit the ball higher over the net with less risk of the ball traveling to a greater distance and landing beyond the baseline. The topspin lob therefore gives the player a greater margin for error. Another advantage of a topspin lob is the fact that the ball is spinning in the same direction as it was traveling when it hit the ground, resulting in less friction from the court surface, which does not slow down the ball as much as a flat or underspin lob. Sometimes when a lob is hit with heavy topspin, and the actual velocity of the shot is slow, the forward speed of the ball actually may increase after the ball bounces.

If the net player manages to get into a position to smash the topspin lob, the problem is not over, because the topspin makes the ball difficult to time as it drops (changes height) quickly. This dipping trajectory of topspin shots is because the top of the ball is spinning in the opposite direction of the air flow whereas the bottom of the ball is moving in the same direction as the air flow. The result is an increased pressure on top of the ball in relation to that on the bottom of the ball, which in effect "pushes" the ball downward.

Because topspin lobs require a severe low-to-high brushing motion up the back of the ball with an almost perpendicular racket face, they can be difficult to time and to execute from either low or high balls.

Half Volley

When a player is delivering a half volley, her reaction, ball judgment, and decision-making skills have not worked as well as she would wish. In an ideal situation, the player would rather have moved forward toward the ball to play a volley or moved away from it to allow space between herself and where the ball bounces to make the timing of the shot easier. However, it sometimes is more effective to play a half volley rather than lunging forward to play a volley with an uncontrolled and very open racket face that may pop the ball up so that the opponent can hit an easy pass. An earlier response to the oncoming ball also would improve the player's ability to interpret the tactical context (situation) as being easy, medium, or difficult. The tactical context when playing a half volley invariably can be described as difficult. As such, half volleys could be described as "emergency control" shots. The sending portion of the skill therefore needs to adapt accordingly. In these countering situations, the first reaction should be one of defense, that is, safety and stability. This is achieved through intense focus on first establishing an optimum contact point, usually achieved by severely shortening the backswing. The angle of the racket face on impact is either perpendicular to the ground or slightly open. The closer to the net the player hits the half volley, the more open the racket face will need to be, as there is a shorter "takeoff runway" before the ball has to clear the net. The racket trajectory (path) moves from low to high through the hitting zone. The angle of the racket path will decrease. The stroke sensation should have a feeling of "catch and push."

Half-Volley Drop Shot

The half-volley drop shot is a specialty shot usually reserved for clay and grass. It is probably one of the most deft of touch shots because it requires precision timing and fine racket-head control.

The contact point for this shot is played closer to the body than for a normal half volley so that a more vertical racket path is encouraged and possible. The racket head is perpendicular to the ground and is moved in a very steep upward

Preparation for the half volley includes a short backswing.

path by the upward movement (elevation) of the legs, hips, and trunk being "locked" together and working as a single unit to help "pop" the ball over the net.

Conclusion

As tennis playing ability increases, the sport evolves into an increasingly high-tempo, fast-moving exchange game in which its participants are required to receive and send the ball in a shorter and shorter space of time. The technical skills needed to achieve this level of performance must relate to both these phases. Specialty shots, as the name suggests, occur infrequently within the game, but ironically their successful execution may well be more attributable to the "technical fundamentals" of the game than the success of the basic strokes. Performance on specialty shots may well be more of a sensitive indicator of the building blocks of sound technique than the ability to hit the basic shots of the game.

Chapter Fourteen

Self-Analysis

Duane Knudson
Pam Shriver

A tennis coach is watching a junior player practice his serve and stops the drill to instruct the player to adjust his toss. At a practice court at the U.S. Open, a tennis coach and a TV commentator intently watch a pro preparing for an upcoming match. These are examples of experts analyzing the technique of a tennis player. This professional skill is called qualitative analysis. What is involved in the qualitative analysis of tennis techniques? How can players use qualitative analysis to improve their own skills and evaluate potential opponents? This chapter will introduce you to the essentials of qualitative analysis and will provide examples of how it can be used to improve tennis technique.

What Is Qualitative Analysis?

Everybody makes subjective judgments about things every day. "I don't think that car is going to stop!" "I think she looks tired; time to run her around." Qualitative analysis is a skill developed by tennis coaches that is built from knowledge of tennis and of movement analysis. In essence, qualitative analysis is a systematic way to observe human movement and make subjective judgments about the best way to improve. The key thing that makes an analysis qualitative is the subjective, non-numerical nature of the process. In this chapter the term "tennis coach" will be used to mean all kinds of tennis professionals. It could be argued that the most important skill of a tennis coach is her ability in the qualitative analysis of a tennis player's technique or the physical competencies referred to by Jim Loehr and Tom Gullikson in chapter 8. We will see that you can improve your "coaching" of yourself or friends by learning to use a comprehensive approach to qualitative analysis of tennis strokes.

Potential of Qualitative Analysis for Improving Tennis Technique

When a tennis coach qualitatively analyzes the strokes of players in a lesson, there are two main benefits that can be achieved. First, correct qualitative analysis leads to faster learning of tennis skills and techniques and, ultimately, improved performance. The second benefit is a reduced risk of injury when appropriate technique is used. A tennis player who just plays matches may refine stroking errors, rather than develop good biomechanical technique. The skilled eyes and mind of a tennis coach, through qualitative analysis, make a major difference in the quality and potential risk of tennis play.

This chapter introduces you to a few concepts in the qualitative analysis of tennis strokes. By adopting these concepts, you can improve your ability to evaluate your own strokes and the strokes of a family member, practice partner, or potential opponent. The chapter cannot provide enough knowledge and experience for you to become an expert on the qualitative analysis of tennis on par with a tennis coach. Most players can, however, improve the qualitative analysis of their own techniques and appreciate the services of tennis coaches.

Kinds of Qualitative Analysis

There are essentially two kinds of qualitative analysis based on when and how the movement is analyzed. Qualitative analysis of tennis strokes is usually based on videotape replay. Most tennis coaches qualitatively analyze strokes as the player is practicing or competing. Live qualitative analysis of tennis strokes is the most difficult because the speed of body movements in tennis is very high. It is difficult and sometimes impossible for human vision to perceive many body motions in tennis. You already may know that you cannot see the ball

Stroke analysis allows players and coaches to focus on each stage of a movement.

strike the tennis court, so the rules about placement of line people and calling balls "in" when in doubt are wise. It is quite common for tennis pros, television broadcasts, and tennis players to use videotape to record tennis strokes so that the replays can be qualitatively analyzed. The main advantages of qualitative analysis of videotape replays are the ability to see the faster parts of the movement using pause and slow-motion features as well as the potentially unlimited number of replays that can be viewed. We also will see that there are limitations to using videotape replay for qualitative analysis. Whatever the setting for the qualitative analysis, it is best to use a systematic approach that will ensure that the analyst sees the big picture of tennis technique.

Seeing the Bigger Picture

"You can observe a lot just by watchin'."—Yogi Berra. The first thing to keep in mind when trying to do an accurate qualitative analysis of tennis technique is a comprehensive vision of qualitative analysis. This bigger picture of such analysis

Self-Analysis

will show that Yogi Berra was wrong and that good qualitative analysis of tennis is more than detecting stroke errors and making corrections ("Watch the ball, bend your knees, that will be $50, please"). The best tennis coaches use a systematic and complex process to evaluate and prescribe changes when qualitatively analyzing strokes. The good analyst is like an experienced physician who weighs all the relevant information, diagnoses the cause of the problem, and intervenes in the most effective and least invasive way. This section will summarize this comprehensive approach to qualitative analysis, which will increase your ability to improve tennis technique.

Arantxa Sanchez-Vicario's service motion.

The qualitative analysis model proposed by Knudson and Morrison (1997) is a simple, yet comprehensive approach that can be applied easily to analyzing tennis strokes. Although this model was written for coaches, it is important for players to understand as well. This complex professional skill can be conceptualized in four main tasks (figure 14.1). First, the coach prepares for the live qualitative analysis by gathering information about the activity and player and preparing an observational strategy. Second, the coach observes the player, using all relevant senses to gather information about performance. The third task may be the most difficult and involves two steps: the evaluation of the strengths and weaknesses of performance and the diagnosis of the movement problem from the many symptoms observed. Fourth, the coach chooses one of many possible interventions to help the player improve. In live qualitative analysis, the tennis coach can return immediately to the observation of the next stroke to monitor the player's progress.

This larger vision of qualitative analysis goes beyond the traditional comparative analysis. Old models of qualitative analysis consisted of comparing a mental image of the ideal stroke technique to the technique visually observed. This old approach leads to tunnel vision, which can miss many key features of the movement and a habit of "detecting errors" and "prescribing corrections." The resulting overemphasis of many small "errors" often results in "paralysis by analysis" in players. Have you ever had a coach with this correction complex who always focused on small, unimportant errors and rarely told you what you

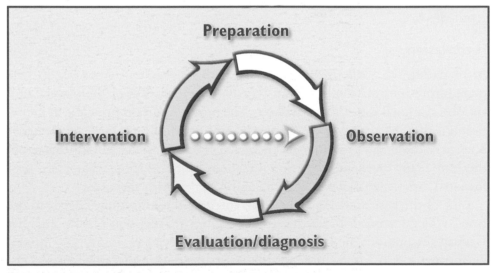

Figure 14.1
The Knudson and Morrison model of qualitative analysis. In on-court analysis the coach or teaching professional will return immediately to observation after providing intervention to the player.

Adapted, with permission, from D. Knudson and C. Morrison, 1997, *Qualitative Analysis of Human Movement.* (Champaign, IL: Human Kinetics.)

Note the critical features of each stroke, such as the forehand.

really needed to do to improve? Let's take a brief look at some important elements in each of the four tasks of a larger vision of the qualitative analysis of tennis strokes.

Preparation

In preparing for qualitative analysis of tennis technique, the analyst gathers prerequisite information on tennis strokes, characteristics of the players, and the observational strategy they will use. The most important principle in preparation is that the analyst must "integrate" (thoughtfully combine) all the sport science research and professional experience in tennis available. Like this book, there are many excellent tennis-specific books based on sport science and professional experience that can help the tennis player with this task.

One of the best ways to organize this integrated tennis knowledge is to define "critical features" for all the strokes and techniques you plan to analyze. Critical features are the key technique points that are necessary for optimal performance. Critical features are the most invariant aspects of tennis technique that are required for safe and effective strokes. Although these critical features can be complex ideas, such as the coordination used in a forehand, you should identify them using simple cue words. The use of simple cue words or phrases makes it possible for the players to remember the key action they are

252

trying to create. This is the beauty of a good cue. Players can focus on one thing or be reminded of one word, and a flood of related information can be attached to this word. In the analyst's mind, these more extensive descriptions also should include the "range of correctness" that is appropriate for each critical feature. This defining in your own mind—the too much or too little for a technique feature of a stroke—makes it easier for you to evaluate it later. Good coaches have an extensive vocabulary of cues, often with several for each critical feature.

Examples of critical features are the four proposed for the beginning instruction and qualitative analysis of the square-stance topspin forehand drive (Knudson 1991). It was recommended that coaches focus on readiness, early and simple racket preparation, body rotation and stroke path, and a moderate and high follow-through. Remember that all critical features will be evaluated in the context of other prerequisite information on the player you are analyzing. Coaches need to be aware of physical and mental characteristics of their players with specific reference to age, gender, and competitive goals.

Analysts can use the information gathered in the preparation task to help develop an appropriate observational strategy. An observational strategy is necessary in tennis because of the visual limitations of observing fast movements of the body and racket. Knowing what to observe and planning how to gather this information in a systematic observational strategy are key components of the next task of qualitative analysis.

Observation

The observation task of qualitative analysis is more than casual visual inspection of a tennis stroke, because good observation is systematic and utilizes all relevant senses. An observational strategy is a systematic plan for gathering all the relevant sensory information about the performance of a tennis stroke. A coach rallying with a player can get kinesthetic (tactile, force, and motion sensations) information from volleying or stroking the player's returns. Suppose you plan to use videotape replay to extend your observational abilities. You might be able to enrich this observation by turning up the sound during replay to use the sound of impact for information on the speed and spin of the stroke. The marks left by footwork on a clay court are another example of how observation can go beyond eyeballing the tennis player. If slide marks are parallel to the baseline rather than angled toward the net, the coach knows that the player was not likely moving at the proper angle to intercept the ball and get more weight into the shot.

To simplify this brief discussion of observation, we will focus on visual observational strategies. Recall that we said the visual perception of movement is severely limited as movement speed increases. The visual tracking of racket and upper extremity in most tennis strokes is extremely difficult. To get the most information out of an overloaded visual system, coaches should plan to focus their attention on key technique points as they observe several strokes. There are many ways to organize an observational strategy (Knudson and Morrison 1997). Common approaches are to focus your attention sequentially on the main phases (preparation, forward swing, follow-through) or different parts of the body (legs, trunk, arms) in the stroke. Another common observational strategy is to observe several performances (five to eight) with observational attention moving from general impressions to more specific critical features. Possibly the best strategy is to focus attention on the critical features ranked in order of their importance to performance for that stroke. Tennis coaches should *not* make judgments on tennis technique based on observations of just a few strokes (one to three) unless the player is doing something dangerous. There always will be small variations in technique and the goal in qualitative analysis is to focus on the most important change—what will improve performance or decrease risk of injury.

Other key elements of a good observational strategy are attention to the situation being analyzed, using several vantage points, and the potential need of extended observational power. Observation of tennis strokes usually should be planned around performances as similar as possible to actual play. Observing

Focus on different phases of the stroke.

serves without the pressure of a return may not provide relevant information for many players. Observation of tennis strokes usually should take place from several vantage points since most strokes are three-dimensional. The appropriate vantage point for a coach to view a particular critical feature is perpendicular to the plane of motion. For example, the distance away from the body that the ball is contacted in the forehand usually should be observed from behind. If the stroke is very fast, the analyst might need to extend observational power by recording the movement with video. It is important to use a very small shutter setting (such as 1/1000 second) to freeze the fast-moving parts of the stroke. Using the pause and jog-shuttle controls on a videocassette recorder (VCR) playback unit will allow the analyst to review the 30 video frames captured each second. Considerable detail in tennis technique beyond live observation can be detected by slow-motion and stop-action review of videotape replay.

Try to observe strokes from different vantage points.

Evaluation and Diagnosis

The third task of qualitative analysis in tennis may be the most difficult and requires two important decisions. First, the coach must evaluate the performance, identifying both the strengths and weaknesses. Second, the coach diagnoses the performance by identifying the underlying causes of the observed strengths and weaknesses. Unfortunately, some tennis coaches still do not use this combination of evaluation and diagnosis of movement but only are familiar with the traditional "detect movement errors," which then are corrected with some form of feedback.

Evaluation involves the careful judgment of identifying the strengths and weaknesses of performance. The careful documentation of the range of correctness of critical features makes it easier to judge what aspects of a tennis stroke

Knudson and Shriver

are a strength or a weakness in achieving the goal of the stroke. Imagine a player with a basic one-handed backhand who tends to contact the ball too close to her body. Using the traditional error-correction approach on the contact point ("Don't hit the ball so close to your body") may be shortsighted. A thorough evaluation may result in a judgment that the basic weight transfer, arm action, and stroke path are all strengths of this player's backhand. Her weakness may be in other areas such as preparatory movements and perception of the spin of the ball being returned. Many factors in the unpredictable environment of a tennis match interact to effect the most appropriate technique. This is why it is necessary to observe several strokes combined with the evaluation of tennis strokes, rather than just identifying things that look wrong.

In diagnosis, the tennis coach faces the challenge of determining what one intervention is most appropriate. Focusing on one aspect of performance to intervene in is critical, because people cannot attend to more than one idea as they make subsequent movements. The diagnosis of the underlying causes of poor performance usually is handled by prioritizing the effect of the possible interventions the coach could use. There are several rationales or approaches to prioritizing the possible intervention. The best approach appears to be a combination of a few of the rationales. We recommend that tennis coaches prioritize tennis technique based on relating actions to previous actions and on the coaches' judgment of the importance of the critical features.

Imagine that a beginning player has been evaluated as weak in generating racket speed through the contact zone on his two-handed backhand. A coach could combine the relating actions to previous actions and the importance of critical features rationale to diagnose the performance. The coach decides if there are previous actions (backswing, forward swing technique, timing, strength) that might be related to the problem (slow racket through impact). If the performer has good timing and adequate strength for the backhand, the coach intervenes in either racket preparation or forward stroke technique based on which is believed to be the most important in the two-handed backhand of most beginners. The common error of a service toss drifting over the player's head usually occurs because of the primarily circular rotation of the tossing arm about the shoulder. If the coach can find what joint actions (shoulder, elbow, or wrist) are the primary causes of the poor toss, he can provide better intervention to focus on the cause of the serving problems.

Intervention

The final task of qualitative analysis of tennis technique is implementing one intervention to improve performance. The most simple of these interventions is the traditional verbal feedback provided to the player. Feedback serves to reinforce correct actions, motivate, and guide the player in more appropriate technique. Sport science research has developed several principles to guide the use of feedback as intervention. If a tennis coach uses feedback as intervention, the research says the feedback should be specific and corrective (telling the person what to do) and the coach should use cue words or phrases, minimize the delay between the movement and the feedback, and use a variety of approaches if unsuccessful. We also know that feedback about the actual stroking movement (knowledge of performance) usually is a more powerful intervention than outcome information about shot success (knowledge of results). A great strategy to use when using feedback as intervention is to "sandwich" any correction between two positive ideas. A coach could praise effort or reinforce some strength of the performance before and after the cue words she wants the player to focus on in the next few strokes.

There are several methods of intervention beyond the traditional provision of feedback that can help tennis players improve. Some examples of these methods are the modification of practice, conditioning, visual models, manual guidance, and overcompensation. For example, exaggeration or overcompensation is a strategy that is particularly effective in situations in which players have difficulty in making a change in technique. Novice players often tend to serve on an incorrect initial trajectory (downward), but players often can get the correct feel and motion if they are instructed to attempt to hit the ball on a straight line to the back fence. This exaggeration of intention usually results in the appropriate vigorous and upward hitting action of a good serve, often placing the first few attempts in the back of the service box. Good coaches use many intervention strategies in their qualitative analyses of tennis strokes.

Summary

The most effective qualitative analysis of tennis strokes requires a broader vision of the process than has been used traditionally. Coaches will be better analyzers of tennis technique if they strive to use the four-task model of qualitative analysis presented here and if they strive to integrate sport science information and experience in these difficult decisions. Important features of this expanded vision of qualitative analysis are preparing for analysis, systematic observation, evaluating both strengths and weaknesses, diagnosing the causes of poor performance, and the thoughtful prescription of a single intervention.

Live Analysis

It is not possible to simulate the qualitative analysis of live tennis techniques in a book, but this section will illustrate how the four-task model of qualitative analysis could be used in the live analysis of a beginning tennis player's serve. In preparing for qualitative analysis of the serve, we adopt the six critical features of the serve proposed by Knudson, Luedtke, and Faribault (1994). They proposed six critical features in an order of importance for the instruction and analysis of beginning tennis players' serves (table 14.1). Assume that live observation of several serves of a beginning tennis player shows actions and results similar to what is illustrated in figure 14.2. For the sake of our analysis, we also will assume that the player used a continental grip and had a good follow-through (not illustrated).

An evaluation of the serve in figure 14.2 indicates that the grip, stance, and follow-through are strengths. The critical features of toss, racket preparation, and continuous upward racket motion are weak. Difficult to identify in this figure is the timing of the serve, in that the racket preparation is long and slow. This, combined with a high toss and the arm not near extension at impact, limits the speed and trajectory of the serve.

Given the three weaknesses identified, the diagnosis implied by the prioritized critical features suggests that modification of the toss might lead to the most improvement. Focusing intervention on a slightly lower toss might force the person to speed up racket preparation to make contact with the ball. This diagnosis is based on a hypothesized association of an action (long preparation and low hitting action) to a previous action (high toss). Not all tennis coaches would agree with this approach to diagnosis. Some coaches might focus the player's attention on a correct upward hitting action, believing that this might lead to greater success, and encourage the player to speed up the racket to hit the ball at a higher point. Ultimately, the diagnosis of any player's performance

Table 14.1

Diagnosis of Tennis Serve by Importance of Critical Features

Critical feature	Rationale
1. Grip	Determines the path of the racket and forearm/wrist action
2. Toss	Determines timing and proper racket path
3. Racket preparation	Affects timing and speed of the racket
4. Continuous upward motion	Determines effective ball trajectory
5. Follow-through	Maximizes racket speed and protects the body
6. Stance	Affects balance, accuracy, and development of racket speed

Adapted from Knudson, Luedtke, and Faribault (1994)

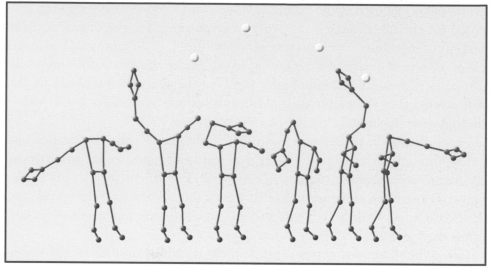

Figure 14.2
A typical serve of a beginning tennis player horizontally spaced to prevent overlapping. Space and time among the images are not uniform.

depends on the coach's and the player's philosophies and the goal for improvement. The tennis player often is interested in short-term results, whereas good coaches need to communicate to players the long-term nature of goals and potential improvement. Attention to a difficult technique change might decrease short-term performance, but it ultimately results in improved performance in the long run.

Video Analysis

Video can be used to record the motions of tennis play for later qualitative analysis. Videotape replay can be used to analyze overall player strategy and tactical responses during match play or to analyze the specific techniques of the movement and strokes of the player. An example of the qualitative analysis of videotape replay is what former tennis touring professionals are hired to do on television broadcasts. In tennis telecasts the commentator often works with a touch screen, so aspects of a player's technique can be isolated with graphics and reviewed for viewers. Freezing Lindsay Davenport's two-handed backhand allows the commentator to point out characteristics of her stroke that contribute to its success. Davenport often has considerable knee bend, as well as good hip and trunk rotation, to create a powerful upward stroke path.

In the past, many tennis professionals did not use videotape replays of practice or matches to analyze and improve their performance. Other sports such as golf, baseball, and football have a longer history of using film and video to

Knee bend and good hip and trunk rotation contribute to the success of Lindsay Davenport's two-handed backhand.

evaluate technique or strategy. More and more tennis coaches are utilizing the power of videotape replay to improve their observation within qualitative analysis. The next paragraphs will summarize some important points in making the most of this technology to extend observational power for qualitative analysis in tennis. The qualitative analysis of videotape replay is particularly effective for stopping and slowing the high-speed movements of the sport that cannot be seen by live observation.

The process of qualitative analysis of videotape replay is quite similar to the live analysis presented earlier. This section summarizes the steps that will allow you to make videos appropriate for qualitative analysis of technique. The setup of the camcorder depends on the purpose of the videotape replay. If the replay will be for immediate, real-time qualitative analysis for the player and coach, the field of view (video picture) should be large with a lot of background features (fence, net, court) that help the analyst see the movement as it appears on the environment. Setup for slow-motion video analysis is different. For slow-motion replay, maximize the size of the player in the field of view with the stroke of interest occurring in the center of the picture. This will allow a better view of the small and fast aspects of the movement while the image is paused.

When setting up a camcorder to record tennis strokes, it is important to put the main movements of interest at right angles to the direction of the camera. If

Self-Analysis

the analyst wants to evaluate the stroke path of a forehand in a vertical plane, the camera should be leveled and placed to the side of the court to capture an image plane (vertical and horizontal) that can be related to the court. You usually should place the camcorder on a tripod as far from the movement as possible and use the zoom lens to get the appropriate field of view. Handheld shots are good for keeping the player in the field of view, but try to avoid excessive camera motion. Perspective can be lost when the camera angles are unknown, so videotape from the top of the stands with moderate panning instead of courtside with extreme changes in camera angle. A limitation of video pictures is that they are a two-dimensional representation of a three-dimensional world, so the motion of objects not moving at right angles to the camera will be distorted. For example, the amount of arm bend in the "back-scratch" position in a serve can look smaller than it actually is from different angles.

Most camcorders automatically will adjust the picture for lighting and white balance. An important feature to check is the shutter. The number of pictures per second is fixed at 30 in off-the-shelf video in North America, but each image will need to be captured over a very short time interval to prevent blurring of fast objects. Set the camcorder shutter to at least 1/500 second or smaller (such as 1/1000 second) if there is enough light.

To replay the video, the most common approach is to use a four-head VCR and a television. The camcorder itself can be used but the larger images on TV monitors are preferable. The feature that maximizes the pause and slow-motion replay function of a VCR is a jog-shuttle wheel, but buttons for pause, frame advance, and slow motion also are effective for reviewing the video. Computer replay of video is becoming more common with video-digitizing cards for analog video, and digital video cameras that can stream video directly into computers. A variety of video replay and editing software programs then can be used to replay the video for qualitative analysis. There are several low-cost software programs specifically designed for the replay of sport videos for qualitative analysis.

Summary

One of the most important tools of coaches for improving tennis performance is the qualitative analysis of tennis strokes. Qualitative analysis can be based on the observation of live or videotaped performances. The best qualitative analysis of tennis strokes uses a larger vision of qualitative analysis than has been used previously. A four-task model of qualitative analysis is recommended for analyzing tennis strokes.

Glossary

angular impulse—The product of the applied torque and the time over which the torque was applied or area under a torque-time curve.

angular momentum—The angular force generated by a body based on its resistance to rotation multiplied by its velocity of rotation.

axis of rotation—The straight line (point) around which all body parts will rotate.

center of gravity—A point slightly above the center of the pelvic region about which all of a person's mass is distributed.

centrifugal force—A pseudo-force equal to and acting in the direction opposite to the direction of the centripetal force (that is, acting away from the axis of rotation).

concentric contraction—Muscle action in which the muscle shortens, causing the attachments to move closer together.

cueing—The observation of body movements that indicate the type and direction of a stroke.

dorsal flexion—Foot movement, articulating at the ankle, upward and toward the anterior surface of the leg.

dynamic balance—Overall body control in moving toward a ball and hitting the shot.

eccentric contraction—A muscle action producing lengthening of muscle fibers while developing tension, as in biceps during arm extension movement; a negative contraction.

elastic energy—When muscles and tendons are stretched they store energy (like an elastic band that is stretched and rebounds) that can be used to assist performance.

horizontal flexion/abduction—The counterclockwise rotation of an abducted upper arm toward the opponent (i.e., in the transverse plane).

internal rotation—Rotation (twisting) of the upper arm forward and toward the opponent (external rotation is rotation away from the opponent).

kinetic chain—A sequence of segmental movements coordinated to provide for the efficient transfer of momentum from one segment to the next (also known as kinetic link or the linked system).

law of acceleration—One of Newton's laws of motion; states that the rate of change of momentum is proportional to the applied force and takes place in the direction of the applied force.

law of action-reaction—One of Newton's laws of motion; states that for every action there is an equal and opposite reaction.

law of inertia—One of Newton's laws of motion; states that a body will continue in its state of motion unless otherwise acted on by an external force or torque.

linear momentum—The linear force generated by a body based on its mass multiplied by its velocity.

momentum—A combination of the mass of the body (body weight) or body part multiplied by its speed.

potential energy—The ability of a body to do work by virtue of its position relative to a reference.

pronation—Rotation (twisting) of the forearm forward and toward the opponent, about its long axis.

supination—Rotation of the palm upward.

torque—An angular force that occurs about a joint.

References

Chapter 3

Cayer, L. 2000. *Developing Tactical Patterns*. Melbourne: Australian Coaches Conference.

Crespo, Miley. 1998. *ITF Advanced Coaches Manual*. London: International Tennis Foundation Ltd.

DTB. 1988. *Step by Step Tennis Skills*. London: Hamlyn.

Tennis Canada. 1998. *Instructor 1 and Instructor 2*. Canada: National Coaching Certification Program.

———. 1998. *Coach 2*. Canada: National Coaching Certification Program.

United States Tennis Association. 1995. *Coaching Tennis Successfully*. Champaign, IL: Human Kinetics.

———. 1996. *Tennis Tactics*. Champaign IL: Human Kinetics.

Chapter 4

Chu, D.A. 1992. *Jumping Into Plyometrics*. Champaign, IL: Human Kinetics.

Ellenbecker, T.S., and E.P. Roetert. 1999. Testing isokinetic muscular fatigue of shoulder internal and external rotation in elite junior tennis players. *Journal of Orthopedic Sports Physical Therapy* 29(5):275-281.

Ellenbecker, T.S., and E.P. Roetert. 2000. The effects of a four month season of collegiate tennis on glenohumeral joint internal and external rotation strength. In review, *Journal of Strength and Conditioning Research*.

Fleck, S.J., and W.J. Kraemer. 1986. *Designing Resistance Training Programs*. Champaign, IL: Human Kinetics.

Kraemer, W.J., N. Ratamess, A.C. Fry, et al. 2000. Influence of resistance training volume and periodization on physiological and performance adaptations in collegiate women tennis players. *American Journal of Sports Medicine* 28(5):626-633.

Roetert, E.P., and T.S. Ellenbecker. 1998. *Complete Conditioning for Tennis*. Champaign, IL: Human Kinetics.

Roetert, E.P., T. McCormick, S. Brown, and T.S. Ellenbecker. 1996. Relationship between isokinetic and functional trunk strength in elite junior tennis players. *Isokinetics & Exercise Science* 6:15-30.

Roetert, E.P., T.S. Ellenbecker, D.A. Chu, and B.S. Bugg. 1997. Tennis-specific shoulder and trunk strength training. *Strength and Conditioning* 19(3):31-39.

Sobel, J., T.S. Ellenbecker, and E.P. Roetert. 1995. Flexibility training for tennis. *Strength and Conditioning* 17(6):43-51.

Chapter 6

Elliott, B.C., R. Marshall, and G. Noffal. 1995. Contributions of upper limb segment rotations during the power serve in tennis. *Journal of Applied Biomechanics* 11:433-42.

Kibler, W.B. 1993. Analysis of sport as a diagnostic aid. In *The Shoulder: A Balance of Mobility and Stability*, ed. F. Matsen, F. Fu, and R. Hawkins. American Academy of Orthopaedic Surgeons.

———. 1995. Biomechanical analysis of the shoulder during tennis activities. *Clinics in Sports Medicine* 14:79-86.

———. 1998. The role of the scapula in athletic shoulder function. *American Journal of Sports Medicine* 26:325-37.

Schönborn, R. 1999. *Advanced Techniques for Competitive Tennis*. Achene, Germany: Meyer and Meyer.

Chapter 8

Burk, C., and J. Kimiecik. 1994. Examining the relationship among focus of control, value and exercise. *Health Value* 18:14-23.

Csikszentmihalyi, M. 1990. *Flow: The Psychology of Optimal Experience*. New York: Harper and Row.

Goleman, D. 1995. *Emotional Intelligence*. New York: Bantam.

Landin, D., and E. Herbert. 1999. The influence of self-talk on the performance of skilled female tennis players. *Journal of Applied Sport Psychology* 2(2):263-82.

Loehr, J. 1990. *The Mental Game*. New York: Plume.

———. 1994. *The Toughness Training for Sports*. New York: Plume.

Martin, K., S. Mority, and C. Hall. 1999. Imagery use in sport: A literature review and applied model. *The Sport Psychologist* 13(3):245-668.

Morgan, W. 1997. *Physical Activity and Mental Health*. Washington, D.C.: Taylor and Francis.

Roetert, P., and T. Ellenbecker, eds. 1998. *Complete Conditioning for Tennis*. Champaign, IL: Human Kinetics.

Seligman, M. 1991. *Learned Optimism*. New York: Knopf.

Thayer, R. 1996. *The Origin of Everyday Moods*. New York: Oxford University Press.

Wurtman, R. 1992. Food and mood. *Nutrition Action* 19(7):5-7.

Chapter 12

Abernethy, B. 1990. Anticipation in squash: Differences in advance cue utilization between expert and novice players. *Journal of Sports Sciences* 8(1):17-34.

Bahamonde, R. 1997. Joint power production during flat and slice tennis serves. In *Proceedings of XV Symposium on Biomechanics in Sports*, eds. J. Wilkerson, W. Zimmermann, and K. Ludwig, 92, Texas Womans University.

———. 2000. Angular momentum changes during the tennis serve. *Journal of Sports Science* 18:579-92.

References

Bahamonde, R., and D. Knudson. 1998. Upper extremity kinetics of the open and square stance tennis forehand. In *Proceedings of 4th International Conference on Sports Medicine and Science in Tennis*, Miami.

Bartlett, R., J. Piller, and S. Miller. 1995. A three-dimensional analysis of the tennis serves of National (British) and County standard players. In *Science and Racket Sports 1*, eds. T. Reilly, M. Hughes, and A. Lees, 98-102. London: E & FN Spon.

Brody, H. 1987. *Tennis Science for Tennis Players*. Philadelphia: University of Pennsylvania Press.

Chow, J., L. Carlton, W. Chae, Y. Lim, and J. Shim. 1999. Pre- and post-impact ball and racket characteristics during tennis serves performed by elite male and female players. In *Proceedings of XVII International Symposium on Biomechanics in Sports*, eds. R. Sanders and B. Gibson, 45-48, Edith Cowan University, Perth, Australia.

Elliott, B., K. Baxter, and T. Besier. 1999. Internal rotation of the upper-arm segment during a stretch-shortening movement. *Journal of Applied Biomechanics* 15:381-95.

Elliott, B., T. Marsh, and B. Blanksby. 1986. A three-dimensional cinematographic analysis of the tennis serve. *International Journal of Sports Biomechanics* 2(4):260-71.

Elliott, B.C., and G.A. Wood. 1983. The biomechanics of the foot-up and foot-back tennis service techniques. *Australian Journal of Sports Science* 3(2):3-6.

Elliott, B.C., R.N. Marshall, and G. Noffal. 1995. Contributions of upper limb segment rotations during the power serve in tennis. *Journal of Applied Biomechanics* 11:433-42.

Groppel, J.L. 1992. *High Tech Tennis*. 2d ed. Champaign, IL: Leisure Press.

Hennemann, M., and D. Keller. 1983. Preparatory behaviour in the execution of a sport-related movement: The return of serve in tennis. *International Journal of Sport Psychology* 14:149-61.

Noffal, G., and B. Elliott. 1998. Three-dimensional kinetics of the shoulder and elbow joints in the high performance tennis serve: Implications for injury. In *Proceedings of the 4th International Conference of Sports Medicine and Science in Tennis*, Coral Gables, FL.

Saviano, N. 1999. The serve. *High Performance Coaching* 1(2):5-8.

———. 2000a. The forehand return of serve. *High Performance Coaching* 2(1):5-8.

———. 2000b. The two-handed backhand return of serve. *High Performance Coaching* 2(2):5-8.

Chapter 14

Brody, H. 1987. *Tennis Science for Tennis Players*. Philadelphia: University of Pennsylvania Press.

Elliott, B., and R. Kilderry. 1983. *The Art and Science of Tennis*. Philadelphia: Saunders College Publishing.

Groppel, J.L. 1992. *High Tech Tennis*. 2d ed. Champaign, IL: Leisure Press.

Groppel, J.L., J.E. Loehr, D.S. Melville, and A.M. Quinn. 1989. *Science of Coaching Tennis*. Champaign, IL: Leisure Press.

Knudson, D. 1991. The tennis topspin forehand drive: Technique changes and critical elements. *Strategies* 5(1):19-22.

———. 1999. Using sport science to observe and correct tennis strokes. In *Applied Proceedings of the XVII International Symposium on Biomechanics in Sports, TENNIS*, eds. B. Elliott, B. Gibson, and D. Knudson, 7-16, Edith Cowan University, Perth, Australia.

Knudson, D., and C. Morrison. 1997. *Qualitative Analysis of Human Movement*. Champaign, IL: Human Kinetics.

Knudson, D., D. Luedtke, and J. Faribault. 1994. How to analyze the serve. *Strategies* 7(8):19-22.

Index

Index

Index

About the Editors

E. Paul Roetert, PhD, is currently the Director of Administration for the United States Tennis Association's USA Tennis High Performance Program. In addition, he serves as Tournament Director of the U.S. Open Junior Tennis Championships. Before re-joining the USTA in November, 2001, Roetert spent two years as the Executive Director of the American Sport Education Program. Prior to that position he spent eleven years as the Administrator of Sport Science for the USTA where he developed the sport science program. He also served as Vice Chairman of the sport science committee.

Roetert is a Fellow in the American College of Sports Medicine (ACSM). He is also a member of the United States Professional Tennis Association (USPTA) and the United States Professional Tennis Registry (PTR). In 1998 he received the PTR's Plagenhoef Award for sport science; in 1999 the Editorial Excellence award from the National Strength and Conditioning Association for his work on the *Journal of Strength and Conditioning Research;* and in 2000 the Outstanding Alumni award from the University of Connecticut.

Roetert holds a PhD in biomechanics from the University of Connecticut. Originally from the Netherlands, he and his wife Barbara reside in Miami, Florida.

Jack Groppel is a cofounder and partner in the highly regarded LGE Performance Systems, Inc., which helps athletes train both mentally and physically to perform at the highest levels of sport. Groppel is an instruction editor for *Tennis* magazine and is in his 13th year as chairman of the sports science committee at the USTA.

Like Roetert, Groppel is a Fellow in the ACSM. He is also a USPTA Master Professional and one of only eight Professional Tennis Registry (PTR) International Master Professionals worldwide. In 1987 the USPTA named him National Pro of the Year. Groppel has also been named to the Midwest USPTA Hall of Fame and has received the International Tennis Hall of Fame Educational Merit Award. He has traveled to more than 45 countries training tennis coaches to teach the game more effectively.

Groppel holds a PhD in exercise physiology from Florida State University. He and his wife Jodie live in Algonquin, Illinois.

About the Contributors

Vic Braden is one of the most recognized tennis instructors in the world. Braden has authored five books, produced countless videos, and hosted several television series. He is a licensed psychologist, author, sports educator and researcher, videographer, and television commentator. Braden got his start as the head tennis coach at the University of Toledo in 1952. After a stint as an elementary school teacher and psychologist, he served on the management staff of the Jack Kramer Professional Tennis Tour and cofounded the Jack Kramer Tennis Club in 1961. He founded the Vic Braden Tennis College in Coto de Caza, California, in 1974 and now has Vic Braden Tennis Colleges in Kissimmee, Florida, and St. George, Utah. Braden served as a member of the Wilson Sporting Goods advisory staff from 1952 to 1999 and as an instruction editor for *Tennis Magazine* from 1974 to 1999.

Howard Brody is an emeritus professor of physics at the University of Pennsylvania where he was the academic and technical advisor to both the men's and women's tennis teams. Brody played varsity tennis and earned his bachelor's degree at Massachusetts Institute of Technology and his master's and doctoral degrees at California Institute of Technology. He has written many papers and articles on the physics of sports, particularly tennis. Dr. Brody is a member of the International Tennis Federation Technical Commission and the USTA Sports Science Committee and Technical Committee, he is a science advisor to the USPTR, and he is on the technical advisory panel of *Tennis Magazine*. His book *Tennis Science for Tennis Players* was published in 1987. In 1996, Dr. Brody received the USPTR Plagenhoef Award for Sports Science.

Donald Chu is a leading authority on power training and conditioning, a former president of the National Strength and Conditioning Association (NSCA), and a frequent contributor to the *National Strength and Conditioning Association Journal*. Chu has been a conditioning consultant for the Golden State Warriors, Milwaukee Bucks, Detroit Lions, and Chicago White Sox as well as a consultant for the U.S. Tennis Association, professional tennis players Todd Martin and Lindsay Davenport, and the U.S. national and Olympic synchronized swimming teams. He is currently the director of the physical therapist assistant program at Ohlone College in Neward, California. Dr. Chu, who earned a PhD in physical therapy and kinesiology from Stanford University, is a professor emeritus of kinesiology and physical education at California State University at Hayward. Chu is a registered physical therapist, a certified athletic trainer through the

National Athletic Trainers' Association, and a National Strength and Conditioning Association—certified strength specialist. He has received many honors, including the NATA's Most Distinguished Athletic Trainer Award in 1995 and the NSCA's President's Award for Service in 1993.

Andrew Coe is the head of product development and technical functions within the International Tennis Federation (ITF), and he has worked with the organization since 1996. Coe has spent more than 20 years in the tennis industry and previously worked for Dunlop Slazenger International. At Dunlop Slazenger, Coe was closely involved with the development of an award-winning racket manufacturing technology, which was used extensively by champions such as John McEnroe and Steffi Graf.

Miguel Crespo is the research officer for the tennis development department of the ITF. Crespo is responsible for the ITF Coaches Education Program and has been involved in the writing of many of the ITF's coaching education publications. He also travels the world conducting coaches' workshops and reporting on the latest developments in the field of coaching. Crespo holds a PhD in sports psychology and a BA in philosophy. He is a former director of the National Coaching School for the Royal Spanish Tennis Federation. Between 1984 and 1989, Crespo was the traveling coach and captain of the Spanish national junior teams. He has taught coaches at all levels and has written articles and books for coaches, players, and officials of the game.

Paul Dent is a national coach for the Lawn Tennis Association (LTA) in the United Kingdom. Dent spent three years as the coaching research officer for the LTA, where he researched physical conditioning, tactics, technical development, mental skills development, and sports medicine. He also worked for five years as the coaching excellence manager for the LTA, where he produced and developed information for the UK's top performance coaches working with the top junior and senior players. Dent has presented at the ITF World Coaches Conference and at the ITF Asian Coaches Workshop.

Todd Ellenbecker is a physical therapist and the clinic director of Physiotherapy Associates Scottsdale Sports Clinic in Scottsdale, Arizona. He is a member of the USTA National Sports Science Committee and a certified USPTA tennis teaching professional. Ellenbecker is the chairman of the American Physical Therapy Association's Shoulder Special Interest Group. He has conducted research and lectured internationally on shoulder and elbow rehabilitation and is the author of two books, *The Elbow in Sport* and *Complete Conditioning for Tennis*. He received his physical therapy degree from the University of Wisconsin at Lacrosse and a master's degree in exercise physiology from Arizona State University.

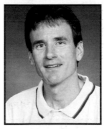

Bruce Elliott is a professor of biomechanics and head of the department of human movement and exercise science at the University of Western Australia. He has published more than 130 articles and written or edited 10 books and 23 book chapters on sport biomechanics. Elliott, a former A-grade tennis player in Australia and a tennis coach, links biomechanics theory with the applied problems of coaching. He has been a speaker at every National Tennis Conference in Australia and has given presentations at the USA National Tennis Conference, International Medicine and Science in Tennis Congress, and at the ITF Asian Conference. He was the inaugural Chair of the Western

Australia Institute of Sport from 1984 to 1994 and the vice president in the Australian Association of Exercise and Sports Science from 1993 to 1995. Elliott was also the scientific chair for the Fifth IOC World Congress on Sport Sciences Pre-Olympic Conference and supervised the biomechanics research projects at the 2000 Games in Sydney for the IOC Medical Commission.

Mary Joe Fernandez has reached the quarterfinal or better in 17 Grand Slams in her career, while capturing 2 Grand Slam doubles titles and amassing 7 singles titles and 19 doubles crowns on the WTA Tour since turning pro in 1986. She captured Olympic doubles gold medals as a member of the U.S. Olympic team in 1992 and 1996. Fernandez was elected to the WTA Tour Players' Council for a fourth consecutive year in 2000. She also serves as a member of the USTA executive board and as a spokesperson for the WTA Tour's F.I.R.S.T. Serve schools program.

Tom Gullikson, the USTA director of coaching, reached at least the third round of all four Grand Slam Championships during his playing career. Gullikson and twin brother

Tim reached the 1983 Wimbledon doubles finals, and he won the 1984 U.S. Open mixed doubles title with Manuela Maleeva. Gullikson joined the USTA Player Development coaching staff in 1988 as a coach for touring professionals. As a USTA Player Development coach, he has coached many top American players such as Jennifer Capriati, Jim Courier, and Todd Martin. Gullikson served as the U.S. Davis Cup captain from 1993 to 1999, captaining the team to the 31st Davis Cup title for the United States in 1995. He also served as the men's coach for the 1996 U.S. Olympic team. He was named USOC Elite Coach of the Year for Tennis in 1996. Gullikson was named the USTA director of coaching in 1997. He is a 1973 graduate of Northern Illinois University.

Patrice Hagelauer is the performance director of the Lawn Tennis Association and previously served as the director of men's tennis at the French Tennis Federation (FFT). Under Hagelauer's coaching direction, French players achieved a total of 24 ATP Tour victories. He worked with Yannick Noah during Noah's 1983 French Open victory and has also coached Henri Leconte and Guy Forget. He was the coach for the French Davis Cup team for 16 years, leading the team to victory twice during his tenure.

Richard "Dickie" Herbst is the general manager of the Longwood Athletic Club, the head coach of the New York Hamptons, and the coach of 1999 Wimbledon semifinalist Alexandra Stevenson. Herbst played tennis at Pepperdine University, graduating cum laude with a bachelor's degree in English before returning to his native New England to coach and develop

programs for tennis clubs. He coached several touring professionals, including five-time Wimbledon quarterfinalist Tim Mayotte and Patrick McEnroe. Herbst was then tapped by the USTA as part of the team headed by Tom Gullikson to develop national junior talent. He served as the national coach for the boys 14s division at the 1998 World Junior Championships.

Jose Higueras, special advisor to USTA Player Development, has been part of the USTA staff since 1988. His primary responsibility is coaching players through the USTA Touring Pro Program. As a coach, Higueras is best known for helping Michael Chang win the 1989 French Open to end America's 34-year drought of men's titles there. Two years later, Higueras helped Jim Courier win the French Open and eventually achieve the number one ranking. In his days as a touring professional, Higueras reached the semifinals of the French Open in 1982 and 1983 and won 15 career singles titles and three career doubles titles. He ranked as high as number seven in the world during his playing career. Higueras won the ATP Tour Sportsmanship Award in 1984.

W. Ben Kibler, MD, is the medical director at the Lexington Sports Medicine Center in Lexington, Kentucky, and is a founding member and former president of the Society for Tennis Medicine and Science. Dr. Kibler is a member of the USTA Sports Science Committee and the medicine advisor to the USPTR. He received the Plagenhoef award for contributions to tennis sports science from the USPTR in 1998. A fellow in the American Academy of Orthopedic Surgeons and the American College of Sports Medicine, he is also a member of the American Orthopedic Society for Sports Medicine and the American Shoulder and Elbow Surgeons.

Duane Knudson, is an associate professor of biomechanics in the department of physical education and exercise science at California State University at Chico. Dr. Knudson is a member of the USTA Sport Science Committee and has done extensive research on the biomechanics of tennis. He is also well known for his research on the qualitative analysis of movement and the application of sport sciences in qualitative analysis.

Jack Kramer has served the sport of tennis from his days as a top player and promoter to his television commentary and innovations in the structure of professional tennis. As an 18-year-old, Kramer was the youngest player in the Davis Cup finals when he played doubles with Joe Hunt against Australia in 1939. After World War II Kramer began to dominate amateur tennis, winning Wimbledon in 1947 and the U.S. singles titles at Forest Hills in 1946 and 1947. He also helped the United States recapture the Davis Cup from Australia in 1946 and defend its title in 1947. Kramer then turned to the professional tennis of the time, dueling Bobby Riggs and then Pancho Gonzalez. In 1952, Kramer took over the promotion of professional tennis. When the open era in tennis began in 1968, Kramer helped devise the Grand Prix structure that was used until the ATP Tour took over in 1990. In 1972, Kramer helped form the Association of Tennis Pros, which was the men's players' union, and served as its first executive director. Kramer also served as a television commentator for more than 20 years.

Jim Loehr is recognized worldwide for his contributions and innovations in training and performance psychology. Loehr has worked with hundreds of world-class athletes, including Jim Courier, Arantxa Sanchez-Vicario, Monica Seles, golfer Mark O'Meara, boxer Ray Mancini, and the NHL's Eric Lindros and Mike Richter. He has appeared on NBC's *Today Show*, ABC's *Nightline*, the *CBS Evening News*, and *CBS Morning News* and has been featured on many other television programs. The president and CEO of LGE Performance Systems, Loehr conducts corporate training programs for hundreds of corporations worldwide. He has authored 12 books and produced several audio and video programs. Dr. Loehr is a full member of the American College of Sports Medicine, the NSCA, the American Psychological Association, and the Association for the

Advancement of Applied Sports Psychology. He has been a monthly columnist for *World Tennis* and *Tennis Magazine* for 10 years and has received the International Tennis Hall of Fame Educational Merit Award.

 **Patrick McEnroe** was selected as captain of the United States Davis Cup team in December of 2000. After helping Stanford University to a pair of NCAA titles, McEnroe spent nine years on the ATP Tour, reaching the semifinals of the 1991 Australian Open and the quarterfinals of the 1995 U.S. Open. He also won 16 doubles titles, including the 1989 French Open doubles title with Jim Grabb, and competed for the United States in Davis Cup play in 1993, 1994, and 1996. Since retiring from professional tennis in 1998, McEnroe has been a television commentator for CBS Sports and ESPN and for the *Imus in the Morning* program. He has served on the ATP Tour Players Council and is a member of the USTA's board of directors. McEnroe also owns the New York Hamptons of DuPont World TeamTennis and is the author of *Tennis for Dummies*.

 **David Miley** is the executive director of Tennis Development for the International Tennis Federation (ITF) and is responsible for overseeing the juniors, veterans, and wheelchair activities of the ITF as well as the ITF Development Program. Since joining the ITF in 1991, he has visited more than 100 countries, advising member nations on all aspects of tennis development, conducting coaches' workshops, and directing junior programs. Miley has also coauthored many of the ITF's coaching education publications, including the *ITF Advanced Coaches Manual* and the *ITF School Tennis Initiative Teachers Manual*. A 1980 business graduate of Lander College in South Carolina and a 1982 graduate of University College at Dublin, Miley was twice the Irish men's doubles champion and is a former nonplaying captain of the Irish men's team.

 **Lynne Rolley** is the USTA director of program development and has coached tennis for more than 25 years. Rolley became the first woman to serve as head coach of a men's NCAA varsity program when she coached the men's tennis team at St. Mary's College in Moraga, California, from 1970 to 1973. As a player, Rolley once ranked in the top 10 in singles and doubles in the United States and was a double quarterfinalist at the 1966 U.S. Nationals with Val Ziegenfuss. She was hired as a USTA national coach in 1988, served as an assistant coach to the U.S. Federation Cup teams in 1993 and 1994, and was promoted to USTA director of coaching for women in 1994. She coached the U.S. women's team at the 1999 Pan American Games. She is a member of the ITF Coaches Commission.

 **Nick Saviano** is the director of the USTA Coaching Education Program. In this role, Saviano directs and runs the USA Tennis High Performance Coaching Program in conjunction with the USPTA and USPTR and is the liaison between the USA Tennis Player Development Program and tennis academies in the United States. He was a touring professional for nine years, earning a top-50 world singles ranking and reaching the round of sixteen at Wimbledon in 1980 and 1982. Twice an NCAA All-American at Stanford, he helped the Cardinal to the 1974 NCAA title. As a coach for the USTA, he has worked with many top American players including Jim Courier, David Wheaton, Todd Martin, Jared Palmer, Vince Spadea, and Justin Gimelstob. Saviano was hired as a USTA national coach in 1988 and was promoted to USTA director of coaching for men's tennis in 1994. He was named the USTA director of technical development in 1998.

Michiel Schapers is the national coach for men's tennis for the Royal Dutch Lawn Tennis Association. Schapers played professional tennis from 1981 until 1993, reaching an ATP ranking of 25 in April of 1988. He reached the quarterfinals of the Australian Open in 1985 and 1988 and made the quarterfinals at the 1988 Olympic Games. In mixed doubles, Schapers reached the finals of the French Open in 1988. He worked as a full-time private coach on the ATP Tour with Daniel Vacek and Alexander Radulescu in 1994 and 1995. He started in his current position in 1995 and served as the Dutch Davis Cup captain from 1998 through 2000.

Pam Shriver ranked among the world's top 10 professional tennis players throughout the 1980s and with Martina Navratilova was part of one of the greatest doubles teams of all time. Shriver reached the U.S. Open final as a 16-year-old amateur in 1978. She has won 21 singles titles and 112 doubles championships, including 22 Grand Slam titles in doubles. Shriver also won the 1988 Olympic gold medal in doubles with Zina Garrison. In 1999, Shriver was awarded the WTA Tour's David Gray Service Award for lifelong service and commitment to the game of tennis. Currently, she is serving her second term on the board of directors of the USTA. She is a former president of the Women's Tennis Association and was a member of the President's Council on Physical Fitness from 1986 to 1992. Shriver is also a minority owner of the Baltimore Orioles, honorary chairperson of the Baltimore Tennis Patrons, and vice president of the International Tennis Hall of Fame. She is a tennis analyst for ESPN, HBO, ABC, CBS, the BBC, and 7 Sport in Australia. Shriver is president of Women's Sports Legends and made her debut on the Virginia Slims Legends Tour in 1996.

Stan Smith dominated tennis in the early 1970s, capturing the U.S. Open in 1971 and Wimbledon in 1972. He was the world's number one player in 1971 and 1972 and the top-ranked American in 1969 and 1971 through 1973. In addition to his 39 singles titles, he captured 61 doubles crowns in his career. Smith and long-time doubles partner Bob Lutz captured four U.S. Open doubles titles between 1968 and 1980. Smith was inducted into the International Tennis Hall of Fame in 1987, and he is a member of the halls of fame for the University of South Carolina, South Carolina, and Intercollegiate Tennis. Smith served as the director of coaching for the USTA from 1988 to 1993, and in 1994 became the USTA's associate director of Player Development. In 1997 he became special advisor/coach of USTA Player Development. He served as the men's tennis coach for the U.S. Olympic team in Sydney. Smith's current associations include his design company, Stan Smith Design, which has designed dozens of top facilities around the world.

Craig Tiley is the head coach of the University of Illinois men's tennis team and the director of tennis at the Atkins Tennis Center. Tiley, a native of South Africa, competed professionally on tennis circuits in Europe, Africa, and the United States. He holds two bachelor's degrees—in economics and business administration—and a master's degree in exercise science. Tiley holds the highest certification from the USPTR and USPTA, serves on the Prince National Advisory Board, is a USTA clinician and Jr. Davis Cup Coach, and has worked as a tennis analyst for Prime Network, TWI, and NBC television. He is also one of the few coaches serving on the USTA National Committee. In 1996, 1998, and 1999 Tiley was named NCAA Regional Coach of the Year and was named the national collegiate coach of the year in 1999. He was named the USPTR National Coach of the Year in 2000. Tiley also coaches several touring professionals and has served as the Davis Cup captain for South Africa since 1998.

Dennis Van der Meer owns and operates the Van der Meer Training Center, where he oversees the technical development of aspiring tour players as well as established WTA and ATP members. Van der Meer founded the United States Professional Tennis Registry and the Van der Meer Tennis University, where more than 10,000 coaches from 124 countries have attended his courses. A native of Namibia, Van der Meer was a leading young South African tennis player before emigrating to the United States in 1960 to become head professional at Berkeley Tennis Club. He has received several coaching awards, including a citation in 1965 from the United States Foreign Affairs Department for his worldwide contributions to tennis. In 1997 he received the Developmental Coach of the Year Award by the United States Olympic Committee. Van der Meer is also a founding and current member of the ATP Tour Coaches Association. He has produced numerous coaching videos and written several tennis books and numerous coaching articles. In 1992 he was designated the first National Master in Tennis by the President's Council on Fitness and Sport.

Frank van Fraayenhoven is the full-time coordinator for coaches education within the Royal Dutch Lawn Tennis Association. He has been involved in the education of coaches for more than 20 years and has worked with coaches and players in more than 50 countries. From 1986 to 1989 Fraayenhoven was a national coach, working with both top juniors and top professionals from the Netherlands. He has written a book (published in Dutch) and many articles on tennis. He has been one of the regular speakers at the European Coaches Symposium during the last 17 years. Today, Fraayenhoven is working with the other Dutch national coaches to produce a new development program for talented players. He is a member of the ITF Coaches Commission.

Ron Woods is the director of the USA Tennis Plan for Growth, a $50 million, five-year effort to recruit new players to the sport. Woods was a professor of physical education and men's tennis coach at West Chester University in Pennsylvania for 17 years before joining the USTA in 1984, where he served for more than 10 years as the first director of Player Development. He was awarded the International Tennis Hall of Fame Education Merit Award in 1997. He was also honored by the United States Professional Tennis Association (USPTA) as 1982 National Coach of the Year and designated a Master Professional in 1984. Woods is a member of the coaching committee of the USOC and is also a member of the United States Professional Tennis Registry.